The Ryder Cup

THE ILLUSTRATED HISTORY

To Margaret M. Hall, who has understood

The Ryder Cup

THE ILLUSTRATED HISTORY

MICHAEL HOBBS

Macdonald
Queen Anne Press

A Queen Anne Press BOOK

© Michael Hobbs 1989

First published in Great Britain in 1989 by
Queen Anne Press, a division of
Macdonald & Co (Publishers) Ltd
6th Floor
Headway House
66–73 Shoe Lane
London EC4P 4AB

A member of Maxwell Pergamon Publishing Corporation plc
Jacket photographs – Front: (left) Bob Thomas Sports Photography
(right) Allsport/Dave Cannon
Back: The Michael Hobbs Collection

Index compiled by David Linton

British Library Cataloguing in Publication Data

Hobbs, Michael, 1934–
   The Ryder Cup: an illustrated history.
   1. Great Britain. Golf. Competitions.
   Ryder Cup, history
   I. Title
   796.352,74,0941

   ISBN 0–356–15537–4

Typeset by MS Filmsetting Limited, Frome, Somerset
Printed and bound in Great Britain by
Butler & Tanner Limited, Frome, Somerset

CONTENTS

Acknowledgements

I should like to thank the PGA of America and the Professional Golfers' Association for their help during my research for this book.

Many individuals have also helped in providing me with original material and I should particularly like to thank David White of the Ellesborough Press, Sarah Baddiel of Golfiana and Bob Grant of Grant Books for lending me rare books and Ryder Cup programmes. Philip Truett, Graham Rowley, Tony Harrold, Brian Wallis and Bruce Critchley are also due my thanks as are Murray Ritchie of the *Glasgow Herald* who supplied me with information on the 1921 match, and Richard Stafford of *Golf World*. Thanks must go to Alan Samson, publisher at Queen Anne Press, and my editor Janet Ravenscroft and picture researcher Donna Thynne for their hard work, professionalism and enthusiasm.

Finally, I should like to thank Peter Alliss, captain of the PGA at the time of the 1987 match and many times a Ryder Cup team member, for contributing the foreword.

The publishers would like to thank the following for their permission to use copyright material:

Aldus Archive/U.S.G.A.: pp 14 top, 22, 37, 40, 53, 59 bottom, 82; Allsport: pp 156, 166 (Dave Cannon), 177 (Dave Cannon); Associated Press: pp 77, 78; Associated Sports Photographers: pp 116 (D. Franklin), 140, 162, 171 bottom; British Library (Colindale) pp 20, 27; Colorific!/Sports Illustrated: pp 89, 90, 95 bottom; Peter Dazeley: pp 20, 130, 131 top & bottom, 132 all, 138, 139, 142 all, 143, 159, 168 top, 171 top; John Frost Newspaper Archive: p 31; The Michael Hobbs Collection: pp 10, 11, 13, 14 bottom, 15, 16, 18 top, 27, 28, 30, 33, 36, 38, 41, 42, 43, 44–45, 54, 56, 59, 61, 63 top & bottom, 64, 65 top & bottom, 75 bottom, 80, 83 top & bottom, 93, 103, 153; Hulton Deutsch Collection: pp 12, 13 top, 17 top & bottom, 18 bottom, 23, 24, 25, 33, 34 top & bottom, 46, 48, 50, 51, 60, 69, 71, 74, 98, 114 bottom, 118 bottom; The Illustrated London News: p 85; Stewart Kendall/Sportsphoto Agency: p 141 top; The Bert Neale Collection: pp 67, 72, 75 top (Bob Thomas), 81, 86 (Bob Thomas), 92 top & bottom, 99 (Bob Thomas), 100, 104, 106, 107, 108, 109, 110, 112, 113, 114 top, 121 (Bob Thomas), 122, 123 (Bob Thomas), 124 (Bob Thomas), 125, 135; Phil Sheldon: pp 136, 148; Bob Thomas: pp 154, 157, 161, 172, 173, 176, 178 all, 180, 181; UPI/Bettmann Newsphotos: pp 95 top, 96, 118 top, 119, 127, 128; Yours in Sport/Lawrence Levy: pp 146, 150, 151, 164, 182.

Whilst every effort has been made to trace copyright holders, this has proved impossible in some cases and copyright owners are invited to contact the publishers.

FOREWORD

I am delighted to contribute a foreword to Michael Hobbs's narrative history of competitions between Britain and America (as the teams were labelled in 1921) up to the present day when Ryder Cup matches are held between the United States and Europe.

My family's connection with the Ryder Cup goes back to 1929. My father Percy was chosen for the team, though he didn't actually play a match because he was troubled by a bad back. He also missed out in 1931, when he was ruled out for being based overseas at the Wannsee club in Berlin. The same ruling later applied to Henry Cotton when he worked in Belgium. However, my father played through the rest of the 1930s with great distinction. There wasn't a great gap before I made my first appearance in 1953 and I'm proud of the fact that we are still the only father and son combination to have played in the matches for either side.

Looking back, the results of many of the matches in the post-war period were almost a foregone conclusion but, at least on British soil, we always felt that we went in with a chance. I was always very stirred by the Ryder Cup and played some of my best golf in the matches during the years 1953 to 1969. The fact that I was playing for Great Britain made everything that much more important. There were many great moments which I look back on very fondly: for instance my largely successful partnership with Irishman Christy O'Connor; the thrill of halving my singles with Arnold Palmer at Royal Lytham in 1961, when he was at his peak, and beating him in America two years later. For me, the Ryder Cup had bad moments as well. I lost both my matches in 1953 when we played two over 36 holes, and then the same thing happened in Great Britain's amazing victory at Lindrick in 1957. Was I jinxed? Happily not, for it all went a great deal better from then on.

Michael Hobbs covers the whole scene most thoroughly and has shed new light on little known aspects of Ryder Cup history. I was particularly interested in his discovery that the Ryder Cup encounters go back to 1926 at Wentworth rather than to 1927 in Worcester, Massachusetts.

Reports in *The Times* that Samuel Ryder had agreed to present the trophy some weeks before that 1926 match and headlines calling the event 'The Ryder Cup' during the encounter itself are convincing. I shall have to correct those people who recount the oft-repeated story of the tea party after the 1926 match during which Ryder is, for the first time, supposed to have agreed to present a trophy. He had already made this commitment some weeks earlier.

So, The Belfry in 1989 will host the 29th match and not the 28th. Certainly the 1926 British team was the strongest that could have been put out and was selected by our PGA. Perhaps the United States' team was not made up entirely of America's top golfers, often the case since. For example, there was no Sam Snead or Cary Middlecoff at Lindrick in 1957, and didn't Tom Weiskopf announce one year that he preferred to go hunting?

Today, we are at a fascinating stage in Ryder Cup history. On this side of the Atlantic we are cock-a-hoop and the European team should start favourites in 1989. But there are problems to ponder; is Bernhard Langer's putting twitch incurable? On his 1988 form he would have no chance of making the team, and neither would Sam Torrance, a fellow-sufferer. And where are the new stars? The generation that first came to the fore in the late 1970s – Ballesteros, Lyle, Faldo and Langer – who all performed so well when quite young, are currently being followed up only by José-Maria Olazabal. At the time of writing, the 1985 hero, Manuel Pinero, and José-Maria Canizares seem to have faded away. But perhaps the same is true in the United States. No giant star has appeared (with apologies to Curtis Strange) to claim the succession to Jack Nicklaus and Tom Watson.

One thing, though, I'm sure of. Our teams will never again be humiliated in the USA as happened until the end of the 1970s and, for a while at least, the United States will not be brimful of confidence in Europe.

Past President of the PGA

INTRODUCTION

The history of international competitions between Britain and the United States goes back to 1921 when the first matches between both the amateurs and the professionals were played at Hoylake and Gleneagles respectively. It was a grave shock to British self-esteem when her amateurs were thrashed by Bobby Jones and his team-mates, but the world was set to rights again shortly after this by some of the grand old men of British golf – including Vardon, Taylor and Braid. This result, however, was misleading. The United States had not assembled quite their best team possible. While US amateurs won the Walker Cup year after year with ease, American-based professionals such as Hutchison, Barnes and Hagen began to demonstrate superiority by winning the Open Championship.

No more professional matches between the two countries were arranged for some years until Samuel Ryder became interested in golf. He thought British professionals should be able to cope with the rampant Americans in matchplay and also win the Open Championship. He engaged Britain's best player, Abe Mitchell, as his personal professional so that Mitchell could concentrate on his golf rather than deal with the needs of members at North Foreland Golf Club. Alas, Mitchell would never win the Open. Another of Ryder's ideas was a great deal more successful; in April 1926, *The Times* announced that Ryder had presented a trophy for matchplay competition between Britain and the United States. The first match for the

Ryder Cup took place at Wentworth a few weeks later, early in June. Ryder's faith in British professionals was justified by their easy victory.

This was a false dawn, however. The British PGA had picked as good a side as they knew how but the United States were not at full strength, good though their team was. But a pattern had been set of good British performances on home soil, win or lose, while in the United States there was only abject failure. As the years passed, American teams became almost as successful on British courses as at home. This changed only with the growth of the European Tour and the emergence of not just one (a Cotton or a Jacklin) but several stars of world stature such as Severiano Ballesteros, Bernhard Langer, Nick Faldo, Sandy Lyle and Ian Woosnam. This book is the story of those matches, from 1921 to 1987. I have treated them sometimes briefly, sometimes in considerable detail, depending on their interest – one close encounter is surely worth three one-sided meetings.

I would like to end with a few explanations. It has been accepted for many years that the Ryder Cup began in 1927 but research has shown this to be untrue. I must also apologise for speaking of 'Britain' and 'British' throughout. This is not national chauvinism on my part – 'Great Britain and Ireland' is rather too many words compared with 'US'. Later, I switch to 'Europe' rather than the term 'Great Britain and Europe' (always an oddity which suggests

the British Isles are a separate continent) for the same reason. Alert readers consulting their bible, the *Golfer's Handbook*, may notice that the order of match results as I give them sometimes differs from theirs, especially for the early years but at other times also. I have given the results in the order that the matches were played, with the winning team's scores in the left-hand column. The full names of players are given with their singles results. A player who did not appear in the singles has his name in full in the pairs.

A history of the Ryder Cup is long overdue and I hope this book will fill the gap. The future of the event from the perspective of 1989 seems very exciting. It is unlikely that the United States will ever regain her past dominance and Europe may indeed be the stronger side for at least the next few years. Whatever happens, the Ryder Cup from now on promises a succession of thrilling encounters.

Above *The man who began it all, Samuel Ryder, stands between J. H. Taylor (left) and Walter Hagen (right)*

BEGINNINGS (1921–1927)

1921

The idea of international matches between the USA and Britain began in America. Who should be given the most credit is doubtful. A man with the unlikely name of Sylvanus P. Jermain of the Inverness Club in Toledo, Ohio, thought such a match would be a good idea. It could be called the Ross Cup as Walter Ross, president of the Nickel Plate Railroad in Cleveland, had indicated that he would foot the bill for a trophy. Nothing seems to have come of this and Ross missed the bargain price immortality that was later to go to Samuel Ryder.

Perhaps earlier James Harnett also became enthusiastic about the idea of sending a team of Americans over the Atlantic to play a match against British professionals as a prelude to competing in the Open Championship. Much more came of this. At a meeting, on 15 December 1920, of the American PGA, Harnett, who was a circulation manager for *Golf Illustrated*, proposed that he and the PGA raise money to send a team to Britain. John Mackie, the retiring president, opposed the idea. He decided the project was a gimmick thought up by immigrant British professionals who wanted to get a free trip home. But the motion was passed. Each man was to get his expenses and $1,000, and foreign-born players would be eligible as long as they had been living in the USA for five years and intended to become US citizens. *Golf Illustrated* is credited with putting up all or most of the money.

Across the Atlantic, the *Glasgow Herald* had started a big money tournament in 1920. Total prize money was £650 and the winner, George Duncan, took home £160. In the words of the

George Duncan demonstrates his follow-through for a photographer

The course at Gleneagles in Scotland was the scene, in 1921, of the first international golf match to be held between professionals

Glasgow Herald, this was 'the largest individual amount that has ever been offered in a professional golf tournament'. From the start, the event was held at the new Gleneagles King's course, before the hotel had been built. Even so 'ample accommodation' was provided for competitors and others as sleeper carriages were moved into Gleneagles Station.

The following year came the *Herald*'s equivalent to the $1 Million Sun City Challenge. The event became 'The *Glasgow Herald* 1,000 Guineas Tournament'. The event, so important in its day, has now disappeared from the record books. It too played its part in what would eventually become the Ryder Cup series. As a *Glasgow Herald* writer put it five years later, 'It

was under the auspices of this tournament that the first professional match between Great Britain and America was played.'

Played on 6 June 1921, it came about a fortnight after the first international of any kind between Britain and America. This was held between amateurs at Hoylake on 21 May, and produced a dominating performance from the Americans who won by nine matches to three. Many would date the clear superiority of US golf from this forerunner to the Walker Cup, rather than Francis Ouimet's freak defeat of Harry Vardon and Ted Ray in the play-off for the 1913 US Open. Vardon and Ray were still good enough for the Gleneagles match. The other members of the British team were J. H. Taylor, George Duncan, Abe Mitchell, James Braid, Arthur Havers, James Ockenden, James Sherlock and Josh Taylor. Containing six past or future Open champions, it was as strong a British team as could have been selected.

The team representing America was Jock Hutchison, Walter Hagen, Emmett French, Freddie McLeod, Tommy Kerrigan, C. W. Hackney, Wilfred Reid, George McLean, Charles Hoffner and Bill Mehlhorn. How good were they? Of the first two in the team, there can be no doubts. In America, Hutchison in this period was always a likely winner of the Open, being 2nd in both 1916 and 1920 and 3rd in 1919. He lost the final of the PGA in 1916 and won the championship in 1920. He also won the other major event of the USA, the Western Open, in 1920 and 1923. Hagen was, quite simply, one of the greatest players in the history

Ted Ray was at Gleneagles for the Glasgow Herald *1,000 Guineas event in 1922 (right)*

Some of the British team at Gleneagles in 1921. (Back row) Abe Mitchell, Harry Vardon, unknown, Sandy Herd, unknown and, seated, Ted Ray, J. H. Taylor and George Duncan

Left *'Wild Bill' Mehlhorn was the only American golfer to win his singles in 1926*

Below *Walter Hagen, one of the greatest golfers of all time, stands on the far left in the back row with members of the American team which took part in the international match in June 1921*

of golf. The remaining members, however, were not quite in his class, but, taking them in order, French twice finished in the top five of the US Open in the 1920s and was the losing PGA finalist in 1922. McLeod was US Open champion in 1908, finished 3rd in 1914 and 2nd in 1921. Of the remainder of the team, 'Wild Bill' Mehlhorn, so-called because he often wore a Buffalo Bill hat on course, was by far the best player. He finished high in the US Open several times, won the 1924 Western Open and lost to Hagen in the final of the 1925 PGA. The others did not make any real impact on golf history though both George McLean and Wilfred Reid threatened to win US Opens.

The performance of the US team in the 1921

Harry Vardon drives off, watched by Ted Ray (with pipe and baggy jacket) and James Braid. All three men played in the first international match

British Open, which followed soon after, is also significant. Hutchison won, Kerrigan was 3rd and Hagen tied 6th. Mehlhorn finished ten strokes behind the winner, Hackney 12 and both McLean and French were 13 behind in joint 26th place. Hoffner and McLeod at least managed to qualify to play all four rounds, the only one to fail being Wilfred Reid. British results were similar, with only James Sherlock failing to qualify. Havers was 4th and Duncan, the title-holder, was 5th.

Before play began, the Gleneagles course came in for severe criticism. The fairways were ragged and the bunkers unkempt – it seems that the greens staff had not scythed the sides. There was coarse grass on the greens and the man from *The Times* commented, 'The sand used in the bunkers is of the wrong type, being far too gritty and full of shells'.

For Britain, Duncan and Mitchell led off against Hagen and Hutchison. Both teams had put forward their strongest pairings. The match was all square after nine holes but the Ameri-

Harry Vardon and Sam Ryder at the 1929 match

and J. H. Taylor, who had both won the Open five times, then came to the last dormy 1 but Hackney holed a good putt to win the hole and halve the match. The last two British pairs won, to give a 3–0 result.

In the singles, the two players with the highest reputations led off for their countries so it was George Duncan, still Open champion and winner of the first *Glasgow Herald* tournament the year before, against Jock Hutchison, who had been born in St Andrews. Duncan reached the turn in 36 to be 3 up and went to dormy 4 before Hutchison struck back by winning a couple of holes. A half at the 17th gave Duncan the first international singles victory by 2 and 1. Abe Mitchell was a formidable striker. In his match against Walter Hagen he was often 50 yards ahead from the tee and only once needed a wooden club for his second shot. Even so, Hagen's masterly short game enabled him to halve, after a match which see-sawed throughout. The USA won the next two matches, with McLeod winning the last three holes to beat J. H. Taylor 1 up.

That, however, was just about the end of American successes. Only Wilfred Reid won in the next six matches, beating Havers 2 and 1 after being 2 down with seven to go. The other matches all went to Britain to give a 6–3 result for the singles and 9–3 overall. Gold medals, courtesy of the *Glasgow Herald*, were presented to the players to commemorate the event. The US ambassador, who had made the long journey from London expecting a US victory, drove hastily away and the St Andrews character, Andrew Kirkaldy, commented, 'I dinna regard it as a level match'.

All in all, it was a low-key affair. The main target of the invaders was the Open Champion-

cans were 2 up after 13. An iron shot dead by Mitchell at the 17th levelled the match but the pair were in trouble at the 18th and needed a long putt from Duncan to halve both the hole and the match. In 1921, Harry Vardon was still a great player. He and Ray cruised home against French and Kerrigan by 5 and 4. James Braid

ship. Hutchison became the first American-based player to win, followed the next year by Hagen as the first American-born champion. Both the teams in that first match, however, probably regarded the financial benefits of the rest of the week as more important than representing their countries. That *Glasgow Herald* tournament was big money. The top 16 qualified for the matchplay stages after 27 holes strokeplay qualifying. Six of the players who had taken part in the match reached the last eight. In the end, Mitchell was the winner, beating the Australian Joe Kirkwood by 7 and 6 in the final.

Perhaps the US team was not quite at full strength, although, other than Jim Barnes, who was shortly to win the US Open, it is not easy to see who else had an emphatic claim to a place in

Above *J. H. Taylor's medal commemorating the international match in 1921*

Below *Walter Hagen about to attempt to drive the Thames from the roof of the Savoy Hotel where he always reserved a suite*

the side. But the idea of international matches had been both born and tidily launched. Though the Walker Cup quickly became a regular event, the professionals were slow to follow. The idea of American supremacy, however, was established in the years 1922 to 1924, with Hagen finishing 1, 2, 1 in the British Open. Vardon, Taylor and Braid were into their fifties and had no clear successors until the arrival of Henry Cotton in the 1930s, when he was at his peak.

GLENEAGLES, PERTHSHIRE, SCOTLAND 6 JUNE 1921

Britain		United States	
Captain J. H. Taylor		*Captain* Emmett French	
Foursomes			
Duncan and Mitchell (halved)	0	Hutchison and Hagen	0
Ray and Vardon (5 and 4)	1	French and Kerrigan	0
Braid and J. H. Taylor (halved)	0	Hackney and McLeod	0
Havers and Ockenden (6 and 5)	1	Reid and McLean	0
Sherlock and Josh Taylor (1 up)	1	Hoffner and Mehlhorn	0
	3		0
Singles			
George Duncan (2 and 1)	1	Jock Hutchison	0
Abe Mitchell (halved)	0	Walter Hagen	0
Ted Ray	0	Emmett French (2 and 1)	1
J. H. Taylor	0	Fred McLeod (1 up)	1
Harry Vardon (3 and 1)	1	Tommy Kerrigan	0
James Braid (5 and 4)	1	Clarence Hackney	0
Arthur Havers	0	Wilf Reid (2 and 1)	1
James Ockenden (5 and 4)	1	George McLean	0
James Sherlock (3 and 2)	1	Charles Hoffner	0
Josh Taylor (3 and 2)	1	Bill Mehlhorn	0
	6		3

Final score: Britain 9 United States 3.
Three matches halved

1926

After the Gleneagles match, no others took place between British and American professionals for some years although the amateurs of the two countries were much more active. After the 1921 Hoylake match, George Herbert Walker, a recent president of the USGA, in 1922 presented the cup which British and American amateurs competed for annually until 1924. After the international that year, the third for the Walker Cup, it was felt that an annual match was too much of a good thing and, like the future Ryder Cup, the match was played every two years thereafter.

Samuel Ryder, the man who made his fortune when he decided to sell flower seeds in penny packets, became a keen golfer when he was advised to take up the game for the good of his health. He also became interested in professional golf, so much so that he took on Abe Mitchell, who, with George Duncan, was the best post-war British golfer, as his personal professional. This does not seem to have been vanity in the King Hassan of Morocco mould. Ryder's aim is said to have been to relieve Mitchell of the burdens of a club professional's life so as to allow him to concentrate on practice and tournament play and – above all – on winning the Open Championship. Alas, Abe Mitchell was to go down in the history of the game as just about the best British player to fail to win the championship, but Ryder was much more successful in another endeavour: to start a series of internationals for the professionals of the USA and Great Britain and Ireland. Perhaps encouraged by Abe Mitchell, he suggested to the PGA that he donate a trophy for such an event. The PGA agreed and on 26 April 1926, the following announcement appeared in *The Times*:

THE 'RYDER' TROPHY

Mr S. Ryder, of St Albans, has presented a trophy for annual competition between teams of British and American professionals. The first match for the trophy is to take place at

THE "RYDER" TROPHY.

Mr. S. Ryder, of St. Albans, has presented a trophy for annual competition between teams of British and American professionals. The first match for the trophy is to take place at Wentworth on June 4 and 5. The matches will be controlled by the Professional Golfers' Association, but the details are not yet decided.

THE TIMES, MONDAY, APRIL 26, 1926.

Above *The report in* The Times *is proof that the Ryder Cup began in 1926*

Wentworth on June 4 and 5. The matches will be controlled by the Professional Golfers' Association, but the details are not yet decided.

The same day, *The Times* also carried this Reuters report:

AMERICAN PROFESSIONAL TEAM **St Petersburg, Florida** Walter Hagen announces that the United States professionals' team to oppose British professionals in Great Britain this year will be composed of Macdonald Smith, A. Watrous, G. E. Sarazen, L. Diegel, W. Melhorn, T. Armour, R. Cruickshank, A. Espinosa, J. Kirkwood, J. Farrell, J. Barnes and possibly two others in addition to himself. *Reuters Special Service. [Sic.]*

Golfing Monthly for May 1926 also referred to the forth-coming match:

'WALKER CUP' FOR PROFESSIONALS The establishment of a professional international match between England and America to be run on somewhat similar lines to that of the Walker Cup appears to be on the way to accomplishment. Mr Ryder of St Albans, who has done much to further the interests of professional golf during the last few years has presented a valuable trophy for a contest between the two nations to be played alternately in this country and in the US at the time of the Open Championship in the respective countries. Walter Hagen as the recognised leader of the American golfers has

Above *The Ryder Cup. Abe Mitchell was the model for the figure on the top of the trophy which was probably made by Mappin and Webb*

gathered a powerful side to represent his country in the first match to be held towards the end of June. I understand that the venues are to be St George's Hill and Wentworth but surely a much more accessible course than either could be selected in order to give Metropolitan golfers an opportunity of watching the first of what may turn out to be a historic series.

The magazine returned to the story later in the same issue:

The PGA has been requested to select a team of four professionals to play the American team which is being selected by Walter Hagen for prizes amounting to £525. The match will consist of 72 holes, 36 holes to be played at St George's Hill and 36 at Wentworth on consecutive days, dates to be announced later. Each player will play each of the opposing team, and the winning number of holes in each match will be counted for the side. The winning team will be that which scores the highest aggregate number of holes on the two days' play, and the player who has the greatest number of holes to his credit will receive an extra prize.

The idea of deciding matches on the basis of 'numbers of holes up' was sometimes considered more fair than straight wins and losses but, in the end, was abandoned for the first Ryder Cup match in 1926. The format eventually adopted was much the same as for the Gleneagles match and the Walker Cup event.

The first of the US team to arrive were Fred McLeod and Emmett French. Jim Barnes was also over early, together with the Open Championship trophy he had won at Prestwick in 1925 and would defend at Royal Lytham and St Annes. 'Wild Bill' Mehlhorn had travelled over with the US Walker Cup team and gone off on holiday to Paris. On 2 June 1926, *The Times* carried a report about the remainder of the team.

AMERICAN PROFESSIONALS ARRIVE

W. Hagen, A. Waltrous, T. D. Armour, S. Newton, W. Melhorn and J. Sheen disembarked from the Cunard liner *Aquitania* at Southampton yesterday, where they were met by G. Duncan.

The first important match in which they will take part is against a team of British professionals for the Ryder Cup at Wentworth next Friday and Saturday. [*Sic*.]

I should break off here to point out the names of some of the Americans were unfamiliar in Britain and the mis-spellings which I have repeated were as used in the journals quoted. 'J. Sheen', for instance, was obviously 'Joe Stein' and 'A. Waltrous' was shortly to become Al Watrous, the man who almost beat Bobby Jones for the 1926 Open Championship. I have been unable to trace 'S. Newton' in golf history but none of the US team who played in the first Ryder Cup match has a name remotely similar.

Of the team Hagen had originally announced in Florida in April 1926, only six actually played: Barnes, Hagen himself, Armour, Mehlhorn, Kirkwood and Watrous. The team was made up by Cyril Walker (English-born winner of the 1924 US Open), Fred McLeod, Emmett French and Joe Stein. Of Hagen's original choices, it seems that several decided not to come over for the Open Championship, the main reason for the expedition, and therefore ruled themselves out of the first Ryder Cup match as well. These included Johnny Farrell, Gene Sarazen, Bobby Cruickshank and Macdonald Smith. The British PGA made their team choice much later as follows: Aubrey Boomer, Archie Compston, George Duncan, George Gadd, Arthur Havers, Abe Mitchell, Ted Ray (captain) and Fred Robson. As reserves, they selected Ernie Whitcombe, Herbert Jolly and Charles Whitcombe, the first two of whom took part when Walter Hagen requested that the match be played by teams of ten rather than eight. The format eventually decided on was five foursomes over 36 holes on

Above *This was probably the first shot ever played in the Ryder Cup as Abe Mitchell drives from the 1st tee at Wentworth in 1926. Jim Barnes is standing to his left in a Fair Isle pullover*

Left *Tommy Armour*

the first day, followed by ten singles on day two, again over 36 holes. Every team member played twice. Each team led off with their strongest players and it seems that members went out in ranking order so the British finished their line-up with Whitcombe and Jolly.

On 4 June 1926, the first match out in Ryder Cup history was between Abe Mitchell and George Duncan for Britain, against Walter Hagen and Jim Barnes for the United States. It took place at Wentworth, which, incidentally, Barnes hadn't seen before. The British pair quickly won the first two holes but Hagen countered with a fine shot to the green on the 3rd which resulted in a win from a birdie 3. For a while there was cut and thrust, with Britain always in the lead and going 3 up on the 9th. The first round ended in comedy. Barnes almost had the American ball on the green with his second shot while Mitchell pulled his iron

shot well left. Duncan then found he had no niblick (about equal to an 8) in his bag and asked if he could borrow Mitchell's. When told this was against the rules of golf, he decided to try to play a skidding shot with a wood through a bunker and on to the green. Instead, his ball was caught up in sand. Mitchell then failed to get out but Duncan holed out at their second attempt for a 5. The Americans chipped weakly and then took three putts. It all meant that the British pair went in to lunch a commanding 4 up.

At the same point, Boomer and Compston were 1 up, Havers and Gadd 5 up but the Americans were doing better in the last two matches. Here, Cyril Walker and Fred McLeod were all square with Ted Ray and Fred Robson while Emmett French and Joe Stein were 1 up on Ernie Whitcombe and Herbert Jolly. After lunch, Duncan and Mitchell ran away with their match. They went to the turn in 33 to be 9 up and then halved the 10th to win the match by 9 and 8. In the other four games, the United States put up sterner resistance but won not a single point. By coincidence, each match went comfortably enough to Britain by 3 and 2 margins. It was a clean sweep. The American

Fred Robson, Freddie McLeod, Ted Ray and Cyril Walker before their foursomes at Wentworth in 1926

caddy Hagen had brought over with him said, 'Why is it that these fellows can play like a lot of world beaters and then when the championship comes – their own championship – they can't hit a balloon?'.

The Times commented as follows on 5 June 1926:

GOLF
THE RYDER CUP
GREAT BRITAIN'S LEAD

The professional international match for the Trophy presented by Mr Samuel Ryder, of St Albans, for annual competition was begun at Wentworth yesterday, when the foursomes over 36 holes were played and Great Britain gained a commanding lead by winning all five of them. With this advantage it is at least probable that the British professionals will win the match and stem the tide of American victories.

After the glorious failure of our Walker Cup team at St Andrews [they had lost only by 6–5] the professionals evidently felt that something was expected of them, but their admirable performance surprised even their most ardent supporters. They definitely out-golfed their opponents and every victory was thoroughly deserved.

The Times correspondent was probably Sir Guy Campbell and not Bernard Darwin, who was at what was considered to be the far more important Amateur Championship. *The Times* went on to hope that in future Ryder Cups:

the foursome will be insisted on, for there is nothing that brings out the true merit of a golfer so well nor is there a better test of team-work. The modern mania for magnifying the individual, even in an event which is definitely a team affair, cannot but tend towards demoralisation.

Demoralising singles it had to be for the second day, however. And demoralising for the Americans in particular. They had another very bad day indeed. Mitchell was again out first for Britain against the Cornish-born Jim Barnes. He was round in 68 in the morning to lead Jim Barnes by 3 up but then swept away in the afternoon to win by an overwhelming 8 and 7. Barnes politely said afterwards that Mitchell had been kind to him – he hadn't sunk any good putts!

Two more big guns were out next, George Duncan and Walter Hagen who, after an Atlantic crossing and much hard liquor, was described as being 'not in touch'. He lost by 6 and 5. Two other dominant victories went to Arthur Havers, 1923 Open champion, who was 6 up after a 69 in the morning against Fred McLeod and went on to win by 10 and 9, and George Gadd. Gadd's opponent, the Australian-born Joe Kirkwood played poor golf. Gadd needed no more than steady golf to be 8 up at lunch and won by 8 and 7 in the end. Considering that the matches were over 36 holes, the other matches were closer, though there were other very comfortable victories by 6 and 5 and 5 and 4. The United States won just one of the ten matches when Bill Mehlhorn got home by 1 up against Archie Compston.

Another American, Emmett French, had a very good chance to win at dormy 1 on the last tee. However, he took three to reach the last green and then missed a putt for the match. Britain had walked all over the opposition to win by 13–1.

But that American caddy proved to be right when the Open Championship followed towards the end of the month. US amateurs Bobby Jones and George Von Elm finished as champion and tied 3rd while Al Watrous was runner-up and Hagen tied with Von Elm. Americans took all the first four places and had seven in the top ten. Abe Mitchell began with two 78s but was still the best British player, finishing joint 5th. Most of the victorious Wentworth team finished well down the field while seven of the ten-man American team made the top 20 and another was 24th.

So, the first Ryder Cup had been played but, like the 1921 Gleneagles match, has largely been forgotten. The reason is very simple; both British and American PGAs seem to have

Walter Hagen drives during the match – note the characteristic position of his back foot

decided to forget it. Instead, the 1927 match at Worcester, Massachusetts is now recorded as the first. Accounts in match programmes and potted histories often include the tale of how the Ryder Cup came to be presented. Although it varies in detail, the fairy tale goes something like this. At the end of play in the Wentworth match on 5 June a few people were sitting around a table having tea. The ones most often mentioned are Emmett French, Walter Hagen, George Duncan, Samuel Ryder and Abe Mitchell. The British golf writer Geoffrey Cousins also claimed to have been present and wrote later, 'Duncan took advantage of the euphoria created by the victory to persuade Samuel Ryder to promise a cup for an official match. I was there during the preliminary discussions.'

Cousins went on to state that there was little interest at the time and that the trophy eventually cost 100 guineas. Other accounts have given the trophy a higher value, Ryder's nephew, Thomas Anderson Davis going to £250 and the PGA £750. Most agree that the cup was made by Mappin and Webb but unfortunately their records have been lost or destroyed as, it seems, have the relevant files of the PGAs on both sides of the Atlantic. As we have seen, however, this story must be nonsense, for how would Samuel Ryder have replied to George Duncan? Perhaps along the lines of: 'George, didn't you hear that I agreed to present a trophy back in April?' and 'Haven't you seen the golf reports over the last few days? You've just been playing in the first Ryder Cup match!'

So, what were these discussions actually about? My surmise is that it would have been logical for them to be concerned with the next match and the pattern thereafter. By this time, there had been two Britain versus USA internationals – both on British soil. The Walker Cup had already been alternating between Britain and the United States for a few years and it was logical that the Ryder Cup event would follow suit. Indeed, Walter Hagen re-

marked that golfing traffic across the Atlantic had been one-way and that the British should make the journey. (Americans had been crossing over to play in the Open Championship since a little before the First World War and in increasing numbers as the years passed. British presence at the US Open had been much more spasmodic and was usually just an incident in an exhibition tour by such leading players as Harry Vardon, Ted Ray or J. H. Taylor.)

The Ryder Cup itself may well not have been made by the time of the 1926 match by the Sheffield factory of Mappin and Webb. After all, it would have been a fairly rushed job – perhaps six weeks from the idea to the finished trophy. In a different case, anyone looking at the Open Championship claret jug trophy and seeing Young Tom Morris's name inscribed first for the year 1872 would image that he was handed it at some brief ceremony after play ended. Not so, the hallmark reveals that the trophy was not made until 1873.

The likelihood is that much the same sort of thing happened with the Ryder Cup. A picture, in fact, exists which appeared in the *Daily Mirror* for 19 May 1927 which shows Mrs Samuel Ryder handing the trophy to George Gadd, a non-playing member of the 1927 British Ryder Cup team. If the Ryder Cup had been made by the time of the 1926 Wentworth match, one would have expected it to have been in the possession of the PGA in London from that time on. The presentation to Gadd, however, suggests that the trophy had only recently been completed in time for the Worcester, Massachusetts, match in early June.

When the Ryder Cup was made is, however, a side issue next to the debate as to whether the first match was held in 1926 or 1927. Why did the professional golfers' associations on both sides of the Atlantic decide that the 1926 match should not count as the first in the series? It would seem that the answer lies in the composition of the teams. There was no problem in retrospect with the British side which was chosen and announced by the PGA and, though there was some slight controversy over one or two members, it was basically the best team that Great Britain could field. But as I have already pointed out, this was not entirely the case with the Americans. Of the players Hagen named at the end of April (12 including himself), six did not actually play. However, the team's performance in the Open Championship at the end of the month showed that they were fit to represent the United States – once they had adjusted to British conditions.

Many later Ryder Cup teams from both countries, for one reason or another, were not the strongest possible. No, the problem the PGAs had to confront once they sat down to

Mrs Samuel Ryder presents George Gadd, a non-playing member of the team, with the new trophy to take to America

think about the future of Ryder Cup internationals was how to define national qualifications for team membership. The US team was made up of golfers who made their living in the United States. The following were undeniably American: Walter Hagen, Bill Mehlhorn, Al Watrous, Emmett French and Joe Stein. Of the remaining five (half the team), Jim Barnes was Cornish-born, Tommy Armour a Scot, Cyril Walker English, Fred McLeod another Scot and, most incongruous of all, Joe Kirkwood was Australian. All had learned to play the game elsewhere before improving their golf in the United States. In a sense, the 1926 US team members represented US tournament golf rather than the United States as a nation.

Players on both sides of the Atlantic were unhappy with this situation. The British did not fancy the prospect of being defeated by

British-born players, whether naturalised Americans or not, and American professionals had always been unhappy that anyone with a Scottish accent was likely to pick up the plum club jobs. Scotland was the home of golf and Scottish immigrants were thought to bring the golfing wisdom of the ages with them.

When the terms for Ryder Cup qualification were eventually decided they laid down that a player must be both born and resident in the country he represented. Though the rules had been only roughly decided by the time of the 1927 match, the Americans referred to their team as 'homebred'. Because the 1926 US team was not, it seems to have been decided to call the 1927 match the first for the Ryder Cup – even though in fact it was not and such US papers as the *New York Times* referred to it as the second match.

In later years, Samuel Ryder declared he was quite willing that naturalised Americans should qualify, and many top US professionals also regarded such stars as Tommy Armour, Jim Barnes, Macdonald Smith and Harry Cooper as 'fully-qualified' Americans but, in Walter Hagen's words, 'PGA politics in America' ruled them out of Ryder Cup matches.

WENTWORTH, SURREY, ENGLAND 4–5 JUNE 1926

Britain		United States		George Duncan	1	Walter Hagen	0
Captain Ted Ray		*Captain* Walter Hagen		(6 and 5)			
				Aubrey Boomer	1	Tommy Armour	0
Foursomes				(2 and 1)			
Mitchell and Duncan	1	Barnes and Hagen	0	Archie Compston	0	Bill Mehlhorn (1 up)	1
(9 and 8)				George Gadd (8 and 7)	1	Joe Kirkwood	0
Boomer and Compston	1	Armour and Kirkwood	0	Ted Ray (6 and 5)	1	Al Watrous	0
(3 and 2)				Fred Robson (5 and 4)	1	Cyril Walker	0
Gadd and Havers	1	Mehlhorn and Watrous	0	Arthur Havers	1	Freddie McLeod	0
(3 and 2)				(10 and 9)			
Ray and Robson	1	Walker and McLeod	0	Ernest Whitcombe	0	Emmett French	0
(3 and 2)				(halved)			
Whitcombe and Jolly	1	French and Stein	0	Herbert Jolly (3 and 2)	1	Joe Stein	0
(3 and 2)	–		–		–		–
	5		0		8		1
Singles				Final score: Britain 13.			
Abe Mitchell (8 and 7)	1	Jim Barnes	0	United States 1. One match halved			

1927

'To win, they will have to play their best, better than they have ever done.' That is what the *Evening News* thought back in May 1927 about the prospects of the British team. The press is a great deal more optimistic in the 1980s as it seems that Europe has a few cards that may turn out to be trumps and the Americans seem to have none. In 1927, however, we had lost our trump – Abe Mitchell. Chosen as playing captain and winner of the last competition before the team sailed – the *Daily Mail* tournament – he dropped out on doctor's orders. Mitchell was the main British hope in the Open Championship for years and a better man still in matchplay. In the British team at Wentworth the year before, he had won his singles against the American number one, Jim Barnes, with ease. Even so, as the *Evening News* quote shows, the British still felt inferior. The reason was the Open Championship. Only George Duncan, in 1920, and Arthur Havers, in 1923, had won it since the war. Americans took most of the high placings and no one doubted that they had the two best players in the world in Walter Hagen and the amateur Bobby Jones.

Although we had lost Mitchell, the founder of the cup matches, Samuel Ryder, had discussed conditions which greatly improved British chances. They were sensible enough – a player had to be born in and reside in the country he represented which had no immediate effect on the choice of the British team. But it meant that the Americans lost Tommy Armour, Jim Barnes, Fred McLeod and Joe Kirkwood from the 1926 Wentworth team. Out also went Harry Cooper, Jock Hutchison and Willie MacFarlane. Four of these had won either the British or US Open and Tommy Armour took the US Open a few days after the Ryder Cup matches; the others were of championship calibre. The Americans had to find new blood.

The British team members seem old by today's standards. The new playing captain, Ted Ray, was 50, George Duncan 44 and Fred Robson 42. Though most of the remainder were a great deal younger, there were no young hopefuls. The seven who met at Waterloo Station included Ray, Open champion in 1912 and winner of the 1920 US Open; Duncan, Open champion in 1920 and Arthur Havers, champion at Troon in 1923. The others had won no great championships, nor would they in the future. The best were Archie Compston and Charles Whitcombe and the others George Gadd and Fred Robson. Herbert Jolly, Mitchell's replacement, left later and they picked up Aubrey Boomer, pro at St Cloud near Paris, at Cherbourg.

Their departure for Southampton and the *Aquitania* was duly photographed but publicity was diminished by a major event: Charles Lindbergh had just landed his *Spirit of St Louis* at Le Bourget outside Paris, having flown the Atlantic single-handed. The world had a new hero. Five days later, the team landed in New York. Back in St Albans, Abe Mitchell had his appendix removed. After a short pause, the team moved to the venue for the Ryder Cup matches: the Worcester Country Club in Massachusetts, a course designed by the great Donald Ross of Dornoch. They had five practice days, plenty of time to find their land-legs (fore-runner of jet lag), learn the course and adapt to American playing conditions. As well as the Ryder Cup, some were hopeful of winning the US Open at Oakmont a few days afterwards.

The undoubted star of the US team was Walter Hagen, then twice winner of both US and British Opens and a four-time PGA champion, and Gene Sarazen wasn't far behind. He had won the US Open and a couple of PGAs. Leo Diegel was a great talent – except in the majors – and was regarded as one of the supreme shot-makers ever. He won the PGA the following two years. Johnny Farrell won

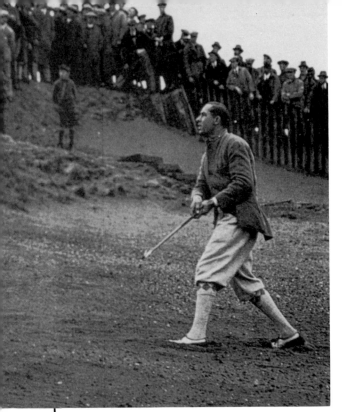

A nattily dressed Walter Hagen recovers from sand

Diegel holed a vast putt for a win on the 11th and then halved the 12th with a 20-foot putt. Not content with that, he next chipped his ball over a stymie for a half on the 13th. Despite these dramatics, the British pair were 5 up at lunch and went further away before winning far from home. Even so, a foursomes result of 3–1 was a major disappointment. The British thought the Americans didn't like this form of golf and couldn't play it and expected to be at least level at the end of the first day.

The singles went worse still. Veteran George Duncan was sent out last because his nerve was expected to hold if there was a tight finish to the match. It did indeed hold; 1 down at lunch and 2 down after 27, he came back and birdied the last to beat Joe Turnesa. It was an encounter fit to settle the Ryder Cup competition in Britain's favour, but alas, that matter was long since decided and Duncan was the only British winner. Charles Whitcombe halved with Sarazen but he had been 5 up after the 15th, back to level after the 25th and then 1 down with a hole to play. Sarazen lost the last to a par. The rest of the team lost and some played none too well. Golden, for example, was round in the morning in 76 but this proved good enough for a lead of 6 up. Al Watrous, out in 33, played the second nine in 45 yet lost only three holes in this stretch. Watrous took 76; like Golden, he too was 6 up. Of the Americans, only Leo Diegel played very well. His 70 was good scoring for 1926 and the days of hickory shafts. It put him 6 up on Ted Ray, who tried a change of putter at lunch.

The Mehlhorn/Compston match was a good one. At lunch they were level and Compston, out in 35 in the afternoon, was 1 up. Although Mehlhorn was 1 up after the 25th, he bunkered his second to the last. Before the invention of the sand iron, one didn't often get down in two from sand, but Mehlhorn did. Against Arthur Havers, Hagen was in top form; only 1 up at lunch he held that position to the 33rd tee. There he drove into the rough and his recovery was still in the rough. He then sent his third into

eight tournaments in 1927, while Al Watrous had been beaten only by Bobby Jones in the 1926 British Open. The remainder of the team was 'Wild Bill' Mehlhorn, Joe Turnesa and Johnny Golden.

In the first day's foursomes, Britain led off with two 'old men', Ted Ray and Fred Robson. They played well. After 18 holes they were level with Hagen and Golden but eventually lost on the 35th green by 2 and 1. At lunch, things were looking bleak; Havers and Jolly were 5 down and our strongest pairing, Duncan and Compston, were 4 down. The Americans had little trouble disposing of them during the second 18. The relatively young pairing of Aubrey Boomer and Charles Whitcombe, aged 30 and 32, respectively, was the success story of the first day. Their opponents, Diegel and Mehlhorn, took a 2-up lead in the shortest time possible but were pulled back to level after seven holes. Boomer and Whitcombe then went ahead for the first time at the 10th. Just after, they were able to overcome a sequence in which

U.S. WINS RYDER CUP FROM BRITISH TEAM

Homebreds Take Six of Eight Singles and Gain Trophy by 9½ to 2½.

CLINCH SERIES AT NOON

Diegel Has Ray 6 Down and Golden's Same Margin Over Jolly Ends All Doubt.

TURNESA IS ONLY LOSER

Bows to Duncan at Last Hole and Sarazen Halves With Whitcombe —Farrell Downs Boomer.

By WILLIAM D. RICHARDSON.
Special to The New York Times.

WORCESTER, Mass., June. 4.— America's homebreds avenged the drubbing that the British professionals gave their pick-up team in England last year by swamping the British professionals in the international matches for the Ryder Cup.

The score was paid off with full interest when the Americans won six of the singles matches at the Worcester Country Club today, halved another and lost only one out of the eight.

Starting with a lead of 3 points to 1 by virtue of their victory in yesterday's foursomes, the homebreds finished the series with a score of 9½ points to 2½. It was not quite as bad a drubbing as the British handed them last year when the score of the first match for the trophy stood 13½ to 1½, but last year England put its full strength into the match while the American side was made up of a number of fill-ins.

Turnesa the Only Loser.

The only member of the American team who went down to defeat today was Joe Turnesa, young Fairview professional, who finished such a close second to Bobby Jones in the open championship at Sciota last year. He lost to George Duncan, the celebrated Scotch star, who won the British open in 1921, but the match went to the last green and Duncan won there by holing a long putt for a birdie 3.

Turnesa led Duncan by two holes going to the twelfth, but a double stymie laid by Duncan there caused the young American to lose a hole that he had won and led to his ultimate downfall on the last green.

The only other match the British salvaged was the one which Charles Whitcombe halved with Gene Sarazen, or rather Sarazen halved with Whitcombe since the British player was 1

up coming to the thirty-sixth, where Sarazen won with a par 4 to halve the match.

Three of the Americans won by long margins. Johnny Farrell, the debonair Metropolitan champion, crushed Aubrey Boomer, star of the British side, by 5 and 4; Johnny Golden swamped his opponent, Herbert Jolly, by 7 and 6, and Leo Diegel smothered big Ted Ray, the British captain, by 7 and 5.

Watrous Also Triumphs.

Al Watrous, the Michigan professional, who played through the series with a split thumb, defeated Fred Robson by 3 and 2; Hagen, the captain of the American side, won from Arthur Havers, former British open champion, by 2 and 1, and Bill Mehlhorn pulled out a victory over Archie Compston, the Manchester giant, by 1 up.

Conditions under which the final matches of the 1927 series were played today were not nearly as good as they were for the Scotch foursome matches yesterday. Auguring perfect weather conditions in the morning when the matches started, the sky clouded around noontime and the afternoon was cold and raw, with a tricky wind that played havoc with many shots. The gallery, however, was larger than yesterday's and the P. G. A. now has a good start toward its fund to be used in sending a defending team to England next year.

Whatever hopes the British team had of atoning for yesterday's unexpected defeat in the foursomes and pulling victory out of the fire by winning the majority of the singles disappeared at noon, when the first half of the thirty-six-hole matches was finished.

Americans Sure to Win.

Even at that early stage the Americans were assured of victory, for Diegel and Golden, the last two members of the team, had their matches in the bag. Diegel, racing around the course in 70 strokes, equaling par, had Ray 6 down, and Golden had Jolly down by the same number of holes.

Counting those two matches won, the Americans had 5 points to the Britishers' 1, and although the remaining six matches were close, the British would have had to win all six to edge out a victory.

No one, however, not even the British, had any idea of that happening, but not one of the Britons gave up until the final putt was holed, and some of them retrieved holes at such an alarming pace as to cause a few shivers.

The only British players who were on the right side of the ledger at the end of the first eighteen holes were Whitcombe and Robson. Whitcombe was 2 up on Sarazen and Robson 1 up on Watrous. Hagen had a one-hole lead on Havers and Farrell and Mehlhorn and Compston were exactly where they started.

America's victory was insured when the Mehlhorn match came up to the last green, for by then Farrell, Golden and Diegel had beaten their men and Bill's narrow-margined victory over Compston lifted their total to 7 points, counting the three points for the foursomes.

The match on which all eyes were focused was that between Farrell and Boomer, and for the first eighteen holes was a beauty. Boomer, playing gorgeously up to the greens, was more than a match for Johnny through the fairway, but the latter was far superior on the greens.

It was there that he eventually broke Boomer's heart. Time and again the Englishman put his ball inside Farrell's on the greens only to stand by and watch his opponent stroke his putts into the hole with unerring accuracy.

Finally, by reason of a few of those heart-breaking one-putters, Johnny reached a point where he was 2 up, but disaster overcame him on the fifteenth and sixteenth holes, and Boomer was able to catch him and finish all square.

Farrell in the Lead.

Early in the afternoon Farrell stole away to a two-hole lead and the finishing touch came on the short eighth when his ball, pushed out to the right, struck the stone wall running alongside the green and bounced onto the edge of the green. Boomer had a beautiful tee shot himself, but it trickled off the green and into a bunker. The result was that he lost the hole to become 3 down and that was the finish of him.

It was typical of the breaks that went against him time after time. Farrell didn't get many, in fact he didn't need many, for he played really excellent golf except for the fifteenth and sixteenth holes in the morning and the second hole in the afternoon. Boomer, however, couldn't get a single one to come his way and the sight of Farrell putting those long approach putts dead to the hole and even dropping a few of them had a depressing effect.

Boomer made his own bed by allowing Farrell to win the first hole, although he was only twenty-five feet from the hole in two, while Johnny was in the rough off the tee. After his second Farrell chipped back to within four feet and after which the Englishman missed a one yarder for the half.

Boomer hit the cup for a 3 on the third and squared the match on the fourth when Farrell dumped a spoon shot into a bunker. Farrell was bunkered again on the long fifth and Boomer won to become 1 up. Then Farrell took the wind out of his opponent's sails by holing a long sixty-footer for a birdie 3 on the seventh after Boomer was close up on his own third from the rough back of the green.

Wins Three in Next Four.

Johnny won three out of the next four holes, Boomer three-putting the tenth from less than seven yards and also the thirteenth. Two down

---

Complete Cards of Players in Ryder Cup Golf Twosomes

FARRELL vs. BOOMER.
Morning Round.
Out—
Farrell ....4 5 4 4 6 3 3 4—36
Boomer ....5 5 4 3 4 3 4 3 4—35
Match all even.
In—
Farrell ....3 5 4 3 4 5 6 4 4—38—74
Boomer ....4 4 5 4 4 4 4 4 6—37—72
Match all even.
Afternoon Round.
Out—
Farrell ....4 6 4 3 5 3 4 4—36
Boomer ....4 6 5 3 6 3 4 4 4—39
Farrell, 3 up.
In—
Farrell 3 5 4 4 3
Boomer 3 5 5 4 4
Farrell, 5 and 4.

MEHLHORN vs. COMPSTON.
Morning Round.
Out—
Mehlhorn ..5 5 4 4 5 4 5 4 4—40
Compston ..4 5 5 4 5 4 3 4 5—41
Mehlhorn, 1 up.
In—
Mehlhorn ..4 4 4 3 5 4 4 5 4—37—77
Compston ..3 4 4 3 4 5 4 4 5—36—77
Match all even.
Afternoon Round.
Out—
Mehlhorn ..4 6 4 3 5 3 3 4 4—36
Compston ..4 6 3 5 4 2 4 3 4—35
Compston, 1 up.
In—
Mehlhorn ..3 5 4 3 5 6 4 4—38—74
Compston ..4 5 4 4 5 4 4 5 4—39—74
Mehlhorn, 1 up.

SARAZEN vs. WHITCOMBE.
Morning Round.
Out—
Sarazen ...4 5 3 4 5 3 4 4 4—36
Whitcombe .5 4 4 3 4 4 4 4 4—36
Match all even.
In—
Sarazen ...4 5 5 4 6 5 4 4 4—41—77
Whitcombe .3 4 4 3 4 5 5 5 5—38—74
Sarazen, 2 down.
Afternoon Round.
Out—
Sarazen ...5 6 5 3 5 2 4 3 4—37
Whitcombe .5 6 5 3 5 3 5 3 4—39
Match all even.

Counting those two matches won, the

In—
Sarazen ....3 4 5 4 4 5 5 6 4—40—77
Whitcombe ..5 4 4 4 4 5 5 5 5—41—80
Match all even.

HAGEN vs. HAVERS.
Morning Round.
Out—
Hagen ....4 6 4 4 5 4 4 3 4—38
Havers ......5 5 4 4 4 3 5 4 4—38
Match all even.
In—
Hagen ....4 5 4 3 5 4 5 5 4—39—77
Havers ......3 4 6 3 6 5 6 5 3—41—79
Hagen, 1 up.
Afternoon Round.
Out—
Hagen ....5 6 4 5 7 2 4 3 5—41
Havers ......5 6 6 3 6 3 5 2 5—41
Hagen, 1 up.
In—
Hagen 3 5 5 4 4 5 5 4
Havers 4 5 5 3 4 6 4 5
Hagen, 2 and 1.

WATROUS vs. ROBSON.
Morning Round.
Out—
Watrous .....5 4 4 2 4 3 4 3 4—33
Robson ......4 5 4 3 4 4 4 3 5—36
Watrous, 3 up.
In—
Watrous .....4 4 5 5 5 6 5 5—45—78
Robson ......3 x 5 4 4 6 5 5 4
Robson, 1 up.
Afternoon Round.
Out—
Watrous .....4 5 4 4 5 4 4 4 5—39
Robson ......5 6 4 4 5 4 5 3 4—40
Match all even.
In—
Watrous 3 4 3 4 4 5 4
Robson 5 4 5 4 5 4
Watrous, 3 and 2.

DIEGEL vs. RAY.
Morning Round.
Out—
Diegel ......4 4 4 2 5 3 4 3 5—34
Ray ....5 7 4 3 5 3 5 4 4—40
Diegel, 4 up.

In—
Diegel ......2 4 4 4 4 5 4 5 4—36—70
Ray ....3 3 4 4 5 5 5 5 4—38—78
Diegel, 6 up.
Afternoon Round.
Out—
Diegel ......5 4 6 3 4 3 4 3 4—36
Ray ....4 5 4 3 6 4 4 2 4—36
Diegel, 6 up.
In—
Diegel 4 4 4 3
Ray 3 5 4 4
Diegel, 7 and 5.

DUNCAN vs. TURNESA.
Morning Round.
Out—
Duncan ......4 4 5 3 5 4 5 5 4—38
Turnesa .....4 5 5 4 4 4 6 4 4—40
Duncan, 2 up.
In—
Duncan ......3 4 5 4 5 5 4 5 4—39—77
Turnesa .....4 4 4 3 4 4 4 5 4—36—76
Turnesa, 1 up.
Afternoon Round.
Out—
Duncan ......4 6 3 5 6 3 4 3 4—38
Turnesa .....5 5 5 4 4 4 3 4 4—38
Turnesa, 1 up.
In—
Duncan ......4 4 5 3 4 7 5 5 3—40—78
Turnesa .....3 4 6 4 5 5 5 5 4—41—79
Duncan, 1 up.

GOLDEN vs. JOLLY.
Morning Round.
Out—
Golden ......4 6 4 3 5 2 4 4 5—37
Jolly ....4 6 5 4 5 4 5 3 6—42
Golden, 4 up.
In—
Golden ......3 4 4 4 5 6 5 4—39—76
Jolly ....4 5 4 3 6 5 6 5 4—42—84
Golden, 6 up.
Afternoon Round.
Out—
Golden ......4 6 4 3 6 3 4 3 4—37
Jolly ....4 6 4 3 5 4 x 3 4
Golden, 7 up.
In—
Golden 2 5 4
Jolly 5 4 4
Golden, 7 and 6.

PAR FOR THE COURSE.

Hole	Yds.	Par	Hole	Yds.	Par
1	335	4	10	155	3
2	570	5	11	400	4
3	325	4	12	450	4
4	325	4	13	195	3
5	450	5	14	350	4
6	180	3	15	555	5
7	450	4	16	385	4
8	175	3	17	460	4
9	405	4	18	555	4
Total	3,165	35	Total	3,275	35
Grand total—6,440 yards; par, 70.					

How The New York Times *reported the American victory in the 1927 Ryder Cup. In the third para, note that the paper describes this as the* second *match for the trophy*

Ted Ray, captain of the losing team, addresses the crowd and the winning US team at Worcester, Massachusetts. The American team members are (left to right) Joe Turnesa, Leo Diegel, Bill Mehlhorn, Johnny Golden, Al Espinosa, Johnny Farrell, Gene Sarazen and Al Watrous

a bunker and was not close to the hole with his fourth. He holed his putt and Havers took 3 to get down. That, more or less, was that – 2 down with three to play.

Of course, there were post-mortems. Why had Britain lost so heavily? George Gadd, who had brought the cup along but was then dropped from the team, said of the Americans, 'They never missed a putt'. He also thought they had 'mechanicalised the game'. Bernard Darwin of *The Times* was of the same opinion, 'They have mastered the art of doing the same thing over and over'. Our men might have flair but the Americans had grooved repeating swings. I think the heart of the problem was rather different. The British players were club pros whose main job was to keep their members happy. The Americans were primarily tournament players which, in the 1980s, they all are. Some, however, thought the British captain had given his opponents a good start by announcing his order of battle to the press so that Hagen was able to line up his team as he wished.

WORCESTER, MASSACHUSETTS, USA 3–4 JUNE 1927

United States		Great Britain and Ireland	
Captain Walter Hagen		*Captain* Ted Ray	
Foursomes			
Hagen and Golden (2 and 1)	1	Ray and Robson	0
Farrell and Turnesa (8 and 6)	1	Duncan and Compston	0
Sarazen and Watrous (3 and 2)	1	Havers and Jolly	0
Diegel and Mehlhorn	0	Boomer and Whitcombe (7 and 5)	1
	3		1
Singles			
Bill Mehlhorn (1 hole)	1	Archie Compston	0
Johnny Farrell (5 and 4)	1	Aubrey Boomer	0
Johnny Golden (8 and 7)	1	Herbert Jolly	0
Leo Diegel (7 and 5)	1	Ted Ray	0
Gene Sarazen (halved)	0	Charles Whitcombe	0
Walter Hagen (2 and 1)	1	Arthur Havers	0
Al Watrous (3 and 2)	1	Fred Robson	0
Joe Turnesa	0	George Duncan (1 up)	1
	6		1

Final score: United States 9
Great Britain and Ireland 2.
One match halved

HOME AND AWAY
(1929–1937)

1929

Despite their major defeat in the USA, the overwhelming British wins in 1921 and 1926 gave cause for hope that things would get back to normal in 1929 when the match was to be played at Moortown, a predominantly moorland course near Leeds. The Americans had financed their trip to England by a series of exhibition matches which had raised some $6,000. Equipment manufacturers had contributed $2,650 and another $2,000 had come in from other sources. I wonder what that would pay for today: bags and slacks?

Although the Americans were now all native-born, their origins were varied indeed. Two were of English extraction, one Irish, two Italian, two German, one Hungarian, one Spanish and one Polish. Johnny Golden, the 'Hungarian', was born in the Austro-Hungarian empire and brought over to the USA as a child. The remainder were born in the USA. Hagen, in January, had announced that foreign-born players should be allowed; after all, they had been permitted to fight in the war.

Walter Hagen (left) returns the Ryder Cup to J. H. Batley of the PGA before the 1929 match

Of the British team, two were non-resident, Percy Alliss having taken a job at the Wannsee Golf Club, Berlin, and Aubrey Boomer was at St Cloud, near Paris. Such players would later be excluded.

Hagen, with his ten-man team consisting of himself as captain, Al Espinosa, Johnny Farrell, Joe Turnesa, Leo Diegel, Ed Dudley, Gene Sarazen, Al Watrous, Johnny Golden and Horton Smith, had decided to try to give every man a game. This was to become normal US practice; if you'd made the team, you deserved to get a game. It was also an indication of US superiority. The British generally had to use

Left *Gene and Mrs Sarazen crossing the Atlantic on the* Mauretania *in the 1920s*

The Americans arrive at Paddington Station on their way to defend the trophy in 1929: (standing l to r) Horton Smith (with scarf), Al Watrous, Johnny Golden, Ed Dudley, Joe Turnesa and Johnny Farrell. (Foreground) Al Espinosa, Gene Sarazen, Walter Hagen and Leo Diegel

the men who were in best form and on this occasion, Percy Alliss and Stewart Burns were described as 'short of practice', a polite form of words meaning 'playing badly'. They played in neither foursomes or singles.

One of the Americans was in trouble; Horton Smith had been winning all the tournaments on the US winter Tour using the new steel shafts. For British soil, he had to accustom himself to hickory shafts, a far more difficult task than changing from one make of club to another, as players frequently do today when well paid to play different manufacturers' clubs with a change of country. He spent many lonely hours in practice. If this was a surprise to British spectators, the sight of the whole US team lined up on the practice ground hitting balls away was a greater one. At this time, the British seemed to prefer playing to hone their games. There was, however, an extra feature that seems quaint today. On 22 April, just a few days before the match began, it was reported that 'the players are undergoing special treatment at the Harrogate Baths'. The Americans, shortly after disembarking from the *Mauretania* had steam baths at Ramsgate. Despite the benefits of 'taking the waters', the US team were chiefly hot favourites because they had dominated the Open Championship from 1921.

The British hoped that a nasty spell of late April weather would ruin those lissome, rhythmic American swings and for the 36-hole foursomes on the first day, 26 April, the weather was indeed very cold but dry and with only a light wind. An observer noted, 'The American players looked less pinched and wore rather fewer sweaters'.

The British threw Charles Whitcombe and Archie Compston, considered their best two individuals, into the top foursomes. They met Johnny Farrell, reigning US Open champion, and Joe Turnesa; the standard of play proved to be the worst of the four matches. The lead shifted from side to side in the morning, with the British getting back to square five times. Compston came in for keen criticism when he lost a hole through hitting the US ball in a bunker when he could have requested it be marked. The British were 1 up, however, on the last tee, when Whitcombe sliced into a gorse bush and Compston could only drop out under penalty. To make matters worse, he then sent the British ball into a greenside bunker. But the Americans were also having trouble; Farrell hooked into the rough and Turnesa followed with another hook close to the palings, leaving Farrell barely room to swing and with the high refreshment tent to carry. He played the shot of the match, actually hitting the flag and finishing a few feet away. All square.

The most dominant performance of any pair came from Leo Diegel, a fine performer in Ryder Cup matches, and Al Espinosa, who was to tie with Bobby Jones for the US Open later that year. By lunch, they were 7 up after a 66. Afterwards, Aubrey Boomer and George Duncan could not get back into the match.

Diegel was attracting more attention than any other single player because of a putting style he had invented. Many of his contemporaries thought him the most talented player in the game but his short putting was always unreliable and dreadful when he had a major championship in his reach. Diegel decided to take the wrists out of the putting stroke (as most players do today) by crouching low from the waist and bending both elbows; his left pointed directly at the hole and his right away from it. Diegel then swung the club so that all movement came from the shoulders and, lo and behold, it actually worked. After Moortown, half the British golfing nation were 'Diegeling', but neither they nor Diegel found that the cramped method worked for long.

In the third match, Abe Mitchell and Fred Robson had a close contest with Gene Sarazen and Ed Dudley. All square at lunch, they managed to jump into a lead afterwards and held on steadily to the end. This meant that the match as a whole was square at 1 point each.

Bringing up the rear for the USA was the strong pairing of Walter Hagen, reigning

Members of the British and US teams who met at Moortown as portrayed by a contemporary cartoonist

British Open champion, and Johnny Golden, a short but straight hitter who could also putt well. They faced E. R. Whitcombe and Henry Cotton, the new young hope of British golf who was making his first Ryder Cup appearance. He played the best golf through the green but, as was so often the case, the Americans holed the putts. At lunch they were 2 up, went 4 ahead afterwards and though they were pulled back won the last two holes, and the match.

Hagen had predicted the result, saying 'I shall win anyway. I always do.'

Was all lost? At the end of the first day such was the general opinion. Americans hardly knew what foursomes golf was; Hagen had to explain the whole procedure to some of his team. The British were quite used to foursomes golf and if we couldn't beat the Americans at 'our' traditional form of the game, there was surely less chance of our doing so in the singles.

The 27 April was Cup Final day (Bolton v Portsmouth) and the crowds at Moortown, who had paid 3 shillings at the gates, behaved on both days as if they were watching football. They cheered whenever an American ball fell into a bunker or a short putt was missed, setting an example which was to be repeated over the years. Hagen brought in Horton Smith and Al Watrous for Golden and Dudley. 'I want to give all the boys a chance', he said. The British captain, George Duncan, put out the same eight players. He had, however, withdrawn his team list when Hagen would not announce his singles players until after the foursomes. Once again, Charles Whitcombe led off and played superbly. In the morning he was round in 68 against par of 76 to be 6 up. That was more or less that for Farrell. J. H. Taylor said he'd never seen better golf.

The second match saw the two captains opposed after Duncan said he would play at number two. Walter Hagen told his team, 'Boys, there's a point for our team right there'. Instead he received what he later called 'a terrific shellacking'. Duncan always felt he had the measure of Hagen in matchplay and he certainly had that day at Moortown. He was round in an approximate 69 in the first round, Hagen trying to hold on with some brave holing out but losing by 10 and 8.

Well though Diegel had played in the foursomes, he was still not satisfied with his putting although he had spent a year trying to perfect his method. For the singles, he tried painting the shaft a different colour. He must have been pleased after holing a putt of some four yards on the first hole for a birdie 4 after driving into a bunker. His opponent, Abe Mitchell, was the best British exponent of matchplay during the 1920s and he kept to his high standards in the morning to be round in 71. Unfortunately it wasn't good enough. Diegel, at a late point, looked likely to have an unbelievable 63 when he pitched apparently dead on the 17th. How-

Right *Horton Smith*

The presentation of the trophy, 1929. Present are (rear, l to r) Archie Compston, Horton Smith, Al Watrous, Johnny Farrell, Al Espinosa (leaning forward), Abe Mitchell, Joe Turnesa, Stewart Burns, Henry Cotton and Ed Dudley. (Seated) Ernest Whitcombe, Gene Sarazen, Percy Alliss, Charles Whitcombe, George Duncan, Samuel Ryder, Walter Hagen, an official, Leo Diegel, Johnny Golden, Aubrey Boomer and Fred Robson

ever, he missed the putt and took 2 in a bunker on the last; only a 65. He went on to win by 9 and 8.

In the next match, Compston always had something in hand on Sarazen and his win levelled the match as a whole. The next British team member was Aubrey Boomer who was 2 down against Joe Turnesa with four to play before lunch but produced a 4, 4, 3, 4 finish to be 2 up. Afterwards he was never behind and eventually won the point that took Britain into the lead.

Twenty-year-old Horton Smith, apparently now used to wooden shafts, levelled the match once more. Although behind in the morning round, he squared on the 18th, getting round a partial stymie in the process. His opponent, Fred Robson, managed to get to 2 up in the afternoon but his game collapsed over the final nine, Smith winning by 4 and 2. The baby of the American team had won. Much now rested on the British baby, Henry Cotton, aged 22. He faced Al Watrous, who had come so close to winning the 1926 British Open. Watrous went out in a dominating 33 but the holes began to come back with Cotton playing steadily. On the 18th, he was only 1 down and then chipped in for a winning 3 from a grassy lane amongst the gorse.

Although Cotton lost the 1st after lunch, he was 2 up after the 8th and unwavering thereafter, winning by 4 and 3. It was all over and the Ryder Cup was regained. The 6 matches to 4 result would have looked even better if Ernest Whitcombe had not allowed Al Espinosa to win the last two holes to halve their match.

Perhaps the Americans had not allowed themselves enough time to 'get their land legs' and accustom themselves to British playing conditions and harsh spring weather. The British triumph certainly looked less convincing after the Open at Muirfield a month later.

Hagen won by 6 strokes; US Ryder Cup team players occupied the first three places; US players took eight of the top ten places though three of these players were not qualified by birth to represent the USA in the Ryder Cup itself. Of the British team, only Mitchell and Percy Alliss, joint 4th, made any sort of showing. Hagen, on his return to the USA with the Open Championship trophy, said he was pleased not to have left both cups behind. Certainly, he'd got the one he cared most about.

MOORTOWN, LEEDS, YORKSHIRE, ENGLAND 26–27 APRIL 1929

Great Britain and Ireland		United States	
Captain George Duncan		*Captain* Walter Hagen	
Foursomes			
Whitcombe and Compston (halved)	0	Farrell and Turnesa	0
Boomer and Duncan	0	Diegel and Espinosa (7 and 5)	1
Mitchell and Robson (2 and 1)	1	Sarazen and Ed Dudley	0
Whitcombe and Cotton	0	Golden and Hagen (2 up)	1
	–		–
	1		2
Singles			
Charles Whitcombe (8 and 6)	1	Johnny Farrell	0
George Duncan (10 and 8)	1	Walter Hagen	0
Abe Mitchell	0	Leo Diegel (9 and 8)	1
Archie Compston (6 and 4)	1	Gene Sarazen	0
Aubrey Boomer (4 and 3)	1	Joe Turnesa	0
Fred Robson	0	Horton Smith (4 and 2)	1
Henry Cotton (4 and 3)	1	Al Watrous	0
Ernest Whitcombe (halved)	0	Al Espinosa	0
	–		–
	5		2

Final score: Great Britain and Ireland 6
United States 4.
Two matches halved

1931

If the Americans hadn't much cared for the weather at Moortown, the British hated it at Scioto, Columbus, Ohio for the return match in 1931. It was the course where Bobby Jones had won the 1926 US Open and where Jack Nicklaus would learn to play golf some 20 years later. The British team was much weakened by the absence of Percy Alliss, Aubrey Boomer and Henry Cotton. Alliss and Boomer had club jobs in Germany and France and were ruled out because they were not British residents. Cotton had refused to agree to a rule imposed by the British PGA that members of the team should share any exhibition money from their six-week tour equally. Nor would he agree to come home on the same ship as the others. The team sailed on 10 June. On 6 June, Cotton, who had tied for the lead in the British Open at Carnoustie after two rounds, was re-invited to join the team – provided that he agreed to the share-out. Always an independent spirit, he again refused so Bert Hodson made up the ten-man team. At around the same time, Herbert Jolly withdrew on the grounds that he was playing badly and the 1923 British Open champion, Arthur Havers, went in his place. Only two of the team were under 30, Hodson and Syd Easterbrook.

The inclusion of American Leo Diegel seemed to break the rules as he was registered as a professional at the Agua Caliente Golf Club in Mexico. However, the problem was solved when it turned out that Diegel lived just across the border in the USA. US team selection had been rigorous and was not finally decided until a day or so before the match. The last four places were filled by the leaders of a four-round qualifying event which let Billy Burke, Whiffy Cox and Craig Wood through. There was then an 18-hole play-off for three who had tied in the next position with Denny Shute succeeding.

The British side that sailed on the RMS *Majestic* was encouraged by good wishes from Samuel Ryder who declared at a farewell banquet, 'I am quite sure we will win. British

strophic. Archie Compston and W. H. Davies were heavily defeated, 8 and 7, by Gene Sarazen and Johnny Farrell. George Duncan and Arthur Havers fared even worse against Hagen and Shute, losing by 10 and 9. There had been a public outcry when Duncan, 1920 British Open champion, was originally omitted from the team. However, he was 48 years old and had won nothing of note for some years. Duncan began well enough with a three-hundred yard drive, while Hagen played a poor tee shot. Even so, the Americans won the hole. They were 5 up after nine holes and a frightening ten ahead at the end of the first round. After lunch, the British did well to stave off the inevitable a while longer and Duncan complained bitterly about the 100 degree heat and humidity. In the third match, Abe Mitchell and Fred Robson jumped straight into a 2-up lead but Diegel and Al Espinosa had squared by the turn and led by 2 at lunch. Even so, the only British point came from this match, by 3 and 1, the fourth game going to the USA.

The result was put beyond doubt by the top two singles on the second day, with Billy Burke and Gene Sarazen both winning by 7 and 6 against Archie Compston and Fred Robson. The second match contained a decisive moment. It was closely contested when Robson put his tee shot on the green at a par 3 while Sarazen hooked violently. His ball clattered into a stack of crates and ricochetted into a refreshment stand. Sarazen found that the ball had settled into a crack in the concrete floor. A refrigerator was moved and Sarazen then chipped through a window to ten feet or so and holed the putt. Robson, imagining his opponent had casually tossed the ball onto the green, equally casually three-putted. Sarazen says that after Robson learned the true situation he never played another good shot. In the third match, W. H. Davies delayed defeat by beating Farrell

golf has taken on a new chapter of its history. They had been persuaded by all sorts of Jeremiahs that they were inferior to the Americans but they are not.' The captain, Charles Whitcombe, sounded rather less confident, 'All members of the team are triers and gentlemen. If we lose, we will lose like sportsmen.'

Cotton and Alliss also travelled to the USA to report on the competition for the press. Perhaps Cotton, in particular, intended to rub in the reason for his non-selection by playing with Alliss in an exhibition match in Columbus.

The British start in the foursomes was cata-

Al and Abe Espinosa with Densmore Shute (centre) pose for a publicity shot

vast empire found the game tolerable in such unfavourable climates as tropical West Africa and Malaya, the desert conditions of the Sudan and Arabia, and the plains of India. After Scioto, however, the British PGA were opposed to the event being fought out in the heat of an American summer and it never was again.

The great British golf writer, Bernard Darwin, summed up shortly after the match, 'The result of the Ryder Cup may be rather disappointing but can hardly be surprising except to those who regard it as a patriotic duty to expect what they know will not happen'. However, he thought the weather was important, 'Cold is the one and only thing that is at all likely to beat the Americans'.

4 and 3 but the next four matches went comfortably to America, Walter Hagen taking the decisive point against Charles Whitcombe. No doubt the captains had agreed to play each other as at Moortown. Playing last, Havers gave some respectability to the match score by beating Craig Wood.

The Scioto result was much the same as the final score of 9 to 2 in Worcester, Massachusetts in 1927: 9 to 3, although in 1927 there was one halved match. It is difficult to believe that the heat had been a decisive factor in the British defeat. After all, British golfers throughout a

SCIOTO, COLUMBUS, OHIO, USA
26–27 JUNE 1931

United States		Great Britain and Ireland	
Captain Walter Hagen		*Captain* C. A. Whitcombe	
Foursomes			
Sarazen and Farrell (8 and 7)	1	Compston and Davies	0
Hagen and Shute (10 and 9)	1	Duncan and Havers	0
Diegel and Espinosa	0	Mitchell and Robson (3 and 1)	1
Burke and Cox (3 and 2)	1	Syd Easterbrook and Whitcombe	0
	–		–
	3		1
Singles			
Billy Burke (7 and 6)	1	Archie Compston	0
Gene Sarazen (7 and 6)	1	Fred Robson	0
Johnny Farrell	0	W. H. Davies (4 and 3)	1
Whiffy Cox (3 and 1)	1	Abe Mitchell	0
Walter Hagen (4 and 3)	1	Charles Whitcombe	0
Denny Shute (8 and 6)	1	Bert Hodson	0
Al Espinosa (2 and 1)	1	Ernest Whitcombe	0
Craig Wood	0	Arthur Havers (4 and 3)	1
	–		–
	6		2

Final score: United States 9 Great Britain and Ireland 3

1933

By chance, the next Ryder Cup match was played on exactly the same dates as Scioto – 26 and 27 June. This time the venue was Southport and Ainsdale in Lancashire. As usual, the USA were handicapped by the fact that British-born players were banned. Samuel Ryder had in fact indicated that he was quite willing for the conditions to be altered so that players who had developed their games in the USA would qualify. In some cases the effect of the rules was absurd; Harry Cooper, perhaps the outstanding US Tour player from the late 1920s to late 1930s, was excluded even though his parents had emigrated from Leatherhead in Surrey when he was only ten years old.

Walter Hagen later wrote that the reason a change was never made was 'PGA politics'. Representing the USA in the Ryder Cup brought financial advantages and perhaps most importantly, it earned the players at least temporary fame for having represented their country. It also meant a free trip to Britain and an opportunity to enter the British Open and possibly a visit to France for more competition

The photographer arranges the 1933 US team to watch Walter Hagen swing: (left to right) Paul Runyan, Ed Dudley, Horton Smith, Craig Wood, Billy Burke, Densmore Shute, Leo Diegel and Olin Dutra

or pleasure. Looking back 50 years and more from a time when golf is much more international, it seems absurd that players were ever excluded because they were not working in club jobs in their native land even though they continued to play in British tournaments. Henry Cotton, at Royal Waterloo in Belgium, was ineligible for the Southport match as was Aubrey Boomer, still in France. Percy Alliss had returned from several years in Germany and was selected.

For the first time, the British PGA nominated a non-playing captain – five-times Open champion J. H. Taylor. There had been a tendency in the press to consider that the Americans were physically fitter than the British but Taylor set about to retrieve the situation. He brought in a physical training specialist, Lieutenant Alick Stark, a son-in-law of Andrew Kirkaldy, from the University of St

Andrews. He had the team out of bed at 6.30 a.m. running on the sands and then gave them all a rub down. The 62-year-old Taylor ran with his team; it certainly sounds more beneficial than taking the waters in Harrogate. Taylor tackled the opposition captain, Walter Hagen, equally effectively. When the time came to exchange team lists in order of play, Hagen didn't appear then another appointment was made and again – no Hagen. Taylor let it be known that if it happened a third time he would call off the match.

They met in apparently friendly spirit, as the picture on page 43 shows. Samuel Ryder appears to be conferring his blessing on the British captain.

The result of all this was that the starter was eventually able to announce, 'Mr Sarazen will drive the first ball for America'. He and Walter Hagen led off against Percy Alliss and Charles Whitcombe.

After nine holes, the Americans were 1 up but fell away to 3 down by lunch. Though the pair were good friends, rumour had it that Hagen had decided to play with Sarazen to demonstrate that they were not enemies, as was widely believed. With ten holes to play, the Americans were four holes to the bad but then there came a swing that was so common in Ryder Cup matches; they proved themselves the stronger finishers. On the 9th, Hagen sank a putt of five yards while Charles Whitcombe missed from much closer. The next two holes went to the USA, Whitcombe missing a tiny putt on the 11th. The following four holes were halved before some ragged play on the 16th. This was the famous Gumbley's, a hole of just

J. H. Taylor (left) and Walter Hagen meet to exchange their orders of battle as Sam Ryder gives Taylor his blessing

under five hundred yards with a carry over large sandhills for the second shot. Hagen played a poor drive, meaning that the Americans could only get home in three. At this point, Alliss sliced into trouble but Whitcombe played a fine recovery to the front of the green. Alliss then putted short and Whitcombe missed the next. The match was all square.

On the 17th, Britain again went into the lead after a hooked shot from the Americans but Alliss threw the last hole away. He put his second shot into a bunker and missed the putt after Whitcombe had recovered to four feet. Brilliant US golf had not brought the recovery. The British took 77 for the second round.

In the second match, Abe Mitchell and Havers gave a splendid display of accurate pitching and firm holing out to lead Olin Dutra and Denny Shute by four holes at lunch. The third match finished level at the same stage when Paul Runyan, a short-game wizard, lofted a stymie on the 18th to draw level with W. H.

Davies and Syd Easterbrook of Britain. Later, however, the British got to dormy 2 up before losing the 17th after a bunkered second shot. Though Craig Wood sent the American tee shot into wild country, Davies did little better on the last, bunkering the tee shot. However, all was well for Britain when the hole was halved in 5.

The fourth match, the two Alfs – Padgham and Perry – against Ed Dudley and Billy Burke was a feast of good play from both pairs. The Americans led at lunch but were pulled back to level after six holes in the afternoon. The Americans eventually got ahead on the 17th when Burke holed a putt of several yards and that was that.

At the end of the first day the score stood at 2–1 to Britain, a useful lead with eight singles, and a visit from the Prince of Wales, to come on the second day. The crowds were enormous; an estimated 15,000 people came to watch, many of whom were keener to see the Prince of Wales than the golf. However, with large crowds

expected in such a holiday area, an army of stewards had been provided. They could be identified by the long bamboo 'lances' they carried with pennants fluttering at the tips. They were not always able to control the crowds, though, who flooded wildly around the course. One spectator, when told his behaviour might upset the players retorted, 'Players be damned. I've come to see the game.' Others were apt to cheer when an American ball found sand or a short putt failed to drop. Years later, Sarazen said that Southport had been more like a carnival ground than a golf course and remarked that the Ryder Cup matches had suffered, particularly in England, from not being played on outstanding courses. In both countries, the choice of course has often been dictated by sponsorship money from a club, individual or some organisation such as a town council.

At lunch, the British team still held its slim lead. The singles stood all square, each team

Ed Dudley, Johnny Farrell, Sir Philip Sassoon, Horton Smith, Olin Dutra and Craig Wood (rear). (Seated) Paul Runyan, Leo Diegel, the Duke of Kent, Walter Hagen, the Prince of Wales, Gene Sarazen, Densmore Shute and Billy Burke

being ahead in three matches and two being square. Two matches looked almost settled. Horton Smith was 5 up on Charles Whitcombe in the last match out, while Abe Mitchell was 5 up on Olin Dutra in the second. This last match was one of the most remarkable ever played in Ryder Cup singles over 36 holes. Dutra opened up with a vast putt to win the 1st but Mitchell replied with a similar length putt to take the 2nd. Playing steady golf, the American gradually crept ahead until he was 3 up after nine but the tide turned on the 11th with a good putt from Mitchell. Dutra then began to be troubled by a hook and the flow of holes was all to the Englishman. The round ended in comedy when Dutra first took 2 to get out of a bunker on the

The state of play near the end of the match

17th and then knocked Mitchell's ball into the hole on the last when trying to avoid a stymie. That was six holes in a row to the Englishman. After lunch, the American won the 1st hole with a very long putt but Mitchell continued to cruise away after this to win by 9 and 8.

Sarazen was playing number one for the USA against Alf Padgham, the British player in the best form. Hagen had wanted to drop him altogether, considering he had played badly in their foursomes, but Sarazen declared that he thought he was performing well. Hagen gave way – after all, Sarazen had won the Open Championships of both Britain and the USA the previous year! Hagen put him out first because he thought he would lose anyway and

Sarazen might as well be the sacrificial lamb against Padgham. Early on, poor putting prevented Padgham from establishing a good lead but he led by one hole after nine before Sarazen sank a number of good putts on the homeward nine. Although Padgham sank a putt from the back of the 18th for a win, he still lunched 1 down. The pattern continued much the same in the afternoon, the future British Open champion hitting the better shots through the green but putting well below Sarazen's standards. The American won the match by 6 and 4.

In the third match, Arthur Lacey took a 2-up lead immediately. Thereafter fortunes swung to and fro until Lacey took 4 to get down from just 50 yards on the 34th and on the next Hagen hit a bad drive but still got his 4 on his 450-yard hole with a good run-up and single putt. This

American singles win made the match level overall. With Smith almost certain to beat Whitcombe in the final match, the next four were vital. The balance then swung towards the United States as Craig Wood beat W. H. Davies in the fourth match.

As far as Britain was concerned the competition now rested on, in order of importance, Percy Alliss, opposed by Paul Runyan; Arthur Havers against Leo Diegel; and Syd Easterbrook, who had lost his first three holes to Denny Shute. Alliss brought home a win first. One up at lunch, he was all square with three to play. He won the 16th and it was suddenly all over as Runyan's attempted explosion shot from sand went out of bounds. Havers, all square with Diegel after the morning's play, produced the better golf in the afternoon and went on to win by 4 and 3. Then came the news that Charles Whitcombe was making a very good fight back from 5 down at lunch. In a tense finish, he went down by 2 and 1. The position was Great Britain 5; United States 5.

Only one match remained out on the course Easterbrook and Shute. After losing those first three holes as a result of poor putting Easterbrook had got back to square before going into lunch 1 down. In the second round, there was nothing in it all the way and the pair came to the last tee level. There were two pot bunkers along the left of the fairway. Both players found sand with their tee shots. Shute went for the green but found another bunker. Easterbrook played safely out, but well short of the green. After both had played their third shots, their balls were a nearly equal distance from the hole, at about five yards. It was Shute's turn to putt first. Hagen was chatting with the Prince of Wales. Should he go over to Shute and tell him to be sure to play safe? After all, a halved match would mean that the USA would retain the Ryder Cup. He decided it would perhaps be an afront to the heir to the throne. Shute set off boldly; too boldly. On the slippery greens, his ball coasted some six feet past the hole. Easterbrook did a little better as his ball stopped about

three, perhaps even four feet away. Shute, to some cheering, missed and to a great roar, Easterbrook holed his. The Ryder Cup was won and British professionals had still not been defeated by Americans on home soil.

Bernard Darwin's earlier remarks about bad weather being essential to an American defeat had proved unfounded; it had been most pleasant for players and spectators alike. Many of those spectators had come for a glimpse of the Prince of Wales, perhaps the most popular royal ever. Two thousand people had clustered around the clubhouse to await his arrival and so many had followed when he had attempted to watch the Hagen/Lacey match that he had given up and walked in. (Hagen, incidentally, had rather grandly introduced the Prince to his British opponent!)

The Prince presented the trophy, saying that as a golfer himself he would rather face a long putt and a tight game than make a speech. J. H. Taylor, trophy in hand, responded by saying, 'I am the proudest man in the British Commonwealth of people at this moment'. He also thanked 'the vast concourse of people for their magnificent behaviour during the past two days'. Well, it could have been a good deal worse but magnificent it was not. Hagen handled the speech demanded of him with his usual charm. It all sounded quite British. He was, for instance, only 'slightly disappointed'. He had 'a place for the cup on the table in the *Aquitania* coming over and we told them to reserve a place going back'.

Both teams shortly went off to St Andrews for the Open Championship where American honour was restored, just as it had been after the Moortown defeat. US players took five of the first six places, Craig Wood and Densmore Shute tying for the championship. The hero of Southport, Easterbrook was the only British player in that top six, taking a seven when in a position to win. In later years he dropped out of the game, even declaring that he hated it. The champion? The scriptwriter got it right: Densmore Shute.

The climax of the 1933 match arrives as Densmore Shute is about to lose the Ryder Cup. Opponent Syd Easterbrook awaits his turn to play

---

SOUTHPORT AND AINSDALE, LANCASHIRE, ENGLAND
26–27 JUNE 1933

Great Britain and Ireland		United States	
Captain J. H. Taylor		*Captain* Walter Hagen	
Alliss and Whitcombe (halved)	0	Sarazen and Hagen	0
Mitchell and Havers (3 and 2)	1	Dutra and Shute	0
Davies and Easterbrook (1 up)	1	Wood and Runyan	0
Padgham and Alf Perry	0	Ed Dudley and Billy Burke (1 up)	1
	–		–
	2		1
Singles			
Alf Padgham	0	Gene Sarazen (6 and 4)	1
Abe Mitchell (9 and 8)	1	Olin Dutra	0
Arthur Lacey	0	Walter Hagen (2 and 1)	1
W. H. Davies	0	Craig Wood (4 and 3)	1
Percy Alliss (2 and 1)	1	Paul Runyan	0
Arthur Havers (4 and 3)	1	Leo Diegel	0
Syd Easterbrook (1 up)	1	Denny Shute	0
Charles Whitcombe	0	Horton Smith (2 and 1)	1
	–		–
	4		4

Final score: Great Britain and Ireland 6
United States 5.
One match halved

1935

In 1935, the British were most perturbed at the thought of playing in the summer heat of America and to avoid it, they were prepared to pass up the opportunity of competing in the US Open. Many had found they could not eat, sleep or play golf in the heat of 1931. The match was arranged for 28 and 29 September at Ridgewood, New Jersey. Once again Henry Cotton, still at Royal Waterloo, was ineligible for the team. It is remarkable how few Ryder Cup matches he took part in, in a span at the top which lasted from the late 1920s to the early 1950s. More remarkable than this though was one aspect of the British team selection; three brothers played for the first and last time. They were the Whitcombe brothers Charles, Ernest and Reg, born in Burnham, Somerset.

On departure, there was the usual optimism. In 1935 far more space was devoted in the press to discussing Ryder Cup prospects, the farewell banquet, and to photographs of the team embarking on the boat train in London than to the match itself. Press agency reports were often relied on and when the results were bad only those of the individual matches were given, perhaps with a comment on an occasional highlight. Unfortunately, there were very few of these for Britain at Ridgewood. After the first three foursomes, which went heavily to the USA, the match was well on its way to an inevitable conclusion but two of the Whitcombe brothers did extremely well, winning the last of the four foursomes by 1 up against Olin Dutra and the interestingly named Ky Laffoon. Because of his high cheek bones, he was once asked if he was of American Indian extraction. Laffoon paused, thought there might be some publicity in it, and said that he was.

The top three foursomes, however, went to the USA very comfortably, no match being closer than 6 and 5. All this from a team that Bernard Darwin, always realistic about British Ryder Cup chances, reckoned the best to have set sail across the Atlantic. Although Charles had won in the foursomes with brother Ernie, he dropped himself from the singles and brought in the future 1939 Open champion, Dick Burton, and his brother Reg Whitcombe who would also be a champion in 1938.

A look at the list of results of the eight singles reveals that the USA lost only one match with a couple halved. However, there were no humiliating margins of defeat for Britain to contemplate over 36 holes; the defeat by 5 and 3 of

Reg, Ernest and Charles Whitcombe shortly before the 1935 match in which all three took part

Dick Burton by Paul Runyan was the biggest. In fact, Britain did far better than the results indicate; despite the burden of entering the singles 3–1 behind, Britain still seemed to have a chance of winning about three-quarters of the way through the singles. But, as was so often the case until the 1980s, the Americans lasted the course better and surged through over the final nine holes. It is debateable why this should happen; the average age of British team members was higher than it is today, but the Americans were also older. A lack of physical stamina was not, therefore, the reason. The Americans, however, were far more used to the rigours of tournament play as the US Tour had

begun to expand and competitions in the British Isles remained limited. It is often said today that an event is won over the last nine holes and that is why the Americans had the edge in the 1935 singles.

The top match, Sarazen versus a new player, Jack Busson, was always close but Sarazen put in a strong finish to win 3 and 2. In the third match out on course, Reg Whitcombe always seemed to have the measure of Johnny Revolta, who was 2 down at lunch. Later he was in the impossible position of 5 down yet Revolta eventually came away to win by 2 and 1. The next game, Olin Dutra against the future 1936 British Open champion Alf Padgham was neck and neck all the way – until Dutra suddenly drew away to win 4 and 2. Oddly, the reverse happened in the only British victory. Percy Alliss was 3 down to Craig Wood after 18 holes but came back to win a tense match 1 up. Following on, Bill Cox gave the best British come-back performance, however, against 1934 Masters champion Horton Smith. He was 5 down after 18 but managed to halve. At the bottom of the order the US Open champion, Sam Parks, faced the recent surprise victor at Muirfield, Alf Perry. The British player looked likely to win on the last green but Parks got a long putt down to halve. The 8–2 result to the United States hardly looked like an improvement from the British point of view, but most agreed that this was the best performance in the United States so far.

This time, there were no British complaints about the weather; there had been rain in the foursomes and it was fine but not hot for the singles. When the competition was over,

Governor Harold G. Hoffman of the state of New Jersey presented honour medals commemorating the match to both teams at a farewell dinner in the Ridgewood club. The US PGA followed up with inscribed wrist watches.

After 15 years in USA versus Britain professional matches, 1935 was the first year Walter Hagen did not play in the singles. After four British Opens, two US Opens and five US PGA matchplay titles, his career was drawing to a close. In 1937, however, he would once again captain the American team.

Members of the 1935 British team: (l to r) Charles Whitcombe, Alf Padgham, Jack Busson, Bill Cox, Ernie Whitcombe, Reg Whitcombe, Ted Jarman, Percy Alliss, Dick Burton and Alf Perry

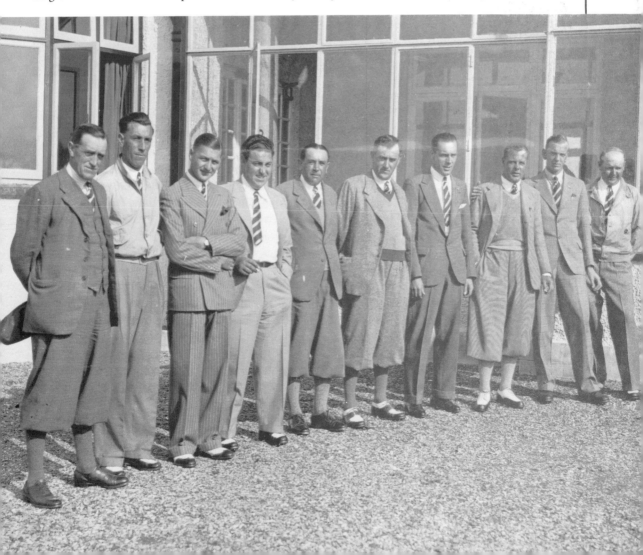

RIDGEWOOD, NEW JERSEY, USA
28–29 SEPTEMBER 1935

United States		Great Britain and Ireland	
Captain Walter Hagen		*Captain* C. A. Whitcombe	
Foursomes			
Sarazen and Walter Hagen (7 and 6)	1	Perry and Busson	0
Picard and Revolta (6 and 5)	1	Padgham and Alliss	0
Runyan and Smith (9 and 8)	1	Cox and Ted Jarman	0
Dutra and Ky Laffoon	0	C. A. and E. R. Whitcombe (1 up)	1
	—		—
	3		1
Singles			
Gene Sarazen (3 and 2)	1	Jack Busson	0
Paul Runyan (5 and 3)	1	Dick Burton	0
Johnny Revolta (2 and 1)	1	Reg Whitcombe	0
Olin Dutra (4 and 2)	1	Alf Padgham	0
Craig Wood	0	Percy Alliss (1 up)	1
Horton Smith (halved)	0	Bill Cox	0
Henry Picard (3 and 2)	1	Ernest Whitcombe	0
Sam Parks (halved)	0	Alf Perry	0
	—		—
	5		1

Final score: United States 8
Great Britain and Ireland 2.
Two matches halved

1937

Southport and Ainsdale was again the venue for the Ryder Cup. Then as now, it was a respected links course but observers considered it had rather too many undistinguished golf holes. Most of the criticism was levelled at the stretch from the 11th to the 14th holes, which were thought to be too short par 4s. (The same criticism is often made of the 9th, 10th and 12th at St Andrews.)

1937 saw the first appearance of two players who had appeared from nowhere and shot to the top. They were Samuel Jackson Snead for the United States, then recognised as the longest good driver ever, and David James Rees of Wales. Always a reliable if not powerful driver of the ball, Dai Rees was enjoying that early period of putting when one just walks up to the ball and knocks it into the hole. Rees could do this even though he had a slicing action at this time in his career.

Britain also had Cotton in the team for the first time since 1929. His prestige as 1934 Open champion had been enhanced by his residence on the Continent but he had returned to be club professional at Ashridge where he opened the most chic pro's shop the British had ever seen – complete with zebra skin seats! Although he had yet to add to his tally of British Open titles, Henry Cotton was recognised by his fellow professionals and the public alike as being a cut above the rest. The reason was not solely the superiority of his play but the fact that he looked the part while some of his fellow British professionals dressed like gardeners, so Cotton said.

One of these was Alf Padgham, who many thought had the best and simplest swing since Harry Vardon. Through the early 1930s the flaw in his game had been putting but Padgham was always an excellent chipper and it occurred to him to play the ball further away from his body while putting – just as for a chip shot. For a season or two he was a great putter and won almost everything in 1936, including the Open Championship.

Ralph Guldahl was the centre of attention at Southport. Although he was at the top of his profession in the second half of the 1930s only and then suddenly lost his game forever, he was the 1937 US Open champion.

Throughout the match there was a cross-gale off the sea for the foursomes and on the second day continuous rain and a chilling wind – the kind of weather that was reputed to favour the British team. Britain led off with the star pairing

Sam Snead went bald young and always wore a hat thereafter

of Cotton and Padgham, the captain Charles Whitcombe probably wanting to make sure of the boost to morale that a victorious start would ensure. They faced Ed Dudley and Byron Nelson. The first nine holes were halved and the next two exchanged. The British then went ahead for the first time on the 14th but lost both the 16th and 17th to lunch 1 down. Their start afterwards of 5, 6, 4 almost put the match beyond reach at 4 down which became 5 down on the 5th. The match came to an end with a sad British 6 on the 16th. Whitcombe's tactic had not paid off; Padgham's form of the previous year had deserted him and the pair might well not have broken 80 on the second round.

The standard of scoring was better in the second match which saw Guldahl paired with the previous year's US Open champion, Tony Manero, against Arthur Lacey and Bill Cox. The Americans were quickly 2 up but the British squared on the 8th. Later, they went 4 up and more or less held this position to lunch,

when they were 3 up. The Americans then made a fast start in the afternoon, winning the first two holes, but were quickly back to 3 down, and after 24 holes, were in the near hopeless position of 4 down with 12 to play. Instead, they levelled after 30 holes and won three out of four holes between the 32nd and 35th to walk in victors by 2 and 1.

With British hopes waning fast, the very experienced Charles Whitcombe went out with the young Dai Rees. They faced what looked like the best US pairing of Denny Shute and Gene Sarazen. The match actually produced the worst scoring of the four, the Americans going round in 77 in the morning, still one

The 1937 US team on an Atlantic liner: (rear) Ed Dudley, Byron Nelson, two officials, Johnny Revolta, Horton Smith, and Henry Picard. (Seated) Gene Sarazen, Sam Snead, Ralph Guldahl, Densmore Shute and Tony Manero

better than the British pair. At this point, the match stood all square. In the afternoon, there was never more than a hole in it either way and on the last, Rees holed a five-foot putt for a half and a halved match. He had got through his ordeal with honour, holing out impressively when his partner left him with quite a lot to do.

In the last match out, with Percy Alliss and Dick Burton facing the Americans Henry Picard and Johnny Revolta, the British pair were 3 up at lunch. By the 8th in the afternoon, the Americans had squared and then went ahead at the 9th but the British came back to win a vital point by 2 and 1.

With the score standing at 2–1 for the United States and with the eight singles to come, the match was fairly evenly balanced, though a good start was vital. The first match was between the two reigning champions, Ralph Guldahl and Alf Padgham. The Englishman held his own for a few holes and then went further and further behind with hardly a suggestion of a rally to lose by 8 and 7.

The British captain made some strange decisions in this match and to lead off with the out-of-form Padgham was one of them. His next, as in the previous match, was to leave himself out of the singles. His choice for the number two position in the singles, Sam King, was also surprising. King had been playing poorly in practice and had not been chosen for the foursomes, but he set off quickly with 3s at three of the first four holes for a 2-up lead. His opponent, Densmore Shute, who had won the two previous US PGA Championships, produced some 3s of his own, however, and quickly squared. Though King held Shute in the morning, he had little else but 5s for the first seven holes of the afternoon and found himself 4 down – a near hopeless position. He then found his best form and managed to square his match with a birdie on the last.

Dai Rees raised British hopes in a match against the formidable Byron Nelson that was exciting all the way but had the lowest standard of golf of any of the singles matches. Nelson's first round was 81 and Rees's 79. Even so, the closing holes were spectacular, with the Welshman moving, in the space of five holes, from 3 down to 1 up. In the afternoon he had 4s at nearly every hole. Although Nelson produced a few 3s he balanced these with a similar number of 5s and 6s to lose by 3 and 1. This made the score USA 3 Britain 2.

As expected, Henry Cotton levelled the match against Tony Manero who, though he had won the 1936 US Open was very much a surprise winner who never achieved much else. Even so, after 27 holes Manero was only 1 down having won the previous two holes. Then Cotton performed majestically and produced figures of 3, 4, 3, 4, 4, 3 to win by 5 and 3. The outcome of the fifth game, between Gene Sarazen and Percy Alliss, became vital. Sarazen began 2, 4, 3 to lead 3 up and went further ahead at the 5th but Alliss brought him back to 1 up by the 9th and was leading by 1 up at lunchtime. With nine to play he was in fact 3 up but the American then put together a string of wins. Walter Hagen had come over to give Gene a pep talk and tell him how important the match was. Alliss really lost the game on the 15th, a par 3. Sarazen, playing first, hit a low hooky shot that ran through the green and up a bank where, legend has it, the ball came to rest in a woman's lap. She leaped to her feet and the ball, of course, came back onto the putting surface. Sarazen holed out for a winning 2. On the last but one hole, Alliss kept himself alive with a putt that grazed past a stymie and toppled in but faced with the same problem on the last hole he couldn't quite do it and lost by 1 down.

With his defeat the match quickly went the same way, each of the last four singles going to the United States. The eventual result was a statistically convincing 7–3 win for the USA. With the definitely nasty weather supposedly heavily in Britain's favour, were there any good excuses forthcoming? Yes: 'the Americans were better equipped than the British players to withstand the elements, for the majority of them wore featherweight, transparent, slackly

Charles Whitcombe (third from left) watches Cotton drive off

fitting oilskins which did not incommode or restrict the swing'.

It was the first US victory on British soil. President Franklin D. Roosevelt received a cable telling him all about it. The president of the US PGA sent the American captain, Walter Hagen, the following message:

To the greatest general in the world congratulations for leading the greatest golfers in the world to a wonderful victory which brings great honor to your country, the PGA and your fellow professionals who are proud of you. Your achievement will go down in golfing history as the greatest of all time; we salute you, admire your courage and honor you as champions and heroes.

These emphatic emotions are in great contrast to the ones felt in post-war years when winning the Ryder Cup, whether at home or away, became a regular achievement for the United States and to be chosen to play was the most important thing.

At the presentation Hagen's notes blew away on the wind and he made a slip in his acceptance speech which nonetheless went down well. He began, 'I am very proud and happy to be the captain of the first American team to win on home soil'. There was muffled laughter and Hagen got the message and quickly held up four fingers to signify his four British Open titles. 'You'll forgive me, I'm sure,' he said, 'for feeling so at home here.' Hagen went on to say that he had brought a great team of American golfers with him and *Golf Monthly* certainly agreed later, stating, 'They were the greatest golfing force which has ever come to this country. They presented a splendid spectacle of athletic youth.' And, as everyone went off to Carnoustie for the Open Championship, British prospects didn't look very rosy.

Indeed, the Americans looked invincible and Horton Smith, Sarazen, Snead, Hagen and Nelson went on to lead the qualifying rounds. It seemed inevitable that one of the US Ryder Cup team would win. However, after a first thrust from Ed Dudley the inevitable US victory drifted away and Englishmen took the first four places. Henry Cotton was again champion and honour restored.

Henry Cotton was chosen to captain the 1939 British team and his men were Dick Burton, Reg Whitcombe, Sam King, Charles Whitcombe, Alf Padgham, Dai Rees and Jimmy Adams. Hagen was again the US captain with Vic Ghezzi, Ralph Guldahl, Jimmy Hines, 'Jug' McSpaden, Dick Metz, Byron Nelson, Henry Picard, Paul Runyan, Horton Smith and Sam Snead in his team. The match was due to be played at Ponte Vedra, Jacksonville, Florida late in 1939. Commander Roe, secretary of the British PGA, had to send his regrets. There was a war on.

Two years later, with no possibility of a match, the US PGA decided to honour their best golfers by choosing a team for a match which could never be. The team was Hagen as non-playing captain, Jimmy Demaret, Vic Ghezzi, Ben Hogan, Jug McSpaden, Lloyd Mangrum, Byron Nelson, Gene Sarazen, Horton Smith, Sam Snead and Craig Wood. This team did play a match, however, against British-born players in America and raised some $25,000 for the Red Cross.

SOUTHPORT AND AINSDALE, LANCASHIRE, ENGLAND
29–30 JUNE 1937

United States		Great Britain and Ireland	
Captain Walter Hagen		*Captain* C. A. Whitcombe	
Foursomes			
Dudley and Nelson (4 and 2)	1	Padgham and Cotton	0
Guldahl and Manero (2 and 1)	1	Lacey and Bill Cox	0
Sarazen and Shute (halved)	0	Charles Whitcombe and Rees	0
Picard and Johnny Revolta	0	Alliss and Burton (2 and 1)	1
	–		–
	2		1
Singles			
Ralph Guldahl (8 and 7)	1	Alf Padgham	0
Denny Shute (halved)	0	Sam King	0
Byron Nelson	0	Dai Rees (3 and 1)	1
Tony Manero	0	Henry Cotton (5 and 3)	1
Gene Sarazen (1 up)	1	Percy Alliss	0
Sam Snead (5 and 4)	1	Dick Burton	0
Ed Dudley (2 and 1)	1	Alf Perry	0
Henry Picard (2 and 1)	1	Arthur Lacey	0
	–		–
	5		2

Final score: United States 7
Great Britain and Ireland 3.
Two matches halved

LAMBS TO THE SLAUGHTER (1947–1955)

1947

There are quite a few candidates for the title of 'greatest British military disaster' but there is little room for doubt in the history of Ryder Cup encounters. The 1947 match at Portland, Oregon, was a total humiliation for the British and when it was all over, the only thing to do was to think up a few good excuses.

How could Britain hope to beat the might of the USA whose players were able to demolish steaks that filled a plate while the British existed on a meagre weekly ration? The journey couldn't have helped. First a long sea crossing followed by a train journey across the continent. There is much talk of jet lag today. In the days of ocean travel it was accepted that it took several days to get the swaying of the ship out of one's sense of balance. The team had to 'get their land-legs back'. Then there was the course which the Americans had had plenty of experience on as their team had competed in the 1946 PGA Championship at Portland and there was also an annual Tour event, the Portland Open. Unfortunately, heavy rain had restricted opportunities for the British team to get to know the terrain.

As in 1931, the weather also gave scope for alibis. In 1947 the sun had shone down almost without interruption on the British Isles. The ball ran a mile, one had to pitch well short of the greens and the putting was on some of the fastest surfaces ever. In Portland, on the other hand, the city had experienced the wettest

October for 65 years and more than an inch of rain fell overnight before play began on 1 November. That morning further torrents came down. Bunkers were often knee deep in water and puddles were very frequent on the fairways. Excuses, excuses, for are not these just the conditions the British winter golfer is well used to while the US Tour has always 'followed the sun'?

Perhaps the man we might have blamed the most in restrospect was an Oregon fruit packer named Bob Hudson. A far more generous Ryder Cup benefactor than Sam Ryder ever was, he had sponsored the event. Without him, the 1947 match might not have taken place.

A few hundred spectators braved the weather to see Ed 'Porky' Oliver and Lew Worsham for the United States and Henry Cotton and Arthur Lees for Britain strike the first shots in post-war Ryder Cup golf. The best ones came from the US players who were 6 up at lunch and went on to win on the 27th by 10 and 9, a record margin for a 36 hole Ryder Cup foursomes. The British pair took two putts per green and the Americans were much sharper. Cotton ruefully claimed to have missed eight putts of less than three yards, some of them very short indeed.

Surprisingly, the teams were level at the lunch interval. But the first two matches out, with British pairs 6 down, were virtual certainties for the USA. Jimmy Adams and Max Faulkner, however, were coping with the most formidable US pairing of Ben Hogan and Jimmy Demaret. After nine holes, they stood 4

Above *The greatest of Ryder Cup benefactors, Bob Hudson (third from the left, front row), is seen with the British team and their manager Commander Roe (standing second from left). They are probably in lumberjack shirts because the match was played in Portland, Oregon*

Left *Byron Nelson, seen a couple of years after his 11 successive wins on the US Tour*

up and were still 2 up at the halfway point. Playing last, Dai Rees and Sam King were 1 up on Byron Nelson and Herman Barron at the same stage. Hogan and Demaret tightened their game going 2 up after 27 holes and, though they were pulled back to level by a British birdie on the 33rd hole, won both the 34th and 36th. Rees and King held their one hole lead until the 29th, which they lost to a birdie and went 2 down over the next two holes. The match ended, 2 and 1 to the USA, when both pairs had 2s on the 35th hole.

So the first day was a clean sweep for the United States, despite Henry Cotton's appeals to both the rules of golf and God before play

began. He first declared that some US clubs had been 'filed up' to produce more backspin but the US captain, Ben Hogan, saw that this matter was attended to. Cotton gathered his team together, sat them down and then held up the bible saying, 'I think, gentlemen, we should have a few moments for meditation'.

For the singles, Hogan demonstrated how strong he thought his team's chances were by dropping out in order to allow Dutch Harrison to play. In this he was following the normal policy of US captains of seeing that everyone got a game. The British have always been more ruthlessly aware of the limitations of their teams; anyone off form or who shouldn't perhaps have been chosen in the first place is usually ignored. Hogan, however, did say that he was 'not playing well' – a polite excuse to conceal the contempt he felt for the standard of British golf. In the singles Harrison, although not playing particularly well, was never troubled by Fred Daly, the current British Open champion. Jimmy Adams matched Lew Worsham, the US champion, for 27 holes but could do little right thereafter. When the next two matches went comfortably to the US the end result was never in question.

The best match was that between Byron Nelson and Arthur Lees; the American was 2 up at lunch after a 70 to Lees' 72. Lees played the third nine in 34 to get back to only 1 down but eventually lost 2 and 1. Cotton was playing sixth and found himself confronted by an opponent whom few fancied in Ryder Cup matches – Sam Snead, who had won the 1946 British Open and had lost the 1947 US Open to Worsham only on the final putt of the 18-hole play-off. Snead was only 1 up after 27 holes but then swept to victory, winning four of the next five holes.

Dai Rees never played a bad Ryder Cup singles game and gave Jimmy Demaret a tense struggle. In the morning, Demaret led by two holes after the first nine but Rees came back in 34 to level the match. After ten holes in the afternoon, the Welshman was 1 up but then the tide turned; like Cotton, he lost four out of five holes – and that was that. The last match out brought the first and only British victory when Sam King beat Herman Keiser. They were level after the first 18 but King went 2 up after 27 and then won both the 29th and 31st. Halves saw him through to his 4 and 3 win.

Although the result – 11 matches to 1 – was catastrophic in British eyes it did lead to more food for Britain. Bob Hudson, at least, thought rationing was part of the problem. In time for Christmas he sent food hampers to all the British players, officials and even camp followers. He was still doing so in 1957!

PORTLAND, OREGON, USA
1–2 NOVEMBER 1947

United States		Great Britain and Ireland	
Captain Ben Hogan		*Captain* Henry Cotton	
Foursomes			
Oliver and Worsham (10 and 9)	1	Cotton and Lees	0
Snead and Mangrum (6 and 5)	1	Daly and Ward	0
Hogan and Demaret (2 up)	1	Adams and Faulkner	0
Nelson and Herman Barron (2 and 1)	1	Rees and King	0
	4		0
Singles			
Dutch Harrison (5 and 4)	1	Fred Daly	0
Lew Worsham (3 and 2)	1	Jimmy Adams	0
Lloyd Mangrum (6 and 5)	1	Max Faulkner	0
Ed Oliver (4 and 3)	1	Charlie Ward	0
Byron Nelson (2 and 1)	1	Arthur Lees	0
Sam Snead (5 and 4)	1	Henry Cotton	0
Jimmy Demaret (3 and 2)	1	Dai Rees	0
Herman Keiser	0	Sam King (4 and 3)	1
	7		1

Final score: United States 11
Great Britain and Ireland 1

1949

Food was the first controversial subject to arise when the American team disembarked at Southampton for the 1949 match at Ganton. Bob Hudson thought the British boys could do with feeding up for the match and brought over $1,349 worth of prime beef. The British Customs officials were not pleased and demanded an import licence. Friends in high places had to be contacted and suitable transport found before the hamper headed north. The gift was not welcomed by all; some thought it smacked of charity. Wives of members of the British team refused the meat at a dinner for the teams, though the players did not.

Ben Hogan, once again the American captain, was not feeling as charitable; like Cotton in 1947, he demanded that the British team's irons be examined. He thought that two of the players, Dai Rees and Dick Burton, had clubs which did not conform to the rules; the grooves, he thought, were too deep. A former captain of the R and A, golf writer Bernard Darwin, had to be summoned from his pre-dinner bath to join a 'panel' inspecting the suspect clubs. Hogan's views were upheld and some clubs had to be filed. Rees considered this a waste of time as the filing roughened the faces and sharpened the edges of the grooves so that they would impart more backspin on the ball.

Hogan was not playing and his choice as captain may have been a sentimental gesture. He had been seriously injured in a car crash the previous February and many thought that he would never play again or at least never be an effective competitor. By the time of the Ryder Cup match, about seven months after his accident, the most he could do was struggle to the 1st tee and the last green.

Another notable absentee was Henry Cotton. Open champion in 1948 for the third time, he had been selected as one of 20 possibles but had withdrawn. Cary Middlecoff, the reigning US champion, was excluded because he had not been a member of the American PGA for long enough. Gene Sarazen remarked that the attitude of his PGA was 'as archaic as the hickory-shafted baffy, the sand tee and the red golfing jacket'. No wonder they never asked him to captain the team!

For once, the foursomes went Britain's way by 3 matches to 1. With Jimmy Adams playing better golf than anyone, his pairing with Max

Above right *All that good American beef – $1,349 worth of it*

Right *Max Faulkner and Arthur Lees examine the irons that Ben Hogan objected to*

Faulkner came through by 2 and 1 against Dutch Harrison and Johnny Palmer. Fred Daly and Ken Bousfield went into a 3-up lead early on and though they were pulled back to square by Bob Hamilton and Skip Alexander, they came again and won very comfortably by 4 and 2.

Charlie Ward and Sam King were thought of as the best balanced British pair but they found that very lively dresser, Jimmy Demaret, and Clayton Heafner in brilliant form. The Americans played their last eight holes in 3, 4, 4, 3, 3, 4, 3, 4 and won 4 and 3. The strongest US pairing of Sam Snead and Lloyd Mangrum lost to Dick Burton and Arthur Lees in a well-fought match. In the 18 morning holes no pair was ever more than 1 up. Burton holed good length putts on the 27th and 28th, while Lees matched him with one from 20 yards on the next hole to give Britain a 2-hole lead. Although Snead and Mangrum fought back, they were still 1 down on the last tee. Burton put his partner safely on the fairway from where Lees cut his second into a greenside bunker. Snead left Mangrum to attempt to hook their second shot around a tree. He hit it and missed the putt which would have won the hole and halved the match.

Hogan had already proved himself a stern captain both over his questioning of the British irons and the way he kept his men hard at practice. After their crushing victory in 1947, they were delighted to be chosen to represent the USA in the Ryder Cup but regarded the match result as certain. Legend has it that Hogan gave them a tongue lashing because of their complacency. Dutch Harrison responded with the most attacking start that had been made in a Ryder Cup singles: 3, 3, 4, 3, 3, 3 or four birdies in the first six holes. This performance destroyed his opponent, Max Faulkner, worried the British side and inspired his fellow Americans. Even so, the top four matches were shared. Dai Rees was round in an approximate 65 in the morning and was 12 under level 4s when he won. His opponent, Bob Hamilton,

Above *Jimmy Demaret: a snappy dresser who would look better in technicolor*

Above right *Arthur Lees on his way to a 7 and 6 beating from Jimmy Demaret, on left of picture*

Right *Ben Hogan and British captain, Charles Whitcombe, shake hands after the match*

was faced with a putt of eight yards or so for a possible win on the 28th and decided he needed some help. 'You up there', he called out, 'come on down and help. But don't send your son this time. It's a man-sized job.' Perhaps there was an answer: Hamilton got the putt.

The last four matches were all lost by Britain, though there was a potentially winning position until close to the end; Rees and Adams had won and Dick Burton led Clayton Heafner by a hole with six to play. Daly, after a 2 on the 10th, led Mangrum. Yet Heafner eagled the 13th to draw

GANTON, YORKSHIRE, ENGLAND 16–17 SEPTEMBER 1949

United States		Great Britain and Ireland	
Captain Ben Hogan		*Captain* C. A. Whitcombe	
Foursomes			
Harrison and Palmer	0	Faulkner and Adams (2 and 1)	1
Hamilton and Skip Alexander	0	Daly and Ken Bousfield (4 and 2)	1
Demaret and Heafner (4 and 3)	1	Ward and King	0
Snead and Mangrum	0	Burton and Lees (1 up)	1
	1		3
Singles			
Dutch Harrison (8 and 7)	1	Max Faulkner	0
Johnny Palmer	0	Jimmy Adams (2 and 1)	1
Sam Snead (6 and 5)	1	Charlie Ward	0
Bob Hamilton	0	Dai Rees (6 and 4)	1
Clayton Heafner (3 and 2)	1	Dick Burton	0
Chick Harbert (4 and 3)	1	Sam King	0
Jimmy Demaret (7 and 6)	1	Arthur Lees	0
Lloyd Mangrum (1 up)	1	Fred Daly	0
	6		2

Final score: United States 7
Great Britain and Ireland 5

level and then won the next three holes as well. Daly was very unfortunate; his morning round of 66 might have given him a dominating lead – but Mangrum had a 65. The American then finished his second round 3, 3, 2, 4, 3. Even so, he won by only a single hole. A win from Daly would have meant a tied match. As it was, the result was 7–5 to the USA.

The next day, the Americans had an unpleasant surprise. With their wallets full of notes, the pound was devalued. The team was to stay to compete in the *News of the World* Matchplay Championship but several team members caught the boat train to Paris instead. As Demaret said, 'All we want of England is out'.

The US team members who made the journey from Ganton in Yorkshire to Walton Heath did not prosper. After four rounds, only Johnny Palmer and Lloyd Mangrum were left and, ironically, both then faced Henry Cotton, the man who had decided not to play at Ganton. He beat Palmer by 2 up and Mangrum more soundly by 4 and 2. In the end, Cotton lost the final narrowly to Rees. Cotton was still a great player and scarcely past his very best. His absence may have cost Britain the 1949 match.

1951

The 1951 match was played early in November on a great course, Pinehurst number 2, in North Carolina. The venue was quite different from, say, the carnival grounds of Southport or, equally, the luxury American country clubs where many Ryder Cup matches in the USA have been played. Pinehurst is a village devoted to golf and here Donald Ross arrived around the turn of the century to 'improve the golf courses'. Though he designed hundreds of courses throughout the United States, this was the course that the Scotsman from Dornoch loved the best.

The British team was charmed by the place which resembled Gullane in East Lothian rather more than Palm Beach or Palm Springs. Even during the golf season, the population at Pinehurst reached only 2,000 or so. It was, and still largely is, a New England village with the benefits of the climate of the mid-South.

The Americans were unhappy; the North and South Tour event which followed the Ryder Cup was long-established at Pinehurst but the promoters had refused to increase the prize money to $10,000. There was also the

oddity of a gap of one day between the four-somes and the singles to allow the teams to attend an American football match at the University of North Carolina but the US team decided to boycott this social event. They were also reluctant to attend what was expected to be the victory dinner.

Though the British press always felt it necessary to make believe a win was possible or even likely, *The Sunday Times* writer Henry Longhurst thought that one foursome and a couple of singles wins were all Britain could expect. In the event, Arthur Lees achieved that almost by himself, becoming the first British player to win both his foursome and single in a Ryder Cup in the United States. Alas, that was nearly the full measure of British success.

The weather changed overnight and when play began it was raining and the mist cut visibility to about four hundred yards. The British led off with their new Open champion, Max Faulkner, partnered by Dai Rees, against Clayton Heafner and Jack Burke. The British

The British team at Waterloo: (front l to r) Jack Hargreaves, Fred Daly, Arthur Lacey (non-playing captain), Dai Rees, Charlie Ward and Arthur Lees. Max Faulkner and Ken Bousfield in the doorway, Harry Weetman behind Lacey, Jimmy Adams behind Weetman and John Panton behind Rees

made some early errors, putting short through the dew-covered greens and were 3 down after nine but a 3, 4, 3, 4 finish reduced their deficit to 2. Heafner and Burke scored better than the 71 that Faulkner and Rees achieved in the morning and hopes of further recovery went after they scored two 5s to 4s from the Americans. The British pair lost by 5 and 3.

The weakest US pair were probably Ed Oliver and Henry Ransom but they faced some good play from Lees and Charlie Ward. A poor start has often been a British failing but on this occasion the British started with three 4s to 5s from the Americans. Though the Americans got the match back to square, Lees and Ward completed the first round in 3, 3, 2, 5, 3, 3 and were round in 69 and 3 up. In the afternoon, they kept their noses in front all the way and won by 2 and 1.

The US captain, Sam Snead, had kept his strength at the bottom of the order. Partnered by Lloyd Mangrum, he never let Jimmy Adams and John Panton into the match and they were unable to do more than hold on as long as possible. This game brought the score to US 2, Britain 1. Fred Daly and Ken Bousfield had equally formidable opposition in the form of Ben Hogan, who was at the peak of his career, and Jimmy Demaret.

Henry Longhurst cabled the following remarks home for his readers:

> Among the gallery in the fourth match, bearing no outward and visible sign connecting him with the proceedings, is a small dark man with grey raincoat, grey cap, grey trousers and inscrutable expression, looking somewhat like a Pinkerton detective on watch for pickpockets. This is the world's greatest golfer, Ben Hogan, participating in a Ryder Cup match. His partner, the normally flamboyant Jimmy Demaret, is concealed in a flowing check ulster with a distinctly Sherlock Holmes air. From time to time they step forward, undress, and give the ball a resounding slam.

Daly and Bousfield did rather less 'slamming' and, reaching the turn in 41, could hardly have been surprised to be 5 down. Thereafter, they did better and reduced the deficit to 3 by lunch before going down on the 15th green in the afternoon.

After the day's pause for football, Jimmy Adams produced little but 5s against Jack Burke but the day's finest match followed: Jimmy Demaret versus Dai Rees. The Welshman started well, quickly going 2 up and was 1 up at the break. After 27 holes, he was still level but Demaret was into a spell of four birdies in five holes which took him into the lead which he held to the end. Years later Rees recalled that Demaret was 11 times in greenside bunkers and ten times down in 2. This statement should be taken with a pinch of salt; rather like Seve Ballesteros today, Dai was reluctant to admit to making a mistake if he failed to win. A sudden wind had blown his ball sideways, a dog had barked, someone had kicked his ball into the rough or, as here, Demaret had an inspired sand iron. This 'it wasn't my fault' attitude, coupled with a belief that one plays well helps to keep the golfer's confidence high. Anyway, Demaret made Rees a present of his sand iron after the match, saying that the Welshman's sand wedge was preventing him from playing finesse shots from bunkers.

Irishman Fred Daly had some success in the third match when he came from behind to halve with Clayton Heafner. Harry Weetman then amazed the Americans with some immense strokes but Lloyd Mangrum won far more of the holes. The outcome of the contest was now no longer in question but the Hogan/Ward match provided a few sights to marvel at. Ward, for instance, managed to lead by 2 after six holes but Hogan squared at the 14th and then led by 2 at lunch. In the afternoon, the close struggle continued. Hogan threatened to get away but Ward came back at him so that after 27 holes he was still only 2 down. But perhaps the 10th, a monster par 5 of almost six hundred yards, was the decisive hole. Hogan drove into the woods, while Ward was comfortably on in 3. Hogan played out and then hit an enormous wooden club shot which barely reached the front of the green. It seemed inevitable that he should at some time hole a very long putt and he certainly did so here, holing from about 25 yards.

John Panton, who had earned praise in practice, could not maintain similar form in the match itself. Coming home in the morning, he had seven 5s and that was just about that – 5 down. His opponent, Skip Alexander, went on to win by 8 and 7. The last match saw the British Open champion, Max Faulkner, facing Sam Snead at the top of his game. Faulkner

Right *Dai Rees in action*

scored better than most of his fellow team members but that wasn't good enough. Snead's morning 67 was 3 strokes better than anyone else managed on either side; it put him 4 up, a lead he maintained to the end.

After the 9–2 defeat, the British team stayed on to play in the North and South event. Hogan, Demaret and Burke were away fast and others withdrew after a round or two. Only Henry Ransom was still at Pinehurst for the fourth round, remarking, 'Well, it looks like I'm the last of the Mohicans'.

Another man who stayed was the British captain, Arthur Lacey. He met a woman at Pinehurst and married her.

PINEHURST, NORTH CAROLINA, USA 2 and 4 NOVEMBER 1951

United States		Great Britain and Ireland	
Captain Sam Snead		*Captain* Arthur Lacey	
Foursomes			
Heafner and Burke (5 and 3)	1	Faulkner and Rees	0
Oliver and Henry Ransom	0	Ward and Lees (2 and 1)	1
Mangrum and Snead (5 and 4)	1	Adams and Panton	0
Hogan and Demaret (5 and 4)	1	Daly and Ken Bousfield	0
	3		1
Singles			
Jack Burke (4 and 3)	1	Jimmy Adams	0
Jimmy Demaret (2 up)	1	Dai Rees	0
Clayton Heafner (halved)	0	Fred Daly	0
Lloyd Mangrum (6 and 5)	1	Harry Weetman	0
Ed Oliver	0	Arthur Lees (2 and 1)	1
Ben Hogan (3 and 2)	1	Charlie Ward	0
Skip Alexander (8 and 7)	1	John Panton	0
Sam Snead (4 and 3)	1	Max Faulkner	0
	6		1

Final score: United States 9
Great Britain and Ireland 2.
One match halved

1953

The West Course at Wentworth was chosen for the 1953 Ryder Cup match. The event was billed as the first international golf fixture to be held in the London area which was not strictly true as both the 1926 Ryder Cup and the Curtis Cup in 1932 had been held at Wentworth.

The American golfers were unfamiliar to British eyes; only four of them had been in the Pinehurst team and just two had played in a Ryder Cup in Britain before. Two American players who were known to the British and who had qualified for the team, Dutch Harrison and Ben Hogan, decided not to play. The ten-man team was indeed one of the weakest the USA had put out but it nevertheless contained at least four great players: Cary Middlecoff, Jack Burke, captain Lloyd Mangrum and Sam Snead.

For the first time, the British team included players with no experience of pre-war golf: Peter Alliss and Bernard Hunt. Both were to play a long role in the Ryder Cup story and both were scarred by their experiences at Wentworth in 1953.

The Americans, who had qualified by accumulating points for tournament performances, were at this time playing in about four times as many events as were held in Britain (not many Britons competed in Continental national championships because they were regarded as unimportant and expensive to compete in). Partly to foster team spirit, 17 possible players were invited to Wentworth for trials and the number was then reduced to ten. While the US team stayed at the Kensington Palace Hotel, which had the marvel of a bathroom in every room, the British players were accommodated at the Dormy House in Sunningdale. Keeping the team under one roof was captain Henry Cotton's idea; he encouraged them to practise intensely, and to have plenty of rest, and made sure they had good food. In the evenings, the players talked together about how to beat the Americans and they came very close

Henry Cotton at Wentworth with some potential team members: (l to r) Arthur Lees, Charlie Ward, Sam King, Bernard Hunt, Harry Weetman, John Jacobs, Peter Alliss and Eric Brown

to winning, after the usual disastrous start in the foursomes.

The first match, Dave Douglas and Ed 'Porky' Oliver against Harry Weetman and Peter Alliss, who at the age of 22 was the youngest player ever to represent Britain, had its comic moments. On the 3rd hole in the afternoon the referee, Admiral Sir Charles Forbes, ruled that the US ball was in a rabbit scrape and the Americans were given a free drop. At the time their ball was almost unplayable at the base of a pine tree and no relief was allowed under the rules of golf from rabbit scrapes – what a howl would go up in similar

circumstances today. At this time, however, referees tended to be good amateur golfers and it was assumed that they knew the rules. That said, one could hardly do better than co-opt the military, the higher ranking the better. In another match, the referee years later confessed to having walked away from an American ball in fear and trembling at having to give a decision when he didn't know the relevant rule about different categories of water hazard. Douglas and Oliver rubbed in their good fortune by ramming home a putt of half a dozen yards to go 3 up when they would almost certainly have been brought back to 1 up.

When the match reached the 35th tee – the famous par 5 at Wentworth which was then measured at 551 yards – America was still 2 up. The US tee shot then sailed out of bounds and Alliss and Weetman needed only a par 5 to level the match. Weetman launched himself into his

A delighted Fred Daly leaves the course after sinking the winning putt in his foursomes

drive which soared upwards and travelled only about pitching wedge distance. With not the slightest chance of getting within pitching distance of the green, Alliss played a safe 5-iron, leaving Weetman another of the same to the green. Alas, Harry lifted his head on the shot and thinned the approach through the back. The Americans played well with their second ball and needed a putt of a couple of yards for a 6. Alliss pitched to four feet. The US got their putt and Weetman missed. The hole was halved and the match lost, by 2 and 1.

Before play began, there had been great surprise that Cotton had decided to omit Max Faulkner and Dai Rees from his foursomes pairings. The decision looked mistaken when the pairings of Eric Brown and John Panton and Jimmy Adams and Bernard Hunt were heavily defeated. They had not played badly but Snead and Mangrum had gone round in 67 and Ted Kroll and Jack Burke in 66 in the morning – formidable scoring. Cotton felt that both Faulkner and Rees were strong individualists and unsuited to foursomes play. Bernard Darwin commented, 'The main point in a foursome is to hit the ball'. Rees, in particular, never played a bad Ryder Cup match in his long career and I feel there would not have been a 7 and 5 or 8 and 7 result if he had been in the line-up.

With three matches gone, British honour was saved by the northern and southern Ireland pairing of Fred Daly and Harry Bradshaw. Daly, the 1947 Open champion, was a little past his best and had been having a bad year with the putter. However, he was able to raise his game for the Ryder Cup. With nine holes to play, the Irishmen were 3 up and although that lead was cut back to just 1 up with three to go, they held the same margin on the 18th tee. On this hole, after Cary Middlecoff had sent the US ball too far right, Walter Burkemo played a superb cut wooden club shot around the trees to the heart of the green. Even so, it wasn't quite enough. Daly toppled a putt in that never seemed to have quite the pace to reach the hole to win the match. Great was the joy at Wentworth and the crowds clustered around the exultant Irishmen; there had been little enough to shout about otherwise all day.

If the Irish were the happiest men at Wentworth, the rest of the team were downcast; surely the match was already lost? Not so, Henry Cotton declared and delivered a fierce tongue-lashing. The next morning at Wentworth, newspaper placards quoted Cotton as saying 'I could kick the team' and his wife, Toots, went round ripping them down. Cotton had certainly called his players 'chicken-livered' and without fight. Cotton sent out his best man for a singles win, Dai Rees, to obtain the good start which was vital at 3–1 down. It was Daly, however, who produced the fireworks for Britain, playing at number two. Round in 66 in the morning – 'The best golf I have ever

played' according to Daly – he had Ted Kroll 6 down and just about out. Daly continued the massacre after lunch to win by 9 and 7.

Rees was all square at lunch. In the other matches, Eric Brown was 2 up, Weetman 4 down to Snead, Faulkner 3 down to Middlecoff, Alliss 1 down to Jim Turnesa, Hunt square with Douglas and Harry Bradshaw 1 up on Fred Haas. There was little cause for hope, with a two match deficit to be made up. On the 16th in the afternoon Rees holed a good putt to get back to only 1 down and his hopes rose when Jack Burke struck a short drive at the 17th. After his second shot, Burke was still 80 yards short of the green. Would he play a high sand iron shot or nudge his ball in with a less lofted club? The answer was that he used the club with the least loft of all – the putter. Burke's ball ran on and on and stopped about nine inches from the hole. The United States won by 2 and 1.

Although Eric Brown beat the American captain, Lloyd Mangrum, in the third match, the eventual result was not in doubt, with Weetman 4 down with only six holes to play and Middlecoff in a comfortable position against Max Faulkner. Suddenly, the formidable Sam Snead came apart. There was talk of a broken bone in his right hand afterwards but, whatever the reason, he began to cut and hook his tee shots deep into Wentworth's woods. Weetman, faced with scores of 6, 4, 6, 6, 5, 5 from Snead, found himself on the last tee 1 up and just held on to win.

With Harry Bradshaw beating Fred Haas by 3 and 2 in the last match out, the result of the 1953 Ryder Cup suddenly depended on the two youngest players, Peter Alliss and Bernard Hunt. Alliss was left 1 down at lunch after a round of 70. He went 1 up on the 15th in the afternoon with a very good approach shot followed by a firm putt into the middle of the hole. After Alliss had driven safely on the next, Turnesa cut his tee shot wildly towards the woods. He was lucky to hit a spectator and his ball stayed in play. Turnesa then hit his second shot at this short par 4 into a greenside bunker.

Jack Burke putting in the Arnold Palmer knock-kneed stance

With the match in his grasp, Alliss was a little short with his pitch – by perhaps 15 yards. Turnesa played out to some three yards while Alliss putted up almost dead. Alas, it was Turnesa who then holed out while Alliss missed from a couple of feet or so away.

Worse was to come. At this stage in his career Alliss was apt to hit flat out on too many shots through the green but he was a secure driver of the ball, relying on a left-to-right shape of shot. On the 17th he aimed down the left but the fade didn't take; he was out of bounds by no more than a yard. A good 4 with his second ball couldn't beat Turnesa's steady par 5. With

fortunes reversed, Turnesa, dormy 1 up, sliced his tee shot at the 18th far into the woods and Alliss followed with a perfect drive. Two shots later, Turnesa was still a pitch short of the green. Alliss, meanwhile, had struck a good 2-iron pin high but some ten yards off the green and around 25 yards from the flag. Turnesa played up to holeable distance for his par 5; Alliss fluffed his little pitch. He was still short of the putting surface yet did well to keep his nerve and get his next attempt about a yard from the hole.

All was not lost. Turnesa missed and Alliss still had his short putt; if he got it, the Ryder Cup would almost certainly return to British hands with Bernard Hunt, behind, likely to win his match. Alliss missed. Playing the last, Hunt had come back from 3 down to dormy 1 up. He

'There goes the Ryder Cup!' – Bernard Hunt misses a short putt in his match against Dale Douglass

US captain Lloyd Mangrum with Cary Middlecoff who took part in his first Ryder Cup contest in 1953

drove well but cut his second. Even so, his opponent Douglas played the hole only moderately. With both on in 3, Hunt had to 2-putt to hold his winning margin. Although he had a long way to go from the back of the green, he coasted his approach putt up to a yard. Like Alliss minutes before, he missed the next. Douglas won the hole, halved his match and the Ryder Cup went to the United States by 6 matches to 5.

Lamentations were heard throughout the land – at least in 1949 Britain had been defeated by a masterly US recovery. This time a lack of British nerve seemed to blame for the final score.

WENTWORTH, SURREY, ENGLAND
2–3 OCTOBER 1953

United States	Great Britain and Ireland	
Captain Lloyd Mangrum	*Captain* Henry Cotton	
Foursomes		
Douglas and Ed Oliver (2 and 1)	1	Weetman and Alliss	0
Kroll and Burke (7 and 5)	1	Jimmy Adams and Hunt	0
Mangrum and Snead (8 and 7)	1	Brown and John Panton	0
Walter Burkemo and Middlecoff	0	Daly and Bradshaw (1 up)	1
	–		–
	3		1
Singles		
Jack Burke (2 and 1)	1	Dai Rees	0
Ted Kroll	0	Fred Daly (9 and 7)	1
Lloyd Mangrum	0	Eric Brown (2 up)	1
Sam Snead	0	Harry Weetman (1 up)	1
Cary Middlecoff (3 and 2)	1	Max Faulkner	0
Jim Turnesa (1 up)	1	Peter Alliss	0
Dave Douglas (halved)	0	Bernard Hunt	0
Fred Haas	0	Harry Bradshaw (3 and 2)	1
	–		–
	3		4

Final score: United States 6
Great Britain and Ireland 5.
One match halved

1955

In 1955 the 'guilty men' of Wentworth, Peter Alliss and Bernard Hunt, did not make the team, whose members were rather mature; only John Jacobs was under 30. Arthur Lees, making his fourth and last Ryder Cup appearance, was the oldest man on the British team, at 47. The Americans were no younger, averaging 37 years old. The selection of the British team was controversial. Surely Henry Cotton was still worth his place, even if aged 48; he had won the Penfold Tournament the previous year and was to continue to be a formidable player in the Open Championship over the next few years. At the other extreme, Peter Alliss represented

the future and was considered the best prospect in Britain at the age of 24. By this time, he had proved he could win, taking the 1954 Daks and the 1955 Dunlop. He expected to be chosen in the last group of three players, the other seven having been selected in mid-season on the basis of five tournament results. But various factors counted against him. He was thought inconsistent and the method of selection, perhaps no bad thing, included penalty points debited when a player failed to qualify for the last day of a tournament. It hadn't helped the Alliss cause that he had failed to qualify for the Open at St Andrews just before the main body of the team was selected. The nod went instead to Johnny Fallon who was not to win a major event throughout his career but had certainly caught the eye at St Andrews, when he finished second behind Peter Thomson. He had looked like winning after reaching the turn in 31 but had taken 39 home, including dropping two strokes on a par 3 when his ball came to rest in a heel mark.

There was no controversy about the choice of Dai Rees as captain. He had played in five Ryder Cup competitions and performed well in each of his singles matches. With his Welsh fervour he might inspire his men to new heights. The venue was the luxurious Thunderbird Ranch and Country Club at Palm Springs, California. The course played to 6,800 yards and the rough was punishing. There was much for the British to adapt to in practice; the greens were Bermuda grass which held the ball. This was American target golf; even a low wooden club shot would stop after the second bounce. Having become used to playing so as to allow for run up to the flag, it was difficult for players to nerve themselves to hit full at it. The Americans enjoyed a considerable advantage in this area of the game as a result. Otherwise, playing skills through and on the green seemed balanced.

As always, the British team was hopeful rather than confident, encouraged by the close contest of 1953 though they must have been

Johnny Fallon tees off at the 1st in glorious sunshine at Thunderbird Ranch, Palm Springs

aware that no team had sailed home from America with their reputation enhanced. As usual there was that strange belief that the British team was the more experienced in foursomes play and might seize a first day lead. In the first match, Johnny Fallon and John Jacobs, unpopular choices for the team, faced Chandler Harper and the diminutive Jerry Barber, who had the best short game on the US Tour. Now forgotten, it was one of the best 36-hole foursomes in the entire Ryder Cup series. Barber lived up to his reputation in full, holing three chip shots during the match. Even so, the British pair were 1 up with seven holes to go but, alas, 3-putted when the chance came to go further ahead. The lead seemed lost when the US ball lay dead to the hole on the 35th. Jacobs, however, followed to four feet and Fallon managed to get the putt down.

On the last, a British win looked certain when Harper sent the American ball just through the green with Jacobs playing another superb iron shot to about four feet. Then came the third chip-in by Barber. Fallon's putt may have been quite short but it was by no means a flat one; he rolled it into the dead centre of the hole. This in fact levelled the match as Eric Brown and Syd Scott had already gone down to Doug Ford and Ted Kroll by 5 and 4. In the third match Lees and Weetman started badly but came home in 31 on the first 18 holes to lunch 1 up. After 35 holes, however, the US led by one hole and Tommy Bolt fired his iron to about four feet on the last to make victory virtually certain. Arthur Lees put his partner ten feet from the hole. When Weetman holed it, British hopes rose but Jackie Burke followed him down to take the match for the USA.

The US had kept their strongest pairing, Sam Snead and Cary Middlecoff, for the last match out, where they faced the British captain and Harry Bradshaw. The Americans dominated the early part of the match but Rees and Bradshaw came back at them over the middle 18 holes of the match with ten 3s. They seemed to lose heart a little, however, when Snead sent his recovery from sand dead and they eventually lost by 3 and 2. The general opinion was that a fairer result would have been level at 2 each after the foursomes. As it was, Britain was 2 points behind with eight singles to play on the second day.

The crowds had been enthusiastic at the standard of play and the turn-out was good. About 3,000 people followed the golf on foot while the British were surprised at the 500 carts on the course. Although it has often been said that it took the US defeat in 1985 at The Belfry to rouse interest in the match in America, this is not wholly true. National passions may not have been aroused but local publicity ensured a good turn-out of spectators.

In the singles, the British team fought well and after some 30 holes were actually winning

Harry Bradshaw watches as partner Dai Rees putts on the second green

on the last day, a fact that is impossible to imagine from the final result, with the Americans winning five of the matches. They were simply stronger at the finish. The outstanding match was between John Jacobs and Cary Middlecoff, the third one out. Jacobs started well to lead but Middlecoff came back to hold a two hole lead at lunch. After 27 holes, Jacobs had squared and then looked unassailable when 2 up with three to play. However, Middlecoff holed a long putt on the 35th to win the hole and in the end Jacobs had to hole from about a yard on the last to win the match. He did so, being round in an approximate 65. It was unquestionably his finest hour as a competitive golfer and he was to return home at least a minor hero, having won both his matches. He was never considered quite good enough to be picked again and had to remain content with his Ryder Cup record. Yet there were to be compensations ahead in his great successes as a teacher, tournament administrator and businessman.

It was Christy O'Connor, a new star in Britain, however, who led the British team. He had played in only five events outside Ireland when he won the 1955 Swallow–Penfold tournament which virtually ensured his

place in the team. O'Connor, quickly recognised as a superb shot-maker, was at times an insecure putter. Even so, he held Tommy Bolt for a while but was still 3 down after the first 18. Then he won two holes back and claims that Bolt lost composure and began tossing clubs into the air. Phil Harris, the singer and bandleader, uttered soothing words to his friend and Bolt went ahead again and won with ease.

Harry Bradshaw gave one of the most mixed performances. Three down after ten he went on to throw six consecutive 3s at his opponent, Jackie Burke. The fifth of these might well have unsettled the American for Bradshaw holed a pitch shot from heavy rough. The Irishman was round in 65 but Burke did not crack and eventually won comfortably enough by 3 and 2.

From the singles order, the best play was expected from Sam Snead and Dai Rees and in the morning Snead did not disappoint; he was round in 66 to be 5 up. Rees fought back in the afternoon with four birdies in the first seven holes. To the turn, he had six 3s and had clawed back to only 2 down. Snead was by no means cracking. On the 7th, he hooked his tee shot up against a tree yet still managed to eagle the hole. For the first nine in the afternoon, he took 36 and that included driving out of bounds on the 9th. However, when a come-back in golf is halted that is very often the end of the recovery. On the 31st hole, Snead was in a greenside bunker but it was he who got down in 2 more, with Rees 3-putting.

Besides Jacobs, the British winners were Lees and Brown so the controversial choices justified both themselves and the selectors. Lees did not play particularly well in the morning but Marty Furgol was off form. Brown had been driving erratically in the foursomes but the sight of an American on the first tee in a Ryder Cup singles usually brought out his best golf. He was 3 up at lunch and virtually finished his man off when he holed a putt of a dozen yards on the 31st.

After the match the method of selection was changed in Britain so that performance over a

Sport and advertising have long been bed-fellows – here Dai Rees models his Pringle shirt

two-year period was the criterion. This did not change the basic problem: the USA could probably field four or five teams that would all beat the best the British Isles could muster. New players were slow to come through because the British PGA would not allow players to compete for prize money until they had been members of the association for five years. This had hampered the development of Eric Brown who, shortly after winning the 1946 Scottish Amateur Championship, turned professional. It meant that very few top young amateur golfers thought it worthwhile attempting to become tournament professionals. After all, at this time only Henry Cotton had earned a great deal of money out of golf. The amateur was better off continuing as he was; his golfing fame meant a well-paid job would very likely come his way. It was all very different in America.

Meanwhile, Bob Hudson had continued to support the event with hard cash and to show their appreciation, the British team presented him with a silver platter inscribed with all their names.

The 1955 US team: (left to right) Cary Middle-coff, Marty Furgol, Chandler Harper, Doug Ford, Lloyd Mangrum, Chick Harbert, Tommy Bolt, Sam Snead, Jack Burke, Ted Kroll and Jerry Barber

PALM SPRINGS, CALIFORNIA, USA
5–6 NOVEMBER 1955

United States		Great Britain and Ireland	
Captain Chick Harbert		*Captain* Dai Rees	
Foursomes			
Chandler Harper and Barber	0	Johnny Fallon and Jacobs (1 up)	1
Ford and Ted Kroll (5 and 4)	1	Brown and Scott	0
Burke and Bolt (1 up)	1	Lees and Weetman	0
Snead and Middlecoff (3 and 2)	1	Rees and Bradshaw	0
	—		—
	3		1
Singles			
Tommy Bolt (4 and 2)	1	Christy O'Connor	0
Chick Harbert (3 and 2)	1	Syd Scott	0
Cary Middlecoff	0	John Jacobs (1 up)	1
Sam Snead (3 and 1)	1	Dai Rees	0
Marty Furgol	0	Arthur Lees (3 and 1)	1
Jerry Barber	0	Eric Brown (3 and 2)	1
Jack Burke (3 and 2)	1	Harry Bradshaw	0
Doug Ford (3 and 2)	1	Harry Weetman	0
	—		—
	5		3

Final score: United States 8
Great Britain and Ireland 4

FALSE DAWN (1957)

1957

The results of the 1953 and 1955 matches gave signs that the gap was closing between the standards of British and American golf. Even so, counting up the final tally of points can be misleading. Only Sam Snead's freak collapse at Wentworth over the closing holes presented Harry Weetman with his singles win and suddenly gave Britain a chance. If 1955 saw the best British performance in the USA at that point, an American defeat was never likely.

Overall, the gulf between British and American standards of play was as wide as ever and the reasons were the same as they had been when the USA established her golfing superiority in the 1920s; America had far more players and those players were far more hardened by continual tournament play than the British. Results in the Open Championship from 1950 to 1960 go some way to illustrating this. Although only one American, Ben Hogan, won during this period few Americans considered entering until Arnold Palmer revived interest in the competition. But did British golfers win? Except for Max Faulkner in 1951, the answer is, no. Golfers from the Commonwealth dominated instead – men like Bobby Locke, Peter Thomson, Gary Player and Kel Nagle. The majority of British players felt that someone from overseas was always bound to win the Open and their confidence suffered. There was the same feeling about the Ryder Cup, whatever patriotic noises the popular press might

Max Faulkner was Open champion in 1951 but lost each of his four Ryder Cup singles matches

make. Dai Rees was quite surprised when Henry Cotton delivered his tongue-lashing after the loss of the foursomes in 1953. The other captains Rees had served under had seemed to expect their team to lose and were not unduly upset when they did.

Judging by the match result, Dai Rees had done well at Thunderbird and he was asked to captain the team again in 1957. Neither country seemed to have a consistent policy on whether to choose a non-playing captain or to pick their best player. The Americans, in little doubt about the result of any match, tended to share the honour around. In 1957 it was Jack Burke's turn and he did not have a particularly strong team to bring over. Ben Hogan and Sam Snead had won the Canada (later World) Cup for the United States the year before but neither was playing in the Ryder Cup. Nor was Cary Middlecoff, US Open champion in 1956. Both he and Julius Boros had gone against US PGA rules by playing in exhibitions instead of the PGA Championship. The Ryder Cup team contained only three US Open champions: Dick Mayer, who had won earlier in the year, Tommy Bolt, who would do so the following year, and Ed Furgol. There were three past or future Masters winners, however, in Doug Ford, Art Wall and Jack Burke, and PGA champions Doug Ford, Lionel Hebert and Dow Finsterwald. Even so, the side lacked familiar names. The US Tour was in a slight trough between the decline of Hogan and Snead and the arrival of the next generation of great players such as Arnold Palmer.

The British team was made up of experienced players with only one newcomer to the Ryder Cup, Peter Mills. Since 1953, Peter Alliss and Bernard Hunt had established themselves as leading British golfers, though Alliss had a reputation for inconsistency and unreliable short putting. Overall, there seemed to be no weak links and many thought that the 1957 team was the best Britain had put out in 30 years.

The choice of the golf course was more

Above *America's Tommy Bolt*

controversial than that of the team; Lindrick in Yorkshire was selected because one of the members, Sir Stuart Goodwin, sponsored the match for £10,000 in the form of an outright gift to the PGA, provided the event was held in the Sheffield area. Doubts were raised at the wisdom of using a course that was bisected by a main road, not just once but twice. It was also considered to be playing to American strengths to use an inland course, especially one only 6,541 yards in length. Too many holes needed only a drive and pitch, and American precision with the wedge was menacing. Few changes, however, were made to the course. Two back

'MINE, I THINK'

Above *A humorous look at the problem*

Right *The order of play*

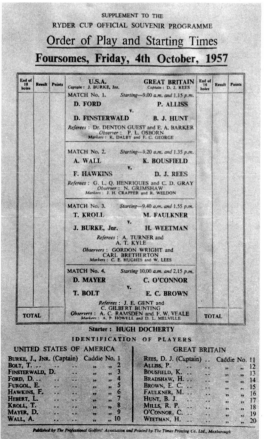

SUPPLEMENT TO THE
RYDER CUP OFFICIAL SOUVENIR PROGRAMME

Order of Play and Starting Times

Foursomes, Friday, 4th October, 1957

End of 18 holes	Result	Points	U.S.A. Captain : J. BURKE, Jnr.	GREAT BRITAIN Captain : D. J. REES	End of 18 holes	Result	Points
			MATCH No. 1. *Starting—9.00 a.m. and 1.15 p.m.*				
			D. FORD	**P. ALLISS**			
			v.				
			D. FINSTERWALD	**B. J. HUNT**			
			Referees : Dr. DENTON GUEST and E. A. BARKER Observer : P. L. OSBORN Markers : K. DALBY and F. C. GEORGE				
			MATCH No. 2. *Starting—9.20 a.m. and 1.35 p.m.*				
			A. WALL	**K. BOUSFIELD**			
			v.				
			F. HAWKINS	**D. J. REES**			
			Referees : G. L. Q. HENRIQUES and C. D. GRAY Observer : N. GRIMSHAW Markers : J. H. CRAPPER and R. WELDON				
			MATCH No. 3. *Starting—9.40 a.m. and 1.55 p.m.*				
			T. KROLL	**M. FAULKNER**			
			v.				
			J. BURKE, Jnr.	**H. WEETMAN**			
			Referees : A. TURNER and A. T. KYLE Observers : GORDON WRIGHT and CARL BRETHERTON Markers : C. E. HUGHES and W. LEES				
			MATCH No. 4. *Starting 10.00 a.m. and 2.15 p.m.*				
			D. MAYER	**C. O'CONNOR**			
			v.				
			T. BOLT	**E. C. BROWN**			
			Referees : J. E. GENT and C. GILBERT BUNTING Observers : A. C. RAMSDEN and F. W. VEALE Markers : A. P. HOWELL and D. L. MELVILLE				
TOTAL					**TOTAL**		

Starter : HUGH DOCHERTY

IDENTIFICATION OF PLAYERS

UNITED STATES OF AMERICA			GREAT BRITAIN		
BURKE, J., JNR. (Captain)	Caddie No.	1	REES, D. J. (Captain) ..	Caddie No.	11
BOLT, T. ...	„	2	ALLISS, P. ...	„	12
FINSTERWALD, D.	„	3	BOUSFIELD, K. ..	„	13
FORD, D. ...	„	4	BRADSHAW, H. ..	„	14
FURGOL, E.	„	5	BROWN, E. C. ..	„	15
HAWKINS, F. ..	„	6	FAULKNER, M. ..	„	16
HEBERT, L.	„	7	HUNT, B. J. ..	„	17
KROLL, T.	„	8	MILLS, R. P. ..	„	18
MAYER, D.	„	9	O'CONNOR, C. ..	„	19
WALL, A.	„	10	WEETMAN, H. ..	„	20

Published by The Professional Golfers' Association and Printed by The Times Printing Co. Ltd., Mexborough

tees were built and another taken out of play. This was because the landowner on whose land it was constructed demanded what was thought a very high fee for its use in the match! Mrs Janet Sidda was also annoyed because club members had occasionally ordered her off what was her own land. As a result the 5th was shortened by 18 yards.

Perhaps recalling that Alliss and Hunt had come to grief at the climax of the 1953 match, Rees sent them out first in the foursomes. The two Englishmen scored as well as any pairing in the British team but lost a close match by 2 and 1. Faced with three 3s to start from Doug Ford and Dow Finsterwald, they lost the first two holes and never managed to bring the match back to square. The Americans Wall and Hawkins started just as well in the second match which saw the British pairing of Rees and Ken Bousfield also 2 down but they managed to square on the 18th but lost both the 3rd and 4th after lunch. However, they lost no more holes, squared the match on the 10th, and then pulled away to win by 3 and 2. This was the win that just kept Britain in the match with a chance of success. In the third match, both Max Faulkner and Harry Weetman felt they had played badly and went down to Ted Kroll and Jack Burke 4 and 3.

For Britain, Eric Brown and Christy O'Connor played par golf but faced what proved the toughest US pair on the day, Dick Mayer and Tommy Bolt. At the time, Mayer may well have been the best player on either side and, in addition to his US Open title, had just won the rich Tam O'Shanter event in Chicago. He looked set to become one of the great players of all time but faded away. Bolt and he went round in 67 in the morning, played the first nine in the afternoon in 32 and then finished Brown and O'Connor off with 3s on the 12th and 13th, holes of 460 and 470 yards. The American pair won by 7 and 5.

With Britain in disarray, there followed what might have been a fatal blow to team spirit. Captain Rees gathered his men together for a discussion on the selection for the singles; Faulkner thought he should not play and Weetman seemed to feel the same. Out they went and in came Peter Mills and Harry Bradshaw. Half an hour or so later Weetman announced he would never again play in a team captained by Rees and the morning papers made a great deal out of this story. The rest of the British team were irritated and made more determined by a man who wrote that a British victory was so unlikely he would bury himself under a ton of compost if he were proved wrong.

Lindrick seemed a different course for the second and final day of the contest; there was an easterly breeze, and the greens had been cut much shorter, to their proper tournament height. Amazingly, the greenkeeper had thought that the Ryder Cup was starting a day later than it did. One result was that some of the Americans took three putts on the 1st but the first shots struck for Britain were not encouraging. Rees felt that Eric Brown was quite capable of beating any American and put him at the top of the order in the hope of making the score 3–2. Brown began by slicing his tee shot into the rough, trapping his second in a bunker and then recovering poorly to be 1 down. Brown then had to scramble for his half on the 2nd. Soon, however, he was in the lead and 3 up after only seven holes. The British, long known for poor starting, led in every match early on except Peter Alliss's against Fred Hawkins.

Perhaps the most remarkable opening was that which saw Christy O'Connor begin with three 3s while Dow Finsterwald began 7, 4, 4 in what proved to be a bad-tempered match. On the 3rd, a par 3, Finsterwald raked his ball back after missing a putt and the referee immediately awarded the hole to O'Connor. Much later, the American got his own back. After he had missed a short putt and been conceded the next he marched off the green, leaving O'Connor to putt out. The Irishman putted to about an inch and then picked up his ball; Finsterwald, legitimately claimed the hole. O'Connor remarks in his biography that at the end of the match the American refused to shake hands.

Perhaps the American team members were annoyed by the behaviour of the Yorkshire crowd. When it was all over, Tommy Bolt remarked, 'They cheered when I missed a putt and sat on their hands when I hit a good shot', to which his team-mate, Ed Furgol, responded, 'Pipe down, we were well and truly licked'.

Furgol's brief analysis tells the whole story. The Americans were not so much beaten as put to the sword. After nine holes, the British were behind in only one match and even there Alliss went on to win the 8th, 9th and 10th to square with Hawkins. Brown was still 3 up on Bolt; Peter Mills, considered the weakest player, was 4 up on Jack Burke, who had brought himself in

Right *The return to Britain of the Ryder Cup trophy was widely covered by the press*

A RYDER CUP FOURSOMES MATCH : Crowds of spectators are gathered round the 18th green on the course at Lindrick Golf Club, in Yorkshire, during the foursomes match between B. J. Hunt and P. Alliss, of Great Britain, and D. Ford and D. Finsterwald, of America. Although the British team lost the foursomes by three to one on the first day, they went on to gain a great victory in the singles, winning six and halving one of the matches. Thus Britain regained the Ryder Cup from the United States for the first time since 1933. It was the third British victory since the series began in 1926. Fine golfing conditions with a moderate south-west wind greeted the players on the second and final day of the tournament. By the middle of the day Britain was well ahead, and the realisation of the impending defeat of the Americans began to dawn on the crowds. The British team played some magnificent golf. Their achievement is all the more remarkable in view of the fact that it was accomplished in the face of having lost three foursomes. The value of the British victory to the competition is incalculable. Having held the trophy for twenty-four years, American interest in the event had appeared to be waning a little. Now, interest will be awakened and the next British team to visit the U.S. will certainly meet resolute opposition.

BRITAIN WINS
THE RYDER CUP

*The Trophy is Regained After
24 Years in America's Keeping*

BACK AT LAST: *Above*—Dai Rees, the British captain, is shouldered by members of his team as he jubilantly holds aloft the Ryder Cup, now in British hands after twenty-four years in America. *On right, above*—The British captain is playing out of a bunker at Lindrick during one of the foursome matches.

PLAY IN PROGRESS ON THE COURSE AT LINDRICK : *Above*—K. Bousfield, Great Britain, sends up a spray of sand as he plays out of a bunker at the 15th green on the course at the Lindrick Golf Club during one of the opening matches of the Ryder Cup tournament. On right—The last ball has been played and Britain has won the Ryder Cup. Amid cheers from the crowds, H. Bradshaw, Britain, and R. Mayer, America, shake hands before leaving the course. They had halved their singles match.

The crowd surges forward at the 18th where the last match – Mayer versus Bradshaw – is still out on the course

when Ted Kroll fell ill. Bousfield was 4 up on Hebert and Rees 3 ahead of Furgol. Both Hunt and Bradshaw were 1 up and O'Connor 2 up. At this time, the situation looked promising but Britain could afford to lose only two of the eight singles and halve one. After 18 holes, the British position was less strong. Though Mills and Bousfield were 5 up and Brown and Rees 4 up – positions from which they surely ought to win – both Bradshaw and Alliss were 1 down, O'Connor all square and Hunt only 1 up. The outcome of the 1957 Ryder Cup depended on the results of these last four matches.

In the afternoon, Brown was brought back to 2 up but went on to win; Tommy Bolt broke a club after his defeat and said he hadn't enjoyed the game; Mills experienced no problems with Burke and won by 5 and 3. Alliss quickly went three behind Hawkins but produced a run of four wins in six holes to lead for the first time but Hawkins went ahead again with 4s at the 14th and 16th, holes of 516 and 486 yards. Hawkins won by 2 and 1 at about the time it

became clear that America had lost the Ryder Cup and was their only singles winner.

The key golf of the afternoon came from Hunt and O'Connor. Hunt went out in 32 to be 5 up and won by 6 and 5. O'Connor won six of the first eight holes; he had lost his lead in the morning through poor putting but a visit to the pro's shop during the lunch interval led to the purchase of a new putter and he holed some very good ones in the afternoon. He won by 7 and 6.

Rees, playing at number five, was never troubled and he went from 4 up at lunch to 7 up after 27. He too won by 7 and 6 and was free to race around the course, in his role as captain, to inspire the team with his good news. Bousfield's match with Hebert produced the decisive moment. When Bousfield stood dormy 4 up and could therefore do no worse than halve, the cup had returned to British hands for the first time since the 1935 defeat.

Soon, just one match remained out on the course, the only one to reach the last green in the afternoon; it featured Irishman Harry Bradshaw against Dick Mayer. Bradshaw had won the first three holes in the morning but the American was 1 up at lunch. A Bradshaw 5 to the American's 6 on the 1st, a four hundred yard par 4, was enough to put him level and there was never more than a hole in it the rest of the way. Bradshaw, in fact, squared on the 14th and the rest of the holes were halved.

Even now, it is hard to see why the United States allowed themselves to be so heavily defeated. No doubt they were overconfident after the foursomes and perhaps the sudden British resurgence in the singles matches shocked them. What couldn't happen, had happened, and it kept on happening.

LINDRICK, YORKSHIRE, ENGLAND
4–5 OCTOBER 1957

Great Britain and Ireland		United States	
Captain Dai Rees		*Captain* Jack Burke	
Foursomes			
Alliss and Hunt	0	Ford and Finsterwald (2 and 1)	1
Bousfield and Rees (3 and 2)	1	Art Wall and Hawkins	0
Max Faulkner and Harry Weetman	0	Ted Kroll and Burke (4 and 3)	1
O'Connor and Brown	0	Mayer and Bolt (7 and 5)	1
	–		–
	1		3
Singles			
Eric Brown (4 and 3)	1	Tommy Bolt	0
Peter Mills (5 and 3)	1	Jack Burke	0
Peter Alliss	0	Fred Hawkins (2 and 1)	1
Ken Bousfield (4 and 3)	1	Lionel Hebert	0
Dai Rees (7 and 6)	1	Ed Furgol	0
Bernard Hunt (6 and 5)	1	Doug Ford	0
Christy O'Connor (7 and 6)	1	Dow Finsterwald	0
Harry Bradshaw (halved)	0	Dick Mayer	0
	–		–
	6		1

Final score: Great Britain and Ireland 7
United States 4.
One match halved

BUSINESS AS USUAL
(1959–1969)

1959

The journey to the Eldorado Country Club, Palm Desert, California was, for the British team, the most testing part of their 1959 Ryder Cup defence. First there was the sea crossing to endure; it was decided to travel on the *Queen Mary* rather than fly across the Atlantic in order to foster team spirit. But the weather was stormy and many of the golfers were sea-sick.

Worse was to follow when the team took to the air. After exhibition matches and a meeting with Bobby Jones in Atlanta, the last leg of the journey was to be a short charter flight from Los Angeles over the San Jacinto Mountains – a hop of about 40 minutes. One result was that golf led the front page of the London *Daily Express* for the first time ever. Another was that Bernard Hunt went down heavily in the foursomes and didn't play in the singles. The twin-engined Convair ran into a storm over the mountains. The pilot tried to find a way through. The plane began to judder, then the movements grew more violent. The climax was a sudden plunge down through the air all the way from 14,000 feet to 9,000.

Bernard Hunt had gallantly given up his seat to an air hostess and was standing in the gangway when the force of the descent almost flung him against the roof. As Hunt clung on to the seat backs the luggage racks emptied and their contents flew upwards. Hunt's shoulders were severely wrenched. Eventually the mad descent came to a stop. The Convair had

escaped disaster by plunging between two peaks and the plane flew onwards towards its destination. Ironically, the airport was closed because of the storm and they had to return to Los Angeles where there was the offer of another flight. Not surprisingly, the captain, Dai Rees, decided to make the journey by Greyhound bus and the team arrived at dawn. One of his team, Ken Bousfield, commented, 'Anzio Beach was never like this'.

The American team looked formidable compared to the Lindrick side; Sam Snead was back, as was Cary Middlecoff. Snead was in excellent form. In 1959 he played four tournament rounds in 259 strokes, including one in 59. On the British side, Peter Mills had come to be regarded as one of the most reliable players but he had to be replaced, when he damaged his back, by John Panton who was flown out but, in the end, was chosen neither for the foursomes nor the singles.

The British team were upset that the Eldorado club had not closed the course so that, during practice, team members were held up by others playing round. Perhaps conscious of the conspicuous wealth all around them, Rees later commented, 'We were paupers in a millionaire's playground!'. A gimmick was also tried which was quite common on the US Tour in those days; in order to get the publicity which comes from freakishly low scoring, tee markers were put forward. The British (and, of course, the Americans) who had been practising from the back tees found their clubbing on second shots

Above *The course at the Eldorado Country Club where Britain lost the cup; she wouldn't regain it for 30 years*

much confused when the markers were moved right forward to much the same length as the ladies' tees when hostilities opened.

Even so, quite a good start was made in the foursomes. The famous British partnership of Peter Alliss and Christy O'Connor met the current Masters champion, Art Wall, and Doug Ford who had previously won the Masters and US PGA. These two were superb putters, which neither Alliss nor O'Connor were, but this was a day when all the short ones went into the middle of the hole. The British pair won by 3 and 2 after the first match had gone to the USA.

The British anchor men, Rees and Ken Bousfield, were then beaten but it looked as if the first day would end level. The final British pairing of Dave Thomas and Harry Weetman were 1 up standing on the last tee. Thomas then launched one of his enormous drives far down the middle. It was the Americans' turn to play their second shots first, with a water hazard to carry. Sam Snead put their ball in. Weetman now made a surprising decision; instead of laying up short of the hazard, he decided to go for the green. However, as a result of Thomas's huge drive, he had only a mid-iron left but he hit the ball just a touch heavily so that it caught the far bank and toppled back into the water. On the hole, both teams were level; Middlecoff pitched to about a dozen feet and Snead holed the putt. The British didn't do as well. The US won the hole and halved the match, gaining a 1-point lead into the singles on the morrow.

Norman Drew, perhaps a sacrificial offering, played number one for Britain against Doug Ford. This time the water on the last worked to British advantage. One hole in the lead, Ford sensibly played short of it with his second. Peter Mills, walking round with his friend, advised Drew that he might as well go for it. Drew then lashed a 3-wood to a foot or so to halve the

match. From there on, British hopes failed; the next four matches went to the US, only Rees putting up much of a struggle, having been 3 down after five played. He nearly halved his match but Dow Finsterwald pitched dead when he had gone through the final green. Then came Peter Alliss with just two lost singles on his Ryder Cup record. He, too, appeared to have lost when he came to the last 1 down, but his opponent, Jay Hebert, hit his second shot into the water and Peter fired a 3-iron safely to the heart of the green to earn a halved match. In the last match, Eric Brown kept his splendid singles (and poor foursomes) record going by defeating Cary Middlecoff 4 and 3.

The result confirmed what everyone thought: Britain may have a chance on home soil, but in America they had no chance. The result was US 7 Britain 2. Afterwards, there

Above *Fashion conscious spectators enjoy the sun as much as the sporting action in Palm Springs*

was renewed talk about the need to strengthen the British team by bringing in golfers from other nations. It was assumed that opening the game up to European players would not make a great deal of difference as only perhaps a couple of golfers would be likely to earn a place in any one year. The Commonwealth, on the other hand, had players of the calibre of Peter Thomson, Gary Player, Al Balding and Stan Leonard. Perhaps golfers from the Commonwealth were never accepted because British tournament players didn't want to lose the prestige and financial returns that came from being picked for the Ryder Cup; if Commonwealth players were to be selected, far fewer British men would earn a place.

ELDORADO, PALM DESERT, CALIFORNIA, USA
6–7 NOVEMBER 1959

United States		Great Britain and Ireland	
Captain Jerry Barber		*Captain* Dai Rees	
Foursomes			
Rosburg and Souchak (5 and 4)	1	Hunt and Brown	0
Ford and Wall	0	O'Connor and Alliss (3 and 2)	1
Julius Boros and Finsterwald (2 up)	1	Rees and Bousfield	0
Snead and Middlecoff (halved)	0	Weetman and Thomas	0
	–		–
	2		1
Singles			
Doug Ford (halved)	0	Norman Drew	0
Mike Souchak (3 and 2)	1	Ken Bousfield	0
Bob Rosburg (6 and 5)	1	Harry Weetman	0
Sam Snead (6 and 5)	1	Dave Thomas	0
Dow Finsterwald (1 up)	1	Dai Rees	0
Jay Hebert (halved)	0	Peter Alliss	0
Art Wall (7 and 6)	1	Christy O'Connor	0
Cary Middlecoff	0	Eric Brown (4 and 3)	1
	–		–
	5		1

Final score: United States 7
Great Britain and Ireland 2.
Three matches halved. (This was the last Ryder Cup in which 36 hole matches were played.)

1961

At the 1961 match at Lytham the Ryder Cup lost its epic 36 hole matches, the four foursomes and eight singles. Individual matches had sometimes produced a landslide result but over 36 holes anyone who wins his singles match is fully entitled to believe that he is the best man on the day. That is why, for example, Eric Brown is still remembered for having played four singles and won them all; that could hardly happen today. Only Larry Nelson has managed to compile a remarkable sequence – and look what happened to him in 1987.

In 1961, 18-hole matches were introduced. At Lytham, there were two sets of foursomes on the first day, four in the morning and four in the afternoon which were followed by eight singles matches in the morning and afternoon.

Alliss and O'Connor gave Britain a good start by beating Doug Ford and Gene Littler in the first match out but the other three morning matches went to the Americans; as a result, the US captain, Jerry Barber promptly dropped his losing pair. Alliss and O'Connor led off for Britain once more in the afternoon, this time facing Jay Hebert and Art Wall who had disposed of Bernard Hunt and John Panton by 4 and 3 in the morning. The British pairing seemed in command, Alliss holing everything of reasonable length and striking his iron shots beautifully at the top of the flag. The match seemed to be theirs on the 15th when the American ball was far into the rough but the tide was turned when O'Connor followed them. The hole was halved and the US won the 16th to lead for the first time. Alliss produced a good long iron to win the 17th and a halved match seemed a fair result with both teams on the last in 2 and both seven yards and more from the hole. Hebert overhit his putt, but dead on line, and down it went; Alliss missed.

The one British victory showed that the Americans, Mike Souchak and Bill Collins, were prone to error at times. Having taken 4 on the 1st, a par 3, they went on to send their tee shots onto the railway at the next two holes. The result of the match was more or less a certainty for Rees and Bousfield when the US took three putts on the 7th. This was the only British success of the afternoon and so the day ended with the Americans holding a 6–2 lead. With 16 singles to come, the British team were still hopeful that there was scope for a Lindrick-type miracle. That miracle came far too late, Britain winning three of the last four matches and halving the other one. In fact, the final result had been decided much earlier; the US

Above left *Neil Coles flicks the ball from a sandy lie at Lytham*

Below left *Dai Rees misses one on the 13th as partner Ken Bousfield watches*

had won three of the first four matches and halved the other, and by lunchtime they led overall by 10–4, Rees and Bernard Hunt having won for Britain.

By this time, Peter Alliss, particularly in the Ryder Cup, had established himself as the best British player; he was now faced by Arnold Palmer in a match to savour. A superstar in America since 1958, he had come close to winning the centenary Open at St Andrews in 1960 and then won the championship at Birkdale about three months before the Ryder Cup match. In the teeth of the gales, he had played what many who watched still consider the greatest golf they have seen.

Palmer took the lead on the 2nd but Alliss levelled on the 3rd and, on the next, he went ahead with a birdie. Palmer got back to even by holing from off the green at the 7th but Alliss immediately went ahead again on the next and when he pitched to a yard on the 10th, with Palmer through the green in a buried lie, he looked about to take a firm grip on the match. With the green sloping away from him, Palmer seemed to have no chance of finishing close, instead he holed the chip. Both players had birdie 3s. The next four holes were halved but Alliss lost his lead on the 15th. Here, Palmer missed the green with his approach shot and was bunkered but then luckily holed out on the second bounce. With the match square, the remaining holes were halved, though Alliss looked as if he might lose it on the last. Here he left himself with a chip of perhaps 40 yards but got it very close and conceded Palmer a putt of more than two feet.

Rees, however, a controversial choice as captain with the players who felt the honour (with accompanying perks) should be shared around, had made one decision which did not work out. He had not used Harry Weetman or Ralph Moffitt on the first day but led off with them in the morning's singles. Both lost – Moffitt by 5 and 4 which is a heavy defeat over just 18 holes. Moffitt was later to be forced out of tournament golf by an odd nervous disability. Many golfers have developed a twitch on short putts, others on the little touch shots from around the green. Moffitt developed a twitch with the driver which meant that he couldn't take the club back. He was dropped for the afternoon, when Dai Rees came to the end of a Ryder Cup career which had lasted close on a quarter of a century. He left in style, winning and losing in the foursomes but beating both Jay Hebert and Doug Ford in his singles.

Ken Bousfield

ROYAL LYTHAM AND ST ANNES, LANCASHIRE, ENGLAND
13–14 OCTOBER 1961

Great Britain and Ireland		United States	
Captain Dai Rees		*Captain* Jerry Barber	
Foursomes (morning)			
O'Connor and Alliss (4 and 3)	1	Littler and Ford	0
John Panton and Hunt	0	Wall and Hebert (4 and 3)	1
Rees and Bousfield	0	Casper and Palmer (2 and 1)	1
Haliburton and Coles	0	Souchak and Collins (1 up)	1
Foursomes (afternoon)			
O'Connor and Alliss	0	Wall and Hebert (1 up)	1
Panton and Hunt	0	Casper and Palmer (5 and 4)	1
Rees and Bousfield (4 and 2)	1	Souchak and Collins	0
Haliburton and Coles	0	Barber and Finsterwald (1 up)	1
	2		6
Singles (morning)			
Harry Weetman	0	Doug Ford (1 up)	1
Ralph Moffitt	0	Mike Souchak (5 and 4)	1

Peter Alliss (halved)	0	Arnold Palmer	0
Ken Bousfield	0	Billy Casper (5 and 3)	1
Dai Rees (2 and 1)	1	Jay Hebert	0
Neil Coles (halved)	0	Gene Littler	0
Bernard Hunt (5 and 4)	1	Jerry Barber	0
Christy O'Connor	0	Dow Finsterwald (2 and 1)	1
Singles (afternoon)			
Harry Weetman	0	Art Wall (1 up)	1
Peter Alliss (3 and 2)	1	Bill Collins	0
Bernard Hunt	0	Mike Souchak (2 and 1)	1
Tom Haliburton	0	Arnold Palmer (2 and 1)	1
Dai Rees (4 and 3)	1	Doug Ford	0
Ken Bousfield (1 up)	1	Jerry Barber	0
Neil Coles (1 up)	1	Dow Finsterwald	0
Christy O'Connor (halved)	0	Gene Littler	0
	6		7

Final score: United States 13
Great Britain and Ireland 8.
Three matches halved

Having thwarted the dreaded Palmer, Alliss played even better in the afternoon and despatched Bill Collins by 3 and 2. The final score was 13 to 8 to the United States. There was much talk that the result might have been different if Eric Brown and Dave Thomas had been in the team. Some took consolation from the fact that five of the 24 matches had been lost by one hole only and three of the singles had been halved. A small swing, they said, would have seen Britain victorious. This reminds me of what a writer once said of Walter Hagen, 'The difference between Hagen and the rest is that he just wins and they just don't'. American Ryder Cup teams continued to benefit from playing in the much more competitive US Tour. The Americans also had a large pool of very good players; their 'second XI' would have easily beaten the British equivalent.

1963

Americans have never been enthusiastic about foursomes golf, which they normally refer to as 'Scotch foursomes'. Increasingly, British golfers at every level have also come to prefer playing their own ball, foursomes remaining a weekly feature at just a few British clubs. At Atlanta in 1963, foursomes remained part of the Ryder Cup but other changes were made to the playing format. The match was extended to three days, to bring in more money. There were four foursomes, held on the morning and afternoon of the first day, followed by the same number of fourballs the second day and then eight singles, both in the morning and afternoon, to complete the event. This raised the number of points at stake to 32, with the potential for an embarrassing score such as the

one that ended the competition.

The first morning, however, went promisingly and finished with the teams level at 1 point each and the other two matches halved, but in the afternoon, the Americans won the lot. The fourballs on the second day went much the same way. There was a creditable result in the morning series: 2–1 to the US and one match halved, but the American team took the first three afternoon matches before Brian Huggett and Dave Thomas managed to halve the last match with Dave Ragan and Bob Goalby.

Standing at 10–2 behind, Britain had a slim chance only as the final day's singles began and that diminished when Geoff Hunt, brother of Bernard, was easily despatched by Tony Lema, who was then at his peak. However, Britain won four of the other seven matches in the morning to the Americans' two. With eight to play, the US led 13–6; the statistics were not encourag-

Christy O'Connor Snr after sinking a 40-foot putt

Below *Welshman Brian Huggett throws his hands up in frustration after losing to Billy Casper and Arnold Palmer*

ing. Then came one of the worst sessions for Britain in Ryder Cup history; Peter Alliss halved with Tony Lema, but the Americans won every other match, giving a match result of US 20 Britain 6, with six matches halved.

Perhaps the only match worth treating in detail from the final day is the Alliss/Palmer match in the morning – a very different encounter from the one at Lytham two years before when Alliss had been a little surprised to find that he had as much length as Palmer. Palmer gave the ball such a furious lash that observers were apt to think him longer off the tee then he actually was. There were no such doubts in this match at East Lake, Bobby Jones's boyhood course, Alliss was much, much shorter than Palmer. He was lifting the club up on the backswing and cutting across the ball in the hitting area. With this kind of action, Alliss was finding the fairways well enough but Palmer was outdriving him every time by about 50 yards. This was not quite the disadvantage it seems as Alliss's irons were going very well indeed and again and again Palmer had to watch as Alliss whistled them in close to the flag before trying to follow suit.

Alliss should have opened up a decisive lead over the early holes but missed a few fairly short putts. After 12 holes, however, he was 2 up and held the same lead with three holes to play. He then lost the 16th and the 17th seemed to be going the same way when Palmer's approach settled about a yard away. Alliss then holed from about four times the distance 'in the loudest silence I've ever heard'. Alliss then halved the last hole and won the match, getting a very long putt with a great deal of borrow stone-dead.

Below *Arnold Palmer at East Lake*

Top *The 14th at Gleneagles, scene of the first international match in 1921* (Michael Hobbs Collection)

Above *Gene Littler at Missouri in 1971* (Bob Thomas)

Left *Peter Alliss follows the flight of his ball at Royal Birkdale* (Gerry Cranham)

Above *Tony Jacklin in a bunker at Muirfield in 1973* (Associated Sports Photography)

Below *Wentworth, scene of the first Ryder Cup match in 1926* (Dave Cannon: All Sport)

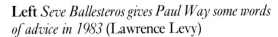

Left *Seve Ballesteros gives Paul Way some words of advice in 1983* (Lawrence Levy)

Below left *Bruce Lietzke and Bill Rogers share an umbrella at Walton Heath in 1981. Rogers clearly finds it all a bit of a bore* (Phil Sheldon)

Below right *Jack Nicklaus at Lytham in 1977* (Peter Dazeley)

Right *Ian Woosnam* (Lawrence Levy)

Left *American Peter Jacobsen watches his shot anxiously* (Lawrence Levy)

Right *Calvin Peete: possibly America's finest black golfer* (Bob Thomas)

Left *Sam Torrance and Howard Clark celebrate their win over Tom Kite and Andy North in the fourballs* (Lawrence Levy)

Left *Craig Stadler of the USA* (Bob Thomas)

Right *The 5th green at Muirfield Village. Sandy Lyle in play* (Bob Thomas)

Below *Howard Clark sets off for the first day's foursomes at Muirfield Village in 1987* (Bob Thomas)

Right *Seve Ballesteros: the world's finest golfer* (Bob Thomas)

Below *America's Curtis Strange met Seve Ballesteros in the match that clinched the 1987 Ryder Cup* (Bob Thomas)

Bottom *Non-playing captain, Jack Nicklaus, discusses the contest with team members* (Bob Thomas)

EAST LAKE, ATLANTA, GEORGIA, USA 11–13 OCTOBER 1963

United States		Great Britain and Ireland	
Captain Arnold Palmer		*Captain* Johnny Fallon	
Foursomes (morning)			
Palmer and Pott	0	Huggett and Will (3 and 2)	1
Casper and Ragan (1 up)	1	Alliss and O'Connor	0
Boros and Lema (halved)	0	Coles and Bernard Hunt (halved)	0
Littler and Finsterwald (halved)	0	Thomas and Weetman (halved)	0
Foursomes (afternoon)			
Maxwell and Goalby (4 and 3)	1	Thomas and Weetman	0
Palmer and Casper (5 and 4)	1	Huggett and Will	0
Littler and Finsterwald (2 and 1)	1	Coles and Geoff Hunt	0
Boros and Lema (1 up)	1	Haliburton and Bernard Hunt	0
	–		–
	5		1
Fourball (morning)			
Palmer and Finsterwald (5 and 4)	1	Huggett and Thomas	0
Littler and Boros (halved)	0	Alliss and Bernard Hunt (halved)	0
Casper and Maxwell (3 and 2)	1	Weetman and Will	0
Goalby and Ragan	0	Coles and O'Connor (1 up)	1
Fourball (afternoon)			
Palmer and Finsterwald (3 and 2)	1	Coles and O'Connor	0
Lema and Pott (1 up)	1	Alliss and Bernard Hunt	0
Casper and Maxwell (2 and 1)	1	Haliburton and Geoff Hunt	0
Goalby and Ragan (halved)	0	Huggett and Thomas (halved)	0
	–		–
	5		1
Singles (morning)			
Tony Lema (5 and 3)	1	Geoff Hunt	0
Johnny Pott	0	Brian Huggett (3 and 1)	1
Arnold Palmer	0	Peter Alliss (1 up)	1
Billy Casper (halved)	0	Neil Coles	0
Bob Goalby (3 and 2)	1	David Thomas	0
Gene Littler (1 up)	1	Christy O'Connor	0
Julius Boros	0	Harry Weetman (1 up)	1
Dow Finsterwald	0	Bernard Hunt (2 up)	1
Singles (afternoon)			
Arnold Palmer (3 and 2)	1	George Will	0
Dave Ragan (2 and 1)	1	Neil Coles	0
Tony Lema (halved)	0	Peter Alliss	0
Gene Littler (6 and 5)	1	Tom Haliburton	0
Julius Boros (2 and 1)	1	Harry Weetman	0
Billy Maxwell (2 and 1)	1	Christy O'Connor	0
Dow Finsterwald (4 and 3)	1	David Thomas	0
Bob Goalby (2 and 1)	1	Bernard Hunt	0
	—		—
	10		4

Final score: United States 20
Great Britain and Ireland 6.
Six matches halved

1965

Harry Weetman had declared during the 1957 Lindrick match that he would never again play under Dai Rees's captaincy and as a result he was banned from British tournament golf for a while. All had been forgiven by the PGA and eight years later Weetman was appointed non-playing captain. The USA honoured Byron Nelson by placing him in the same role, almost twenty years after he had retired from full-time tournament golf. Dai Rees provided match commentary on the television.

The match was being sponsored by a former Royal Birkdale captain Brian Park and great care was taken with the preparations; Park even went to the USA to see if there was anything to be learned about tournament organisation. As a result, the Birkdale Ryder Cup match was the best presented event yet seen in British golf. However, the course and the weather caused problems. It is always assumed that the British

97

will cope better with bad weather than the Americans and at Royal Birkdale the weather was fine. British players are also far more used to links golf than Americans, specially those with little or no experience of playing in the Open Championship. But the weather had been wet and some also said the fairways had been overfertilised – they were certainly not fast running, and tight fairway lies were an exception rather than the norm. The near parkland quality of the fairways meant that, except for the longest hitters, there were difficulties in being up in 2 at perhaps six of the holes. With the Americans superior at getting down in 2 from 60 yards or so, this factor seemed likely to work against the British.

By the time of this match, the layout of the course had reached what may remain its final shape. The short 17th had been abandoned and a very good 190-yard par 3, the 12th, was substituted instead. The finish was now formidable and a long iron or more was needed for the shot to the green at seven of the last eight holes.

Palmer was once again the superstar of the US team, though he was to win no more major championships after his fourth Masters in 1964 – a decline which at the time no one thought possible. Tony Lema was playing almost as well as Palmer; Lema had won the Open Championship at St Andrews in 1964 with slight knowledge of the course but sadly he was to be killed in a place crash within a year. Jack Nicklaus was missing from the US team because he was not eligible under US PGA rules as he had been a professional for a little over three years only. Nicklaus had won the US Open, a US PGA title and the Masters twice and had come close to winning both the 1963 and 1964 Open Championships. Unfortunately, this didn't count.

The US selection system was always worse than the British but this passed unnoticed when the Americans were winning but the shock of defeat in the 1980s has caused rethinking. The US selectors aimed to reward those golfers who

Rival captains Byron Nelson and Harry Weetman at Royal Birkdale

had served their time; they didn't concentrate on fielding the best team because it simply wasn't of vital importance. The Americans did have one team problem at Birkdale, however; Johnny Pott had damaged some rib muscles just before coming over which did not respond to treatment. Should the next in line, Mike Souchak, be flown over? The captain, Byron Nelson, decided to manage with his nine remaining players – another sign of American confidence.

The British start was poor in the foursomes, Lionel Platts and Peter Butler opening with three 5s to three 4s from Julius Boros and Tony Lema. In the following match, however, Dave Thomas and George Will, facing Palmer and Dave Marr, began brilliantly – 4, 3, 3. These starts helped settle both matches. The first British pairing could never quite get back to level terms but took Boros and Lema to the last green. Thomas was in magnificent form in his long game and George Will, also a powerful player, backed him well; they didn't lose a single hole and a birdie on the 13th finished the Americans off. Had the mighty Palmer been humbled? Not really – Dave Marr had played the poor shots.

In the next two matches Bernard Hunt and Neil Coles went 1 up after three holes on Billy Casper and Gene Littler but the Americans won four of the next five holes and steady play on the homeward nine was good enough for victory by 2 and 1. Peter Alliss and Christy O'Connor were always in the dominant position against Don January and Ken Venturi. Two up at the turn, they won three out of four holes from the 11th and that was that.

Though the scores stood level at 2 points each after the morning's play, the British had the better of it. There was once a time when

Gene Littler watches a tee shot by Don January

some club and even international matches used to be settled on the basis of 'holes up'. In this sense, the US totalled 3 up in the two matches they had won while the British were 11 up.

Weetman dropped Platts and Butler for the afternoon and moved his winning pairs into the first two matches out. Thomas and Will again faced Palmer and Marr and what a difference there was; in the 13 holes the match lasted, the Americans had eight 3s, six of these coming in a row from the 2nd to the 7th. Out in 30, they finished the British off with an eagle 3 on the 13th so although the British were only two strokes worse than in their victorious morning, this time out they didn't win a hole. Palmer and Marr were 7 under par.

Alliss and O'Connor had a sterner fight against Casper and Littler. Despite getting to the turn in 31 they were only 1 up and the Americans then squared with a birdie on the 13th. The British pair stuck to par or better,

The sign reads:

HOLE 10
YARDS 393
PAR 4

however, and went on to win by 2 and 1. They were 6 under at the finish – hardly behind the scoring of Palmer and Marr.

Jimmy Hitchcock and Irishman Jimmy Martin lost the 3rd, 4th and 5th and that run was almost enough to account for their losing by 5 and 4 to Lema and Boros, perhaps the strongest US pairing. Coles and Hunt played considerably better than in the morning; they opened up with an eagle and never looked back. Hunt finished the match off, 3 and 2, with a vast putt of some 20 yards to win the hole and match and level the points score at 4 all.

Peter Alliss looks disgusted with his tee shot. In the same fourball are (left to right) Christy O'Connor, Dave Marr and Arnold Palmer

Britain went behind for the first time after the morning's fourballs of the second day which they lost by 2–1 with one game halved. It was in this session that the Ryder Cup was won and lost.

A glance at the scores seems to show that Alliss and O'Connor must have played badly to lose by 5 and 4 while the first two British pairs had at least managed to halve and lose by only 1 hole but the figures are deceptive. Thomas and Will looked in total command for much of their match, going to the turn in 33 to be 3 up. They then won the 10th and Don January had to hole a good putt to halve the 11th. Then things went rapidly wrong. Neither of the British players could get a par on the 12th, a par 3, nor on the other short hole coming home, the 14th. Apart from these failings they went down to a barrage of birdies. From their earlier 4-up position, the British reached the last hole 1 down – and so it remained.

Platts and Butler were also out in 33 and 3 up. Later, they improved to dormy 4 up so that they needed just one half on any of the closing holes to win. Butler seemed to have done it when two very good wooden shots saw him on the 15th green, a hole of 536 yards, but he sent his first putt past the hole and missed the return. The Americans birdied the hole and Littler birdied the last three as well, single-putting each time. The Americans deserved the half; Butler shouldn't have given them the opportunity. The potential for a 3–1 win in the morning for Britain turned into a 2½–1½ loss.

Alliss and O'Connor led off in the afternoon against Palmer and Marr, who had beaten them by 5 and 4 in the morning. First one pair, then the other led with the Americans squaring the match with a birdie on the 15th. The position remained the same on the 18th, a hole of 513 yards, and reachable with a couple of driver shots that day. Alliss was the only one of the four to manage it and he used a 4-wood for his second shot, easing his hands ahead of the clubhead to keep the ball low and turning in the toe. He wasn't even asked to putt in the end.

The match scores were level again but it was the last full point to come Britain's way for some time. Although Platts and Butler managed to get to 4 up after eight they could manage only a halved match. The other two matches were narrowly won by the US and at the end of the day America held a 2-point lead with 16 singles to come.

A great difference in captaincy styles now appeared. Nelson sent out his three best players first, both morning and afternoon: Palmer at number one, followed by Boros and Lema. Weetman, on the other hand, put his strength – Coles, Hunt and Alliss – more or less in the middle. You can see how it all worked out from the match results below; the top three Americans won all 6 points at stake for their country.

After the first four singles in the morning it looked like the Americans had won, the US having an overall lead of 6 points. However, Hunt and Alliss then improved the position by winning the next two matches. David Thomas also seemed to be in a good position at 2 up after nine holes but he then picked up on the 10th, took 6 on the 13th and lost his ball on the 15th. He lost by 2 and 1.

At lunch the Americans were 5 points in the lead and they needed to win only two more matches which happened soon enough as Palmer beat Peter Butler and Boros defeated Jimmy Hitchcock. The two wins came almost simultaneously and the crowds at the home green were treated to the sight of a superb 3-wood from Palmer, precisely shaped to draw round a greenside bunker and stop little more than a yard from the flag. At the same time, Boros won his match on the 17th.

Lema then emphasised the American superiority by playing superbly and beating O'Connor by 6 and 4. Three of the last five matches went to Britain, although it was too late to affect the final result, and Alliss brought his tally to 5 points out of a possible 6. The British total was 11 as against 18 for the United States. Three matches were halved.

When it was all over, the analysis began. Byron Nelson thought his players had been far more likely to get down in two from 60 yards or less. Many observers felt that the Americans were always likelier to hole the putts that really mattered. Others pointed out how close it had all been but the fact remains that the United States had been home and dry after just two singles on the final afternoon.

ROYAL BIRKDALE, LANCASHIRE, ENGLAND 7–9 OCTOBER 1965

United States		Great Britain and Ireland	
Captain Byron Nelson		*Captain* Harry Weetman	
Foursomes (morning)			
Boros and Lema (1 hole)	1	Platts and Butler	0
Marr and Palmer	0	Thomas and Will (6 and 5)	1
Casper and Littler (2 and 1)	1	Hunt and Coles	0
Venturi and January	0	O'Connor and Alliss (5 and 4)	1
Foursomes (afternoon)			
Marr and Palmer (6 and 5)	1	Thomas and Will	0
Boros and Lema (5 and 4)	1	Jimmy Martin and Hitchcock	0
Casper and Littler	0	O'Connor and Alliss (2 and 1)	1
Venturi and January	0	Hunt and Coles (3 and 2)	1
	4		4
Fourballs (morning)			
January and Jacobs (1 hole)	1	Thomas and Will	0
Casper and Littler (halved)	0	Platts and Butler	0
Marr and Palmer (5 and 4)	1	Alliss and O'Connor	0
Boros and Lema	0	Coles and Hunt (1 up)	1

United States		Great Britain and Ireland	
Fourballs (afternoon)			
Marr and Palmer	0	Alliss and O'Connor (1 up)	1
January and Jacobs (1 up)	1	Thomas and Will	0
Casper and Littler (halved)	0	Platts and Butler	0
Lema and Venturi (1 up)	1	Coles and Hunt	0
	4		2
Singles (morning)			
Arnold Palmer (3 and 2)	1	Jimmy Hitchcock	0
Julius Boros (4 and 2)	1	Lionel Platts	0
Tony Lema (1 up)	1	Peter Butler	0
Dave Marr (2 up)	1	Neil Coles	0
Gene Littler	0	Bernard Hunt (2 up)	1
Billy Casper	0	Peter Alliss (1 up)	1
Tommy Jacobs (2 and 1)	1	David Thomas	0
Don January (halved)	0	George Will	0
Singles (afternoon)			
Arnold Palmer (2 up)	1	Peter Butler	0
Julius Boros (2 and 1)	1	Jimmy Hitchcock	0
Tony Lema (6 and 4)	1	Christy O'Connor	0
Ken Venturi	0	Peter Alliss (3 and 2)	1
Dave Marr (1 up)	1	Bernard Hunt	0
Billy Casper	0	Neil Coles (3 and 2)	1
Gene Littler (2 and 1)	1	George Will	0
Tommy Jacobs	0	Lionel Platts (1 up)	1
	10		5

Final score: United States 18 Great Britain and Ireland 11. Three matches halved

1967

Dai Rees was brought back to captain the 1967 match which was held at the Champions club, outside Houston in Texas; it was hoped that his optimism and energy would be infectious. He also had the benefit of leading the only British team to win the Ryder Cup since 1933. The United States' choice was the man with the most authority in golf – Ben Hogan.

Hogan came off much the better of the two in the team introductions during the pre-match dinner. Rees spoke first, naming each member of his team and listing their achievements man by man. Sometimes, alas, there wasn't very much to tell; none of his players had won a major championship and only two, David Thomas and Christy O'Connor, had come close – in the Open Championship. Then came Hogan's turn. He asked his team to rise to their feet and then said, 'Ladies and gentlemen, the finest golfers in the world'. And then they all sat down again. Jack Nicklaus still wasn't in the team, despite having won two US Opens, one British Open, one US PGA and three Masters;

The 1967 British team: (back, l to r) Tony Jacklin,
Peter Alliss, David Thomas, Bernard Hunt, George
Will, Christy O'Connor. (Front) Malcolm Gregson,
Hugh Boyle, Dai Rees, Brian Huggett, Neil Coles

the rules of the US PGA would not allow him to
participate.

Britain had a potential new star in the team in
Tony Jacklin who had become a household
name not so much by winning the Dunlop
Masters at Royal St George's but by holing in
one at the 16th under the eyes of the television
cameras. It helped him to a final round of 64.

Mark McCormack put the British prospects
very much in focus when he wrote, 'Americans
playing on their home ground are no more likely
to lose to the British than Boston is likely to
apologise for the tea party'.

Hogan was a disciplinarian; he decreed that
his team must be in bed by 10.30 p.m. and that
they should attend no social events. He decided,
that since it was optional, they should all use the
small British ball. If they preferred not to, he
declared, they hadn't enough sense to be in the
team anyway. Watching his team on the practice ground at Champions, he remarked, 'I've

never seen so many god-awful shots in my life'.
What he thought about the British players is not
recorded. Arnold Palmer arrived in his personal
jet and immediately objected to the idea of
using the small 1.62 ball. Hogan's reply was,
'Who said you were playing?'.

Unlike Dai Rees, who asked everyone's
opinions about, for example, who should be
paired in foursomes or fourballs and what the
singles order should be, Hogan made his decisions alone. And he never explained his reasons.
The team loved him; they knew just where they
were with Hogan and what they had to do: win.
Those that lost in the morning could expect a
'rest' in the afternoon – but not too many
Americans lost at Houston.

There was one successful British pairing in
morning and afternoon foursomes – David
Thomas and the young Tony Jacklin. They
won twice, first against Doug Sanders and Gay
Brewer and in the afternoon against Gene
Littler and Al Geiberger. The best Britain
could manage in the remaining six matches was
one half. With two days still to go, the end result
was virtually a foregone conclusion. Humiliation followed in the eight fourballs. This time,

in their two matches, the successful Thomas/ Jacklin pairing managed just one halved game. In terms of the total British performance this almost ranked as a glittering success. That half, coming in the last match of the afternoon, prevented a clean sweep by the United States and at the end of the day they led by 10 points.

In the singles, Neil Coles, who, because of a fear of flying, had taken a weary eight days to make the journey to the Champions, had a good day, beating Doug Sanders twice. The rising Tony Jacklin, however, sank in both his games. Bernard Hunt, who twice stepped on to the last tee dormy 1 up, lost the hole both times with bogeys. This was almost as bad as one freak happening in the previous day's fourballs; Hugh Boyle and George Will were 4 up on Palmer and Boros after an outward nine in 30. Boyle was then the only player on the 10th green in two. He 3-putted, the United States won the hole and then fired some birdies of their own.

After the match, with its 21–6 scoreline, the post-mortems began. The British lagged their putts, the US banged them at the hole and seemed confident – and successful – in holing the 4 or 5 footers they often had back. This boldness seemed to run right through American play. You had to get the birdies to win on the US Tour; in Britain a more cautious approach seemed to bring rewards. (The US Tour still awards prizes for the most birdies and eagles but there's nothing for the man with the fewest bogeys.)

Again there were discussions about a formula which would produce a team to give the Americans a run for their money. The gap between standards of play was widening, not narrowing as had once been hoped. It might help if Bob Charles of New Zealand and Peter Thomson, Bruce Devlin, Bruce Crampton and other Australians could be brought in to the British side. It was still assumed that the inclusion of continental players would do little to strengthen the team. The British captain, Dai Rees, thought that reducing the team numbers to

Above *Bernard Hunt: 'Do you want to try this one, Peter?'*

eight might help to strengthen the side because while Britain might have a handful of good players there were always a couple, at least, who performed well below international standards. He felt improvement of wedge technique would also help. Players should stop flicking at the ball with their hands and develop a method where the knees flowed with the stroke, a style introduced by Byron Nelson a quarter of a century earlier. Some British players, Rees included, thought the American size 1.68 ball should become compulsory in British tournaments. Because the small ball does not veer to left and right as drastically when mishit, British players concentrated on trying to hit it straight. Americans, instead, aimed to draw or fade the ball, according to taste, and this brought a more consistent and effective pattern to their play.

Commonwealth players were not introduced to Ryder Cup play, but action was taken over the 1.68 ball. The PGA announced that it would be used in tournament play in 1968.

CHAMPIONS, HOUSTON, TEXAS, USA, 21–22 OCTOBER 1967

United States		Great Britain and Ireland	
Captain Ben Hogan		*Captain* Dai Rees	
Foursomes (morning)			
Casper and Boros (halved)	0	Huggett and Will	0
Palmer and Dickinson (2 and 1)	1	Alliss and O'Connor	0
Sanders and Brewer	0	Jacklin and Thomas (4 and 3)	1
Nichols and Pott (6 and 5)	1	Hunt and Coles	0
Foursomes (afternoon)			
Boros and Casper (1 up)	1	Huggett and Will	0
Dickinson and Palmer (5 and 4)	1	Gregson and Boyle	0
Littler and Geiberger	0	Jacklin and Thomas (3 and 2)	1
Nichols and Pott (2 and 1)	1	Hunt and Coles	0
	5		2
Fourball (morning)			
Casper and Brewer (3 and 2)	1	Alliss and O'Connor	0
Nichols and Pott (1 up)	1	Hunt and Coles	0
Littler and Geiberger (1 up)	1	Jacklin and Thomas	0
Dickinson and Sanders (3 and 2)	1	Huggett and Will	0
Fourballs (afternoon)			
Casper and Brewer (5 and 3)	1	Hunt and Coles	0
Dickinson and Sanders (3 and 2)	1	Alliss and Gregson	0
Palmer and Boros (1 up)	1	Will and Boyle	0
Littler and Geiberger (halved)	0	Jacklin and Thomas	0
	7		0
Singles (morning)			
Gay Brewer (4 and 3)	1	Hugh Boyle	0
Billy Casper (2 and 1)	1	Peter Alliss	0
Arnold Palmer (3 and 2)	1	Tony Jacklin	0
Julius Boros	0	Brian Huggett (1 up)	1
Doug Sanders	0	Neil Coles (2 and 1)	1
Al Geiberger (4 and 2)	1	Malcolm Gregson	0
Gene Littler (halved)	0	David Thomas	0
Bobby Nichols (halved)	0	Bernard Hunt	0
Singles (afternoon)			
Arnold Palmer (5 and 3)	1	Brian Huggett	0
Gay Brewer	0	Peter Alliss (2 and 1)	1
Gardner Dickinson (3 and 2)	1	Tony Jacklin	0
Bobby Nichols (3 and 2)	1	Christy O'Connor	0
Johnny Pott (3 and 1)	1	George Will	0
Al Geiberger (2 and 1)	1	Malcolm Gregson	0
Julius Boros (halved)	0	Bernard Hunt	0
Doug Sanders	0	Neil Coles (2 and 1)	1
	9		4

Final score: United States 21
Great Britain and Ireland 6.
Five matches halved

1969

In 1969 Britain had the services of a man well used to the big ball – Tony Jacklin. He had won a tournament in America in 1968 and in 1969 had become the first British player to win the Open Championship since Max Faulkner at Royal Portrush in 1951. To match Britain's new star, the United States fielded Jack Nicklaus for the first time, more than seven years after he had won his first Tour event, the 1962 US Open. However, since the US team was selected on the basis of players' performances over two years, it did not include either the current Masters or US Open holders, respectively George Archer and Orville Moody. As neither of them was in the superstar bracket the team was not weakened.

The British had changed their selection process to a compromise; six men were picked because of their tournament performances and

the remaining six were chosen by team captain Eric Brown, Dai Rees and Tom Haliburton. They selected young men; besides Jacklin there were Maurice Bembridge, Brian Barnes, Peter Townsend (then considered as promising a player as Jacklin) and Bernard Gallacher. The Americans had generally been competing in tournaments for a long time but were virtually unknown in Britain. Two, Ken Still and Dave Hill, were to make an impression on British spectators.

Royal Birkdale was the venue for the 1969 competition and, sticking to its recent policy of asking elder statesmen to captain their teams, the US PGA put forward Sam Snead. The British captain, Eric Brown, made an immediate impact when he instructed his players not to help look for US balls in the rough. He pointed out that looking for golf balls was tiring and that one could also be penalised for accidentally treading on an opponent's ball. On the first point, he may have been right, if discourteous, but he was wrong on the rules.

As the first foursomes match went out in the morning, the weather was thought to favour the United States because there was not a breath of wind. Brown had put experience at the head and tail of his line-up, with youth in the middle. Coles and Huggett began against Ray Floyd and Miller Barber. Though down early on, the English pair levelled on the 9th, held it, and then suddenly the match was theirs as they won the 13th, 14th and 15th. Gallacher and Bembridge were faced by birdies from Trevino and Still on the 2nd and 3rd but levelled on the 8th and went ahead on the 10th. The first of several incidents involving Ken Still came on the 13th when Bembridge, about to drive, asked Still to move out of his line of vision. The American responded by making a performance of moving

other players and caddies from where they stood.

When it was Still's turn to drive, he hooked his tee shot into the rough and from there Trevino moved it under the lip of a bunker. When Still attempted to force the ball out, it appeared to strike his shoulder – Trevino thought so but Still didn't reply to his query. Trevino made up his own mind and told Still to 'pick it up'. (Though Trevino was a new star in golf, he immediately qualified for Ryder Cup selection because, unlike Nicklaus, he had served his time as a PGA member.)

That match also went to Britain but the best play from any pairing came from Jacklin and Townsend in the third match, playing Dave Hill and Tommy Aaron. They quickly went 2 up and the Americans did well to hang on until the 17th. At this hole of just over five hundred yards, Townsend lashed a 3-wood to a couple of yards and Jacklin holed the eagle putt for a 3

Left *Raymond Floyd in his first Ryder Cup match. He is captain of the 1989 US team*

Right *Dave Hill plays a pitch shot*

and 1 victory. They were 7 under par at that point, needing a par at the last for a 66. Bringing up the rear, the old firm of Alliss and O'Connor almost made it a clean sweep. With never more than a hole in it either away, the British squared with a 2 on the 14th and the remaining holes were halved. From the British point of view, this run of success was like Gleneagles 1921, Wentworth 1926 and Ganton 1949. Was it too good to last? The afternoon did indeed go less well. Sam Snead's language to his men was reportedly ripe at lunch and they responded.

Although Neil Coles and Brian Huggett were quickly 2 up against Dave Hill and Tommy Aaron, the Americans had reversed the position at the turn. But the British squared at the 536-yard 15th, winning with a 6 to an American 7. The game remained level to the last hole where Hill's shortish putt for a birdie 4 ran round the cup and eventually fell in. The British took 5. The second match also went to the United States.

Bernard Gallacher and Maurice Bembridge were up against the best US player, Lee Trevino, and Gene Littler. The British got into a one-hole lead at the 5th with a birdie but the Americans immediately came back by winning three holes in a row. The British, however, gave themselves a chance right at the end by winning the 17th and going to the last just 1 down. Alas, Gallacher then drove into the rough and that was about that.

Then came the young stars, Open champion Tony Jacklin and Peter Townsend facing Billy Casper and Frank Beard. The British pair were down or no better than level all the way but took a lead on the 17th for the first time. Both pairs birdied the last, with Townsend floating a pitch shot stone dead.

In the last match, Bernard Hunt and Peter Butler, playing debutant Jack Nicklaus and Dan Sikes, were 1 down after the 4th and all the holes were then halved until the 16th, which the British pair won in par. Both pairs then took unimpressive 6s on the 510-yard 17th and Nicklaus followed up by hooking his drive on

The young Jack Nicklaus seen in 1962: he didn't qualify for the Ryder Cup until 1969

the last into the rough. His partner forced it out near the green and Nicklaus wedged to a couple of feet with the British about eight yards away, also in 3: match to the United States.

Though Britain led at the end of the first day by a point, the Americans had stemmed a tide that might have flowed strongly against them in the afternoon. Jacklin and Townsend, with two victories, were the best pairing on either side.

For the second day's fourballs, captain Eric Brown decided to split his successful partnership – a decision many thought absurd. His reasoning was that a Jacklin/Townsend pairing meant that his best eggs were in one basket. The other point of view was that he'd broken up a pairing who felt they could beat the world. Happily for Brown, Jacklin was in such good form during the 1969 Ryder Cup that any partner would have suited him in fourball play. Playing last in the morning with Neil Coles, Jacklin put Britain into a 6–4 lead and, with the same partner in the afternoon, halved. Townsend won with Christy O'Connor and lost with Peter Butler.

As play began on the second day, the air was again still as O'Connor and Townsend went out against Dave Hill and Dale Douglass. In an up-and-down struggle in a low-scoring match, the key was the British finish. Though they dropped a stroke on the 14th, a par 3, they were 6 under par on the other back nine holes, with birdies on three of the par 5s and an eagle on another. Even so, they won by only the narrow margin of 1 up. The second match was halved and the third went to the United States, with Brian Barnes and Peter Alliss, who had not dropped a shot on any hole but were always behind, managing to level on the 15th. Trevino

then sank a long putt on the 17th to snatch the lead back and both pairings then birdied the last. The best scoring came in the last match out. Both teams were out in 32 and the match square. In the end, a Coles 4 on the 510-yard 17th was the difference. The British now led 6–4. Sam Snead, who had not played Nicklaus in the morning foursomes on the first day, dropped him from the afternoon fourballs. In this session, the United States came back once again. They won the first two matches out and the remaining two were halved.

It says much for the standard of behaviour in professional golf that the worst incident ever in the Ryder Cup took place in the afternoon match between Brian Huggett and Bernard

Dan Sikes drives watched by Jack Nicklaus and his caddy, and opponents Peter Butler and Bernard Hunt

Christy O'Connor Snr sinks a long putt to win his foursomes against Dave Hill and Dale Douglass. Partner Townsend is delighted

Gallacher of Britain and Dave Hill and Ken Still. Even so, it was hardly serious, although enough harsh words were spoken for officials and fellow team members to make their way towards the quartet to calm the frayed tempers.

The trouble began on the 7th green when Huggett pointed out that Hill had putted out of turn when he knocked a fairly short second putt into the hole. Meanwhile Ken Still, because he could not improve the fourball score, had picked up his own ball. Thinking the hole had been awarded to Britain, he swept off to the next tee shouting, 'Hell, if you want to win this badly you can have the hole'.

In effect, the American pair had conceded the hole although Hill's ball could have been replaced. Still later said that the referee had announced, 'Loss of hole' at some point in the

confusion. As the match moved away down the 8th, Still had words with the referee, and Huggett said his piece to Still. Many in the crowd heard what was said and began to boo as Dai Rees tried to calm the Huggett/Still dispute. More was to follow. On the very next green, Still sent his first putt past the hole and decided to putt out; he thought he had the chance to show his partner the line to the hole. Bernard Gallacher, baby of the British side, prevented this, legitimately, by conceding Still's putt and picking his ball up. Ken Still then claimed he should not have touched an American ball and had therefore forfeited the hole, which was incorrect. Eventually, Dave Hill holed for his birdie to win the hole and bowed ironically to the crowd. This put the US 2 up once more and they went further ahead on the 9th, Britain came back, however, by winning both the 11th and 13th. The American pair had the last word with their clubs. Dave Hill struck two superb shots to the 510-yard 17th and holed his eagle putt for a 2 and 1 victory. Hill wouldn't shake hands with the referee but Still later apologised for losing his self-control. All four said they were now the best of friends and put the incidents down to the effects of the heat of the battle.

Besides the US win in this match, Billy Casper and Frank Beard had won the first game out as a result of a stronger finish and the other two matches were halved. After two days, the teams were level at 6 wins each. Tony Jacklin had been involved in three of those wins and a halved match. Surprisingly, after Nicklaus's long-delayed debut, Sam Snead had played him in only two of the matches – perhaps he wanted him fresh for the last day where he sent him out last of his eight singles players both morning and afternoon. To lead off, he used Trevino and Hill.

Peter Alliss played his last Ryder Cup match at number one against Trevino. Alliss took the first two holes with birdies but Trevino produced a spurt of his own to go ahead on the 10th and eventually won by 2 and 1. Alliss asked to be dropped for the afternoon; although he had been 2 under par at the end, his putting was poor. Meanwhile, Dave Hill had been producing the best golf of anyone. Against Peter Townsend he went to the turn in 32 with four birdies and went on to win by 5 and 4.

With the United States now leading for the first time, Neil Coles faced Tommy Aaron, a future Masters champion. After ten holes Coles was 2 up but then suddenly lost the next three holes. His finish, however, was remarkable; on the 16th he holed a birdie putt of about five yards to square and then followed by hitting a fairway wood dead at the 17th for an eagle. When both birdied the last, Coles was left 1 up. It was a vital victory; British spirits might otherwise have dropped when Barnes lost by the same margin although he had been 2 up with four to play. His opponent, Billy Casper, finished with four birdies in a row. While this was happening, though, the tide had begun to turn. Christy O'Connor won well out on the course and Maurice Bembridge, 4 up with six to

play, looked good for another point but Ken Still won four of the next five holes. On the last tee, the pair were level again but the British player finished with a birdie 4 while Still, surprisingly, took 6. Peter Butler held on to his lead over Ray Floyd but the match went to the final green and birdies from both players left Butler the winner by 1 up.

The star attraction was the match between the new Open champion, Tony Jacklin, and the greatest golfer of all – Jack Nicklaus. After the first five holes had been halved, Jacklin took the lead with a par on the 533-yard 6th and went 3 up after the 12th. Although Nicklaus then produced an eagle, Jacklin replied with wins on both the 14th and 15th to win by the decisive margin of 4 and 3; Nicklaus had helped by missing three short putts during the round. Britain had won the last four matches to take a 2-point lead into the afternoon series; they needed three wins and a halved game from the eight singles to win the Ryder Cup.

Players on both teams were now under strain and feeling tired and though many of the matches were close, the scoring was seldom particularly exciting. Dave Hill went out steadily against Barnes. That was good enough for a 3-up lead and, though he had four 5s on the homeward nine, he increased his lead to win by 4 and 2. Hill had had a very good Ryder Cup.

Gallacher, who had not played in the morning, was faced by Lee Trevino. Down twice early on, Gallacher was 1 up at the turn and 2 up after the 12th; pars at the 14th and 15th won him both holes and the match. The young Scot had been in full control of his long game and holed out tenaciously so that only $2\frac{1}{2}$ points were needed from the remaining six matches.

Miller Barber, playing Bembridge, went to the turn with no fireworks at all, just pars and one bogey. Bembridge, however, produced a shower of 5s and 6s to be out in 42 and the American then finished him off with a couple of birdies to win by 7 and 6. Two and a half points were still needed and it looked like one could be coming from Peter Butler when he went 3 up

Some two months before the 1969 match, Tony Jacklin won the Open Championship. His late wife Vivienne shares the moment

after four holes, but Dale Douglass squared at the 10th. From this point, however, Butler produced all pars or birdies – until the par-4 16th where he took 5. Even so, that was good enough for a half and the match. Britain needed just 1½ points from O'Connor, Huggett, Coles and Jacklin.

Gene Littler was quickly ahead against O'Connor and, though the Irishman levelled, Littler was 3 up after a birdie 2 on the 12th. O'Connor won the next two holes but he made mistakes thereafter and Littler ended up the winner by 2 and 1. Neil Coles, often a man to bank on for a point in Ryder Cup singles, began 5, 6 and struggled to the turn in 40 to be 2 down to Dan Sikes, who had birdied nothing and dropped shots here and there. The match eventually went to the United States by 4 and 3. This was a turning point – suddenly a British victory depended on a win and a half from just two matches still out on the course: Brian Huggett versus Billy Casper and Tony Jacklin against Nicklaus.

The first of these was a close struggle all the way with first one man then the other leading. Huggett went behind again on the 10th and five holes were then halved. Huggett squared at the 16th, however, when Casper was twice bunkered. On the par-5 17th, Huggett had to struggle for a half when Casper chipped dead for his birdie, leaving Huggett having to hole from five feet. They went up the 18th still level and both found the green of this 513-yard hole in 2. After Casper had putted, Huggett had a putt of about ten yards to win his match but he was a little too bold, leaving himself four to five feet past. As he considered the problem, a great roar came to him from around the 17th green. Obviously, Huggett thought, Jacklin had won. Huggett needed this putt to win the Ryder Cup; he got it, shook hands with Billy Casper and collapsed in tears in the arms of his captain, Eric Brown, and Dai Rees. After all, he had just brought the cup back to Britain. Or so he thought.

What had been going on behind? The

Jacklin/Nicklaus match was an up-and-down struggle. The first three holes were halved in uninspiring figures before Nicklaus went into the lead with a 2 on the 212-yard 4th but Jacklin got back to level with a birdie of his own on the 6th and then briefly led with another on the 8th. Then a 6 on the 9th, to Nicklaus's bogey 5, saw the match square again and with some exchange of holes, it was level as they played the 16th where Jacklin dropped a shot to go behind. On the 17th, both drove well but Jacklin did not strike his 5-iron to this 510-yard hole any too well. Even so, he made the green, helped by a useful bounce, yet was a long way from the hole. Nicklaus flew in a soaring 7-iron much nearer the hole.

A few minutes later came the reason for the roar: Jacklin had holed his long putt, later measured at 55 feet, for an eagle 3. It must have been a blow for Nicklaus but he can take them just as well as he can hand them out – he missed his medium length putt, though. The time was about 6 o'clock and their match and the whole Ryder Cup series was level. I wonder whether Jacklin and Nicklaus were thinking about winning the cup for their country, or worrying about losing it. However, both hit good tee shots and Nicklaus put his approach in the middle of the green, about five yards from the hole. Jacklin's 8-iron flew straight at the flag but ran on to the back of the green to settle perhaps ten feet further from the hole than Nicklaus's As the light faded, Jacklin's putt ran straight at the hole but with never quite enough pace; it stopped a couple of feet short.

Nicklaus then tried to win the Ryder Cup outright for the United States; he hit the ball firmly at the hole, but a little off line, so that it eventually stopped some four feet past. Nicklaus took his time satisfying himself about the line and then, despite the memory of his poor short putting in the morning, found the middle of the hole. The United States would not lose the Ryder Cup and nor, it seemed, would Britain. Nicklaus strode straight over to Jacklin, gave him his putt, and said, 'I don't think you would have missed that putt but in these circumstances I would never give you the opportunity'.

The crowd warmed to Nicklaus, and Jacklin later sent him a letter of appreciation; Nicklaus's team-mates were less enthusiastic.

Brian Huggett is congratulated by Billy Casper after sinking a testing putt to square their match

And so the match ended with the honours shared but there was no real doubt that Britain should have won and perhaps deserved to. Faced by only par golf from Hill, Barber and Littler, Barnes and Bembridge had played badly and Coles had some bad holes. Just a half from any of those matches would have meant a British victory.

The cup did not return to the United States immediately; Sam Snead decided to leave it behind for 12 months. Eric Brown, with his enthusiasm for youth, thought that Britain might win in America in two years' time if young players carried on improving. He said, 'I have no doubt that this result will stop further suggestions that future Ryder Cup teams should contain overseas players to even up the battle. This sort of talk has been killed for ever.' He was to be proved wrong.

Tony Jacklin's battle with Jack Nicklaus was a thrilling end to the contest. (Below) captains Sam Snead and Eric Brown share the trophy

ROYAL BIRKDALE, LANCASHIRE, ENGLAND 18–20 SEPTEMBER 1969

United States		Great Britain and Ireland	
Captain Sam Snead		*Captain* Eric Brown	
Foursomes (morning)			
Barber and Floyd	0	Coles and Huggett (3 and 2)	1
Trevino and Still	0	Gallacher and Bembridge (2 and 1)	1
Hill and Aaron	0	Jacklin and Townsend (3 and 1)	1
Casper and Beard (halved)	0	O'Connor and Alliss	0
Foursomes (afternoon)			
Hill and Aaron (1 up)	1	Coles and Huggett	0
Trevino and Littler (2 up)	1	Gallacher and Bembridge	0
Casper and Beard	0	Jacklin and Townsend (1 up)	1
Nicklaus and Sikes (1 up)	1	Hunt and Butler	0
	–		–
	3		4
Fourballs (morning)			
Hill and Douglass	0	O'Connor and Townsend (1 up)	1
Floyd and Barber (halved)	0	Huggett and Alex Caygill	0
Trevino and Littler (1 up)	1	Barnes and Alliss	0
Nicklaus and Sikes	0	Jacklin and Coles (1 up)	1
Fourballs (afternoon)			
Casper and Beard (2 up)	1	Townsend and Butler	0

Hill and Still (2 and 1)	1	Huggett and Gallacher	0
Aaron and Floyd (halved)	0	Bembridge and Hunt	0
Trevino and Barber (halved)	0	Jacklin and Coles	0
	–		–
	3		2
Singles (morning)			
Lee Trevino (2 and 1)	1	Peter Alliss	0
Dave Hill (5 and 4)	1	Peter Townsend	0
Tommy Aaron	0	Neil Coles (1 up)	1
Billy Casper (1 up)	1	Brian Barnes	0
Frank Beard	0	Christy O'Connor (5 and 4)	1
Ken Still	0	Maurice Bembridge (1 up)	1
Ray Floyd	0	Peter Butler (1 up)	1
Jack Nicklaus	0	Tony Jacklin (4 and 3)	1
Singles (afternoon)			
Dave Hill (4 and 2)	1	Brian Barnes	0
Lee Trevino	0	Bernard Gallacher (4 and 3)	1
Miller Barber (7 and 6)	1	Maurice Bembridge	0
Dale Douglass	0	Peter Butler (3 and 2)	1
Gene Littler (2 and 1)	1	Christy O'Connor	0
Billy Casper (halved)	0	Brian Huggett	0
Dan Sikes (4 and 3)	1	Neil Coles	0
Jack Nicklaus (halved)	0	Tony Jacklin	0
	–		–
	7		7

Final score: Great Britain and Ireland 13
United States 13. Six matches halved

NO CONTEST (1971–1981)

1971

Britain had some new young men for the 1971 match – Harry Bannerman, John Garner (who played only once) and a player who was to prove a very good performer in Ryder Cup matches, Peter Oosterhuis. Seven of the team were still in their twenties and some thought this a good omen as the team flew off for the Old Warson Country Club, St Louis, Missouri. Others thought it rather more significant that the USA were fielding four of the greatest players in the modern game – Jack Nicklaus, Arnold Palmer, Billy Casper and Lee Trevino – and tried to take comfort from the thought that Dave Stockton had a weak long game (but was the best putter on either side!) and Mason Rudolph was unimpressive. Overall, it was a very formidable team.

The British team: (l to r) captain Eric Brown, Brian Huggett, Brian Barnes, Peter Oosterhuis, Peter Townsend, Bernard Gallacher, Peter Butler, Christy O'Connor Snr, Tony Jacklin, Maurice Bembridge, John Garner and Harry Bannerman

The British, for their part, had little hope of winning but were confident that they would not disgrace themselves. In Tony Jacklin they had a major-championship winner who, the previous year, had become the first British player since Ted Ray back in 1920 to win the US Open. Trevino, however, was the majors form man: he had won US, Canadian and British Opens in quick succession in 1971.

In the foursomes on the morning of the first day, Britain made an excellent start; Coles and O'Connor were square with Casper and Miller Barber at the turn but then won the next two holes. Though they took 7 to lose the monster 590-yard 12th hole, Coles immediately struck back by holing a long putt for a 2 on the next, after which Casper missed from a few feet. After a succession of halves, they ran out winners by 2 and 1.

Townsend and Oosterhuis played very good golf in the next match and Palmer hit a decisive shot on the last to win with Gardner Dickinson. His 6-iron went 20 feet or so past the flag and then spun back to no more than a foot.

In the third match, Frank Beard and Charles Coody went 3 down after six holes to Maurice Bembridge and Peter Butler and then 4 down after ten. All this despite the fact that the British pair had recorded not a single birdie. The Americans later pulled themselves together to win back a couple of holes but then lost the 620-yard 16th to a 4 and that was that.

In the last match out, the American captain, Jay Hebert, had tried an experimental pairing of long-hitting Jack Nicklaus with short-hitting Dave Stockton. He thought that Nicklaus would be able to blast long drives away when it was his tee shot or still reach the greens from Stockton's drives. The way the course worked out, Nicklaus would be taking the tee shot on all the par 3s, after which Stockton's putting would pull in the 2s. Too much strategy of this sort seldom seems to pay off in foursomes. Nicklaus missed the par 3s and even he couldn't hit his tee shots far enough for Stockton to reach the par 5s in 2. Without a birdie on their card, Jacklin and Huggett were 4 up after ten holes and won comfortably.

Britain had made easily their best start in the USA, leading by three matches to one. In the afternoon the momentum was maintained for a while, as Bernard Gallacher and Harry Bannerman beat Casper and Barber in the first match. Palmer and Dickinson then beat Oosterhuis and Townsend although the Englishmen held a narrow lead most of the way before losing 1 down. The next match ended in a half when Jacklin chipped in from nearly 20 yards off the last green for a par the Americans couldn't match. Hebert changed his strategy over who to partner with Jack Nicklaus. This time he gave him a long hitter, J. C. Snead, and it worked a lot better. The Americans had only one 5 on their card when they got home by 5 and 3 against Bembridge and Butler, themselves only 1 over par on a course measuring over 7,200 yards.

The day ended with Britain 1 point in the lead. Could the first victory on US soil lie ahead? It didn't seem so after the morning's fourballs, where strategy again played a part. With hindsight, it seems that the British captain made errors. Eric Brown was a loner, unlike Hebert, in his decision-making; he consulted no one, left out Jacklin, changed his pairings – successful or not – from the foursomes and brought in John Garner for his first Ryder Cup match. Not surprisingly, Brown came in for criticism when the British lost all four matches.

A famous incident occurred in the Palmer/ Dickinson versus Oosterhuis/Gallacher fourball. When 1 up on the 208-yard 7th, Palmer cracked a superb 5-iron into the heart of the green. Awestruck, Gallacher's American college-boy caddy sidled up to Palmer and said something like, 'Jeez Arnie, what you hit there?' 'A 5', came the answer. That did it. The British were penalised loss of hole under Rule 9a, just as if Gallacher had asked the question rather than his caddy. It is said that Gallacher heard neither question nor answer, though he apparently changed his choice of club from a 4-iron to

Arnold Palmer and Jack Nicklaus line up a putt

which went all the way and had been on the losing side in them all!

In the last match out, Charles Coody and Frank Beard were running away with it after five holes when they were 4 up. Neil Coles then had four birdies in a row to square on the 9th. A gallant effort, yes, but all seemed lost when the United States took both the 12th and 13th. Again Coles brought the teams level with birdies on the 16th and 17th. On the last, O'Connor had a very good chance of a birdie to win the match but this putt stopped on the lip. Thus the day ended with the United States leading by 4 points.

Tony Jacklin no longer enjoyed competing in the Ryder Cup; he didn't like the way unrealistic hopes were expressed about the British team's chances. Also, in strong contrast to what was to happen in the 1980s, he was an individualist rather than a team man. He

Tony Jacklin in 1971: he didn't enjoy Ryder Cup matches in those days

a 3. The British pair were two down. Palmer asked that the penalty be dropped but . . . well, rules are rules and the British lost that match by 5 and 4.

The British put up a better struggle in the afternoon. Gallacher and Oosterhuis put their disappointments behind them and beat Casper and Trevino by one hole in the first match but Jacklin and Huggett, together again, lost to Snead and Gene Littler by 2 and 1. Then followed some of the best scoring of the day. Nicklaus and Palmer reached the turn in 30 only to find themselves 1 down to Peter Townsend and Harry Bannerman. The next four holes were halved and Nicklaus then hit a wedge from the rough stone dead to square the match which continued level until Nicklaus holed a putt of about four yards on the last for both the hole and the match. Peter Townsend had by this time been involved in four matches

thought Britain had no real chance in the United States and didn't relish being associated with failure. He was out against Trevino – his Nemesis in the British Open in 1972 – and went 4 down after five holes. Thereafter he had some luck which involved hitting a tree which stopped his ball going out of bounds and then entangling his ball in the flag with too strong an approach shot later on. His ball fell down dead to the hole but in the end Trevino still won.

Things then went better for Britain with a halved match followed by a couple of wins. In the fifth match, though, Peter Townsend didn't get to the last green and Jack Nicklaus beat him by 3 and 2. Of the remaining matches, one was lost and two halved. Harry Bannerman made a strong impression while halving with Palmer. His large cigars gave him an air of lordly confidence, justified when he went 2 up on the 12th. In the end, though, he let Palmer off the hook when he could not par the last.

All in all, the morning's eight singles had produced a creditable British performance but they were 5 points in arrears with the final eight singles to go. The chance of a recovery seemed to fade when Trevino, first out in the afternoon, dismissed Huggett by 7 and 6 but, as the pattern of play developed, Britain led in all the other matches except two. They had no margin for individual error, but the errors came. Neil Coles, for instance, had been 3 up against Nicklaus after three holes but then it all went wrong. Although Nicklaus managed only two birdies over the next ten holes, he won eight of them – and the match.

The Jacklin/J. C. Snead match had been a good contest; Jacklin holed a vast putt across the 17th green to square the match rather as he had done against Nicklaus at Birkdale in 1969. However, this time he failed to par the last hole and Snead won the decisive point.

Britain made the score quite respectable; they finished level in the afternoon singles and

level in the match – if you discount the fourballs, which they had lost by 6–1 with one match halved. The overall result was US 16 Britain 11 with five halved games.

Jacklin was not the supreme player he had been at Birkdale, this time taking $1\frac{1}{2}$ points out of a possible 5. Perhaps the achievements of some of the British team in the singles should be highlighted. Outstandingly, Peter Oosterhuis defeated both Gene Littler and Arnold Palmer by the decisive margins of 4 and 3 and 3 and 2 respectively. Barnes also won twice, against Mason Rudolph and Miller Barber, and Harry Bannerman and Bernard Gallacher both came out with a win and a half. If the rules had gone against Gallacher in the fourballs, they went in Bannerman's favour in his match against Gardner Dickinson. On the 7th green, the American's caddy picked up his ball close to the hole before Bannerman had conceded the short putt. The Scot had wanted the ball to remain in position because it might have helped him with his own putt. Instead, he was awarded the hole.

In the post-mortems which followed, the fact that Britain had produced her best performance ever in the USA tempered the criticism but Eric Brown came in for most of what there was because of his fourball combinations on the second day. Critics found it strange that, as John Garner had been picked for the team only at Brown's insistence, he had played the young man just once, when Garner had looked very under-powered. Brown also seemed to have a low opinion of Maurice Bembridge whom he played in both foursomes, when Bembridge was involved in a win and a loss, but not in the singles.

Brown was not asked to captain again, although his teams had produced the best result in Britain since 1957 and the best ever on US soil. However, it is fair to say that in Britain, as in the USA, there has always been the feeling that the honour of captaincy should be shared around. Some surprising people have not captained a Ryder Cup team – players with distinguished playing careers and long experience of the pressures of the match. Gene Sarazen would have made an immensely popular captain but was never chosen because of what he believed was 'PGA politics'.

OLD WARSON, ST LOUIS, MISSOURI, USA 16–18 SEPTEMBER 1971

United States		Great Britain and Ireland	
Captain Jay Hebert		*Captain* Eric Brown	
Foursomes (morning)			
Casper and Barber	0	Coles and O'Connor (2 and 1)	1
Palmer and Dickinson (2 up)	1	Townsend and Oosterhuis	0
Coody and Beard	0	Bembridge and Butler (1 up)	1
Nicklaus and Stockton	0	Huggett and Jacklin (3 and 2)	1
Foursomes (afternoon)			
Casper and Barber	0	Bannerman and Gallacher (2 and 1)	1
Palmer and Dickinson (1 up)	1	Townsend and Oosterhuis	0
Trevino and Rudolph (halved)	0	Huggett and Jacklin	0
Nicklaus and Snead (5 and 3)	1	Bembridge and Butler	0
	3		4
Fourballs (morning)			
Trevino and Rudolph (2 and 1)	1	O'Connor and Barnes	0
Beard and Snead (2 and 1)	1	Coles and John Garner	0
Palmer and Dickinson (5 and 4)	1	Oosterhuis and Gallacher	0
Nicklaus and Littler (2 and 1)	1	Townsend and Bannerman	0
Fourballs (afternoon)			
Trevino and Casper	0	Gallacher and Oosterhuis (1 up)	1
Littler and Snead (2 and 1)	1	Jacklin and Huggett	0
Palmer and Nicklaus (1 up)	1	Townsend and Bannerman	0
Coody and Beard (halved)	0	Coles and O'Connor	0
	6		1
Singles (morning)			
Lee Trevino (1 up)	1	Tony Jacklin	0
Dave Stockton (halved)	0	Bernard Gallacher	0
Mason Rudolph	0	Brian Barnes (1 up)	1
Gene Littler	0	Peter Oosterhuis (4 and 3)	1
Jack Nicklaus (3 and 2)	1	Peter Townsend	0
Gardner Dickinson (5 and 4)	1	Christy O'Connor	0
Arnold Palmer (halved)	0	Harry Bannerman	0
Frank Beard (halved)	0	Neil Coles	0
Singles (afternoon)			
Lee Trevino (7 and 6)	1	Brian Huggett	0
Jesse Snead (1 up)	1	Tony Jacklin	0
Miller Barber	0	Brian Barnes (2 and 1)	1
Dave Stockton (1 up)	1	Peter Townsend	0
Charles Coody	0	Bernard Gallacher (2 and 1)	1
Jack Nicklaus (5 and 3)	1	Neil Coles	0
Arnold Palmer	0	Peter Oosterhuis (3 and 2)	1
Gardner Dickinson	0	Harry Bannerman (2 and 1)	1
	7		6

Final score: United States 16 Great Britain and Ireland 11. Five matches halved

1973

In 1973 the Ryder Cup competition was held in Scotland, at Muirfield, for the first time. Changes were made to the format: foursomes started off each of the first two days with fourball play in the afternoon but the pattern of the singles remained the same – eight singles morning and afternoon.

Team selection methods remained broadly the same, which meant that the Americans could not field two of their rising stars, Lanny Wadkins and Johnny Miller. The latter had won the US Open in June with the help of a remarkable last round of 63. Two others worth a place – though their names have since faded from memory – were Jerry Heard and Grier Jones. Though the British system meant that the top 12 point scorers in tournament play were chosen, the selectors had an option to omit two or three in favour of men in form which they chose not to do. The US team was regarded as formidable indeed although three members just struggled in by scoring enough points in the nick of time. These were Palmer, Casper and J. C. Snead.

The British captain, Bernard Hunt, professed himself confident of victory; he felt the use of the big ball in Britain since 1968 meant that his players could strike as well as the Americans. He thought that young American players 'have hardly a decent swing amongst them' and won only because of nerve and tight short games. Correctly, he pointed out that many quickly fade away after early successes. Hunt noted that British players were better able to cope in hot weather now that golf was becoming more international and British golfers were competing in Africa, the Far East and Australia.

Hunt's doubts probably centred on the fact that he had six good players, perhaps even eight or nine, but what would he do about the remaining three or four? He decided that, unlike Eric Brown, he would always try to put out a strong pair, rather than matching a weak player with a strong one. Anyone who was not

Arnold Palmer

good enough or too short a hitter, 'just won't get a game'. In the event, John Garner didn't play and Clive Clark and Eddie Polland had only one and two games respectively. The United States was captained by Jackie Burke who remarked that he might not be re-admitted to America if he lost again – a reference to the 1957 defeat at Lindrick when he was captain – and he did have some cause for worry. The US PGA did not get their team to a hotel until noon on Monday after an over-night flight so they had only two practice days in which to learn the course.

Once again, the British players performed well in the foursomes. Hunt had put Brian Barnes with Bernard Gallacher, to achieve power allied with a fine short game. Trevino,

Bernard Gallacher played over 30 matches during his Ryder Cup career

paired with Casper, was in a strange mood; early on Trevino asked if he could swap clubs with Casper and later wanted to change his putter. Of course, both moves are against the rules of golf. On the second occasion, Trevino said he might snap the putter 'accidentally'. Throughout his career, Trevino found talking a means of releasing his nervous tension. This match went to Britain and the 'old men' – Christy O'Connor playing his tenth Ryder Cup, and Neil Coles – beat the new British Open champion, Tom Weiskopf, and Jesse Snead. Then came the strongest British pairing

of Jacklin and Oosterhuis against Chi Chi Rodriguez and Lou Graham, both new to Ryder Cup golf. After Jacklin and Oosterhuis had squared at the 16th they looked about to win the 17th but Rodriguez holed from about ten yards and the match was halved.

Next came the United States stars, Palmer and Nicklaus, against the unpromising British pairing of Eddie Polland and Maurice Bembridge who would have had a tough time anyway but Polland played poorly. The Americans were 6 up after 11 and the match ended soon afterwards. Then came the new British Achilles' heel – fourball golf. Barnes and Gallacher were again first on the tee and produced fine golf – all 4s and 3s and a couple of 2s as well. Tommy Aaron and Gay Brewer were 5 down after ten holes and eventually went down by 5 and 4, the worst US performance in fourball Ryder Cup golf at the time.

Bembridge, after suffering at the hands of Palmer and Nicklaus in the morning, was soon facing them again, alongside Huggett this time. Bembridge proved to be the strong man of the match. He sank a good putt on the 1st for a half and thereafter hit most of the decisive shots which included a 6-iron to within a couple of feet of the 6th to square the match; a 3 at the 7th to take the lead; an eagle at the 9th; and a chip-in at the 14th. Britain won 3 and 1.

The third match again involved Jacklin and Oosterhuis, facing Weiskopf and Casper. Between them, the British pair managed to get to the turn in 28 with seven birdies but the Americans, getting a few of their own, were 3 down. Casper put the US back into the match with good putts to win the 12th and 13th but they lost the 15th to a par and that was about that. Some spectators who had come to watch Weiskopf, the new Open champion, were surprised by his poor iron shots. Britain lost only the final match and so ended the day with a 3-point lead. There had been confidence that a British victory was imminent and fears that the Ryder Cup could hardly be worth playing for if defeat continued to follow defeat for Britain.

After dinner that evening, a severe blow struck the British camp – Bernard Gallacher went down with a stomach virus and he remained in bed the following day. Gallacher, a good matchplayer who was always desperately keen to beat the Americans, was a great loss. Hunt had to bring in men who were either off form or in whom he had little confidence. Furthermore, the most successful British pairing was broken up. As if to emphasise this, Barnes was again out first, with his new foursomes partner Peter Butler. After five holes, they were 3 down to Nicklaus and Weiskopf which was still the position as Nicklaus and

Tommy Aaron lost his singles match in 1973 to Tony Jacklin

Butler stepped on to the 16th tee to play the tee shots. Nicklaus seemed to settle the match with an iron right over the flag and just a few feet past. Butler then holed out with his tee shot and the fluke recovery went even further when he holed a long putt to win the 17th. Then the miracles stopped. However, the British regained momentum with another win from Jacklin and Oosterhuis. Bembridge and Huggett then won easily against the American pairing of Lou Graham and Chi Chi Rodriguez, who had seven 5s and a 6 to finish.

The morning ended with almost errorless foursomes play from Casper and Trevino which Coles and O'Connor could not quite match. At this point the important thing from the British point of view was that they had maintained a 3-point gap. British hopes were high – after all, this was a slightly better position than at lunch on the second day at Birkdale in 1969.

Barnes and Butler were out first in the fourballs again. The British were in a good position, mainly as a result of some very long putts from Barnes, and were 1 up after the 8th. With the match level on the 17th tee, a par 5, only J. C. Snead could birdie the hole and Palmer made sure of the match with a birdie on the difficult last hole.

The British pair, Jacklin and Oosterhuis, did little wrong against Gay Brewer and Billy Casper but ran into golf which would be hard for any pair to beat. When the match finished, the US pair needed a couple of 4s for a better ball score of an approximate 62. Significantly, Casper remarked in the press tent afterwards, 'As for Jacklin, he looks like a fellow who's dead beat'. He may well have been right; the strain on Jacklin was extreme. Though Oosterhuis was moving in that direction, Jacklin was the only world star in the British team. All eyes were on him and he was expected to 'do it for Britain'. The population of the United States, on the other hand, remained largely unaware of the Ryder Cup so that no American was burdened with the hopes of the nation.

Above *Tony Jacklin*

Hunt omitted two of his 'old men' from the fourballs, because he wanted them fresh for the singles, which meant bringing in Clive Clark and Eddie Polland who were likely to lose. As the luck of the draw had it, they faced Nicklaus and Weiskopf, who fired five 3s at them in the first seven holes and went on to win by 3 and 2. Huggett and Bembridge then managed a half with Homero Blancas and Trevino, despite their moderate putting. The Americans had caught up and it looked like the Ryder Cup was lost that afternoon as there was little reason to hope that Britain could match the strength of the United States over 16 singles matches.

Barnes, again leading off, had shot his bolt. He had no fewer than nine 5s against Casper and later remarked, 'He was fitter than I was. It's becoming just a commando course now.' At the time, Casper was very overweight and in his early forties while Barnes was 28. In the second match, Gallacher reappeared from his sick bed to face Tom Weiskopf. It was close for a long time, Gallacher even managing to square with a bogey 5 on the 10th. He was 2 down on the 17th tee, however, and though Weiskopf then hit a poor tee shot into the rough, Gallacher topped his second shot to lose 3 and 1.

Peter Butler continued to play badly against Homero Blancas and went down without a fight. Three points gone and the match was fast slipping away. Then came Jacklin facing the current Masters champion, Tommy Aaron, who was suffering from a bad back and was in poor form. He lost 3 and 2 to Jacklin. It was the only win for Britain that morning but the main damage was done by the losses at the head of the order. Three of the remaining games were halved (Coles missing from a yard on the last to beat Brewer), including Bembridge's match with Nicklaus, where both played poorly, and par was often good enough to win a hole. O'Connor lost to Snead and complained of feeling 'tired and stiff', another indication that the United States were going to last the distance better than the Britons.

There had been mutterings because Brian Huggett had not been selected for the morning games. Now 3 points behind, Hunt at last moved Brian Barnes from the number one position and sent Huggett out. After six holes, Blancas was 2 up but Huggett did little wrong thereafter. Huggett played the six holes from the 11th to the 16th in 3 apiece and won. Barnes then lost to Jesse Snead. He complained afterwards that too few British players had played too many matches. 'I'm so tired I just couldn't concentrate' he said. Gallacher was again played in the afternoon but began disastrously

Dave Hill played in only one game in 1973 – the foursomes with Arnold Palmer

by losing four of the first five holes – all to pars. He had declared himself fit to play but the fact that he was trounced by Brewer by 6 and 5 suggests that he was anything but.

The Ryder Cup was lost once again. After this match, there was little talk of superior American putting or mastery of the wedge but the Americans had lasted the course better. Although Trevino, for instance, said he was 'whacked out' at the end, Coles 'looked even more tired and he played real bad'.

Near the end, there was a sentimental moment for the spectators to savour; O'Connor, at 48, was almost certainly playing in his last Ryder Cup. He finished by getting down in 2 from sand at the last and halving with Weiskopf. Oosterhuis finished on an ebullient note. He said, 'I've heard that a lot of the boys are tired out, but I'm feeling strong. I could go out and play another 18 holes right now.' The fact that he had beaten Palmer 4 and 2 probably had something to do with his resilience.

The BBC coverage came in for criticism. Snead's afternoon win against Barnes in the second match out had settled the destination of the Ryder Cup but this was not revealed in the commentary, presumably to keep patriotic interest alive.

Arguments about the future of the contest began again. Should Britain allow in golfers from the English-speaking world? Reduce the size of both the teams and/or the number of matches? The fact was that no change in formula could counteract the power of the winners of major championships in the US team and the all-round strength of the American side – even if the teams were reduced to four men a side.

MUIRFIELD, GULLANE, SCOTLAND 20–22 SEPTEMBER 1973

United States		Great Britain and Ireland	
Captain Jack Burke		*Captain* Bernard Hunt	
Foursomes (morning)			
Trevino and Casper	0	Barnes and Gallacher (1 up)	1
Weiskopf and Snead	0	O'Connor and Coles (3 and 2)	1
Juan Rodriguez and Lou Graham (halved)	0	Jacklin and Oosterhuis	0
Nicklaus and Palmer (6 and 5)	1	Bembridge and Eddie Polland	0
Fourballs (afternoon)			
Aaron and Brewer	0	Barnes and Gallacher (5 and 4)	1
Palmer and Nicklaus	0	Bembridge and Huggett (3 and 1)	1
Weiskopf and Casper	0	Jacklin and Oosterhuis (3 and 1)	1
Trevino and Blancas (2 and 1)	1	O'Connor and Coles	0
	–		–
	2		5
Foursomes (morning)			
Nicklaus and Weiskopf (1 up)	1	Barnes and Butler	0
Palmer and Hill	0	Oosterhuis and Jacklin (2 up)	1
Rodriguez and Graham	0	Bembridge and Huggett (5 and 4)	1
Trevino and Casper (2 and 1)	1	Coles and O'Connor	0
Fourballs (afternoon)			
Snead and Palmer (2 up)	1	Barnes and Butler	0

Brewer and Casper (3 and 2)	1	Jacklin and Oosterhuis	0
Nicklaus and Weiskopf (3 and 2)	1	Clive Clark and Polland	0
Trevino and Blancas (halved)	0	Bembridge and Huggett	0
	–		–
	5		2
Singles (morning)			
Billy Casper (2 and 1)	1	Brian Barnes	0
Tom Weiskopf (3 and 1)	1	Bernard Gallacher	0
Homero Blancas (5 and 4)	1	Peter Butler	0
Tommy Aaron	0	Tony Jacklin (3 and 1)	1
Gay Brewer (halved)	0	Neil Coles	0
Jesse Snead (1 up)	1	Christy O'Connor	0
Jack Nicklaus (halved)	0	Maurice Bembridge	0
Lee Trevino (halved)	0	Peter Oosterhuis	0
Singles (afternoon)			
Homero Blancas	0	Brian Huggett (4 and 2)	1
Jesse Snead (3 and 1)	1	Brian Barnes	0
Gay Brewer (6 and 5)	1	Bernard Gallacher	0
Billy Casper (2 and 1)	1	Tony Jacklin	0
Lee Trevino (6 and 5)	1	Neil Coles	0
Tom Weiskopf (halved)	0	Christy O'Connor	0
Jack Nicklaus (2 up)	1	Maurice Bembridge	0
Arnold Palmer	0	Peter Oosterhuis (4 and 2)	1
	–		–
	9		3

Final score: United States 16 Great Britain and Ireland 10. Six matches halved

1975

For the 1975 match at Laurel Valley in Pennsylvania, the strength of American golf was illustrated by their major championship performers. Seven of their team members had won the US Open, three had won the British Open, two had Masters titles and four were US PGA champions. The recent winner of the British Open at Carnoustie, Tom Watson, was not qualified to play because he had not been a PGA member long enough.

Against this, Britain had a fading Tony Jacklin with his 1970 US Open and 1969 British title. There was also an oddity; Palmer was non-playing captain of the United States. His wins in the Spanish Open and British PGA that summer would have made him a leading qualifier for the British side!

For this match, there was little bombast from the British press. The US team was thought very strong indeed, the British weak – an attitude reflected in the betting shops throughout the nation where no money was being accepted on a US victory. The most one could do in this respect was place a bet on the final score. The shortest odds were on the prospect that the US would take about 2 points to every 1 from the British but even that level of British performance seemed unlikely after the foursomes on the morning of the first day. Over the years Britain had settled into a pattern of jumping into an early lead before seeing it gradually or dramatically eroded on the following days; this time all four matches in the morning went to the United States.

It started with the early heroes of Muirfield – Bernard Gallacher and Brian Barnes – facing Nicklaus and Weiskopf. They were quickly brushed aside by the American pair who were 5 under par when the match ended after 14 holes. Although the other British defeats were not quite as overwhelming, the scoreline read US 4 Britain 0 at lunchtime. Barring miracles, the contest was already over. It is possible to win from that position when you think you have the

Brian Barnes, after missing a ten-foot putt during the foursomes match against Nicklaus and Weiskopf

best team; it's much less likely when you've been trying to persuade yourself that there's at least an outside chance.

The afternoon began better, however. The strong pairing of Jacklin and Oosterhuis, who had lost to Al Geiberger and Johnny Miller in the morning foursomes, this time beat Casper and Floyd 2 and 1. The next three matches saw Barnes and Gallacher gaining a half against Nicklaus and Bob Murphy but the others were lost. For the British team, supporters and press it was acutely embarrassing: one win and a halved match against six US successes. In both camps, people were saying that the important thing was friendly competition, tradition, meeting new people, making new friends and all the other clichés that had been clutched at since US dominance began in 1947. However, nearly 30 years is a long time to be saying the same thing. The players, throughout, remained fairly satisfied; it was the only time that a team was picked to represent the professional golfers of their respective countries. The British PGA never gave any serious thought to the bringing in of other nations. There was some mention that Sam Ryder had given his golden chalice under certain terms – but that was eventually dismissed without too many backward glances. During the 1930s, it would have been easy enough to let members of the British Empire in, but by the 1970s there was no easy formula. The Commonwealth would have lacked any good South Africans and would otherwise bring in two or three Australians and Bob Charles from New Zealand. The concept of the European Tour lay ahead.

On day two, Palmer, who had apparently an ambition to have his team win every match and achieve a 32–0 score, totally changed his pairings. The order of play was also changed, with fourballs leading off and foursomes following.

The process of US victory slowed, but only a little. Jacklin, paired with Oosterhuis in the morning fourballs, halved and won with Barnes in the afternoon foursomes. Eamonn Darcy and Guy Hunt halved their fourball. The day went to the United States by 5–1 with two halves.

At 11–2 going into the singles of the final day, there were no prospects of drama and Brian Barnes provided the main story. Perhaps Britain had, in the end, won some kind of moral victory, for Barnes beat Jack Nicklaus twice. To add to that, Peter Oosterhuis, in the 1970s Britain's most reliable performer, beat both Johnny Miller and J. C. Snead in a day. Unfortunately, the remainder of the team picked up just three halves throughout the day, and wins from Tommy Horton and Norman Wood when the match result was already settled.

When it was all over, Hale Irwin commented that the US had been rather below their best. Palmer tried to be polite about the contest, saying that there were only a few points between the two teams (Britain lost 18–8). But

Above '*I thought it would break from the right*'

Palmer thought the fun had gone out of the contest somewhere on the morning of the final day. Even then, it had long ceased to matter. No one I have heard of took a picture of the historic moment when, yet again, the United States won the Ryder Cup. For the record, though, it came when Tom Weiskopf beat Guy Hunt by 5 and 3 in the second-to-last morning singles. Despite the match being so one-sided, the spectator turnout was reasonable – considering the lack of interest the event is always said to arouse in America; over 21,000 attended play.

Would the formula ever change? There was little impetus from the Americans who were quite happy to be selected to represent the United States of America. The PGA on the other side of the Atlantic was also quite happy, as were its members, to choose teams representing the geographical British Isles. Those golfers likely to be picked did not want to lose their places and a new formula might exclude them.

After the 1987 Ryder Cup victory with those honorary Englishmen Seve Ballesteros and Bernhard Langer, it seems a long way back to the rather drear days of 1975. Ballesteros had come to the public's notice as a difficult-to-credit phenomenon in the 1976 Birkdale British Open. Following this the British PGA would probably have liked to include him in the 1977 Ryder Cup match at Lytham. At last, there was a European who would not merely strengthen the team but who was a world class golfer. With the European Tour developing fast, there was new motivation for bringing continental European players into the contest – despite the original wishes of Sam Ryder. He had not, in fact, done a great deal more than present the golden chalice and thereby earn himself a kind of immortality. In contrast, few remember much about Mr Walker and his trophy for the amateurs on both sides of the Atlantic.

LAUREL VALLEY, PENNSYLVANIA, USA 19–21 SEPTEMBER 1975

United States		Great Britain and Ireland	
Captain Arnold Palmer		*Captain* Bernard Hunt	
Foursomes (morning)			
Nicklaus and Weiskopf (5 and 4)	1	Barnes and Gallacher	0
Littler and Irwin (4 and 3)	1	Wood and Bembridge	0
Geiberger and Miller (3 and 1)	1	Jacklin and Oosterhuis	0
Trevino and Snead (2 and 1)	1	Horton and O'Leary	0
Fourballs (afternoon)			
Casper and Floyd	0	Oosterhuis and Jacklin (2 and 1)	1
Weiskopf and Graham (3 and 2)	1	Darcy and O'Connor Jr	0
Nicklaus and Murphy (halved)	0	Barnes and Gallacher	0
Trevino and Irwin (2 and 1)	1	Horton and O'Leary	0
	6		1
Fourballs (morning)			
Casper and Miller (halved)	0	Oosterhuis and Jacklin	0
Nicklaus and Snead (4 and 2)	1	Horton and Wood	0
Littler and Graham (5 and 3)	1	Barnes and Gallacher	0
Geiberger and Floyd (halved)	0	Darcy and Hunt	0
Foursomes (afternoon)			
Trevino and Murphy	0	Jacklin and Barnes (3 and 2)	1
Weiskopf and Miller (5 and 3)	1	O'Connor and O'Leary	0
Irwin and Casper (3 and 2)	1	Oosterhuis and Bembridge	0
Geiberger and Graham (3 and 2)	1	Darcy and Hunt	0
	5		1
Singles (morning)			
Bob Murphy (2 and 1)	1	Tony Jacklin	0
Johnny Miller	0	Peter Oosterhuis (2 up)	1
Lee Trevino (halved)	0	Bernard Gallacher	0
Hale Irwin (halved)	0	Tommy Horton	0
Gene Littler (4 and 2)	1	Brian Huggett	0
Billy Casper (3 and 2)	1	Eamonn Darcy	0
Tom Weiskopf (5 and 3)	1	Guy Hunt	0
Jack Nicklaus	0	Brian Barnes (4 and 2)	1
Singles (afternoon)			
Ray Floyd (1 up)	1	Tony Jacklin	0
Jesse Snead	0	Peter Oosterhuis (3 and 2)	1
Al Geiberger (halved)	0	Bernard Gallacher	0
Lou Graham	0	Tommy Horton (2 and 1)	1
Hale Irwin (2 and 1)	1	John O'Leary	0
Bob Murphy (2 and 1)	1	Maurice Bembridge	0
Lee Trevino	0	Norman Wood (2 and 1)	1
Jack Nicklaus	0	Brian Barnes (2 and 1)	1
	7		6

Final score: United States 18
Great Britain and Ireland 8.
Six matches halved

1977

In 1977 there was some change to the organisation of the matches. Splitting the day into a morning and afternoon pattern was dropped. Foursomes, however, were retained, although some US players would have liked to see them abandoned; tradition won the day. The playing format, then, was made up of five foursomes on the first day, followed by five fourballs on the second day. With a total of only ten points at stake, pessimists about British chances could be reasonably sure that there would still be something to play for on the last day when ten members from each of the 12-man teams faced each other in singles.

One other factor very slightly improved British chances: the fewer matches there were, the greater Britain's chance of seizing an early lead and hanging on to it. The shorter the period of time the better. Britain could also ambush the American team as it cruised to a seemingly inevitable victory. The British always seemed to find something to feel encouraged about after a bad day; in 1975, it had been Brian Barnes's two wins in a day over Jack Nicklaus. This time hope came in the form of the new 'white hope' of British golf, Nick Faldo, who had yet to win his first important tournament as a professional. He was paired with the experienced Oosterhuis in the foursomes against 1975 US Open champion Lou Graham, and Ray Floyd, who had won the Masters in brilliant style the year before. Faldo began shakily but all went well from that point on. Both the British men played well, Oosterhuis making his normal contribution on the greens.

Captain Huggett had remembered the good start which Gallacher and Barnes had made in the Muirfield Ryder Cup and sent this pair out first. After a close contest they were just ahead

A victorious Dave Stockton with Jerry McGee

Above *Eamonn Darcy*

with a 1-point lead; instead, they were behind 1–4.

On the second day, Faldo continued as Britain's hero. That looping willowy swing (far more attractive than the workman-like one he emerged with nearly ten years later) seemed to waft his drives past the American ball. He and Oosterhuis took the lead on the 2nd and were never seriously threatened by Nicklaus and Floyd, winning 3 and 1. But if they could do it for Britain, no one else could. Only one match was even close; the young pair of Ken Brown and Mark James nearly got a half against Hale Irwin and Lou Graham. The United States were 5 up in each of the other three games when the holes ran out.

The new format provided the British side with a chance when they went into the final day

Below *Ken Brown and Mark James*

with five holes left but they lost the next four to go down by 3 and 1. Alas, this was all too much the pattern of the day. The second pair out, left-handed newcomer to the Ryder Cup, Peter Dawson, with the senior member of the team, Neil Coles, were 2 up with three to play against Dave Stockton and Jerry McGee. Stockton holed two huge putts on the 16th and 17th to level the match and the British then made matters even worse by playing the last hole badly. Britain had lost two matches that seemed to be going her way.

Then came the Faldo/Oosterhuis success followed by the disappointment of Tony Jacklin and Eamonn Darcy managing only to halve when they too had been 2 up with three to play. In the fifth and final match Jack Nicklaus and Tom Watson were never troubled by Mark James and Tommy Horton. 'If only' was the comment most frequently heard. Certainly Britain should have gone into the second day

131

Above *Ray Floyd and Jack Nicklaus on their way to defeat in the fourballs by Peter Oosterhuis and Nick Faldo (below)*

Above *The great Tom Watson*

with the ten singles remaining. However, with a 5-point lead already, the Americans had little left to do in order to win. Before those singles began, Brian Huggett had done the almost unthinkable; he dropped Tony Jacklin, a mainstay of the team since his first Ryder Cup appearance in 1967. There had been a brief row out on the course, when Huggett seems to have said that Jacklin should have been out supporting the team more. He had not played well over the first two days – only Faldo and Oosterhuis had – but though Jacklin's great days were over and he was no longer a world star, it would be difficult to argue that the other ten players that Huggett sent out were better golfers.

This was a young British Ryder Cup team which included several players with a very good future – Nick Faldo, Mark James, Ken Brown and Howard Clark. Clark it was, looking very nervous against an equally confident Lanny

Wadkins, who led off. Wadkins was always in charge of this match, as was Lou Graham facing Neil Coles. With those two matches going early to the United States, thoughts of a British victory quickly became absurd. It was a strange captaincy decision as Huggett had not thought highly enough of Clark to play him in either foursomes or fourballs. His most likely winners were Faldo and Oosterhuis (who had never been beaten in a singles). Huggett played them last, a tactic which is all well and good in a tight finish which was not the situation in 1977. Playing at nine and ten, the two enhanced their reputations by winning but they could not change the outcome of the competition. Though Oosterhuis's opponent, Jerry McGee, was not someone who will feature high in the history of golf, Faldo was playing the world's number one, Tom Watson. In 1977 he had won the Masters – with Nicklaus doing all he could

to stop him – and then came a memorable encounter at Turnberry in the British Open where Nicklaus played superlatively but Watson was a stroke better. At Lytham and St Annes Faldo came out top; he parred the last hole, which Watson didn't, to win 1 up.

On the American side, only Lanny Wadkins came through with three wins (although others played two games and won them both). Faldo and Oosterhuis did the same for Britain, winning three of Britain's total of 7 to 12 for the United States. Twenty years had gone by since the last British win, one of only three since 1927. Everyone agreed that there had been too little golf at Lytham. Although the ten singles occupied ample time on the final day, having only five matches out on course on each of the other two days had proved an unsuccessful experiment. The only advantage was that the match was still undecided by the third day.

ROYAL LYTHAM AND ST ANNES, LANCASHIRE, ENGLAND
15–17 SEPTEMBER 1977

United States		Great Britain and Ireland		Hill and Stockton (5 and 3)	1	Jacklin and Darcy	0
Captain Dow Finsterwald		*Captain* Brian Huggett		Irwin and Graham (1 up)	1	James and Ken Brown	0
					–		–
Foursomes					4		1
Wadkins and Irwin (3 and 1)	1	Gallacher and Barnes	0	*Singles*			
Dave Stockton and McGee (1 up)	1	Coles and Dawson	0	Lanny Wadkins (4 and 3)	1	Howard Clark	0
Floyd and Graham	0	Faldo and Oosterhuis (2 and 1)	1	Lou Graham (5 and 3)	1	Neil Coles	0
Ed Sneed and January (halved)	0	Darcy and Tony Jacklin	0	Don January	0	Peter Dawson (5 and 4)	1
Nicklaus and Watson (5 and 4)	1	Horton and James	0	Hale Irwin	0	Brian Barnes (1 up)	1
	–		–	Dave Hill (5 and 4)	1	Tommy Horton	0
	3		1	Jack Nicklaus	0	Bernard Gallacher (1 up)	1
Fourballs				Hubert Green (1 up)	1	Eamonn Darcy	0
Watson and Green (5 and 4)	1	Barnes and Horton	0	Ray Floyd (2 and 1)	1	Mark James	0
Snead and Wadkins (5 and 3)	1	Coles and Dawson	0	Tom Watson	0	Nick Faldo (1 up)	1
Nicklaus and Floyd	0	Faldo and Oosterhuis (3 and 1)	1	Jerry McGee	0	Peter Oosterhuis (2 up)	1
					–		–
					5		5

Final score: United States 12
Great Britain and Ireland 7.
One match halved

1979

For the 1979 match at The Greenbrier at White Sulphur Springs in West Virginia, the number of points at stake was 28, as opposed to 20 at Lytham. It was no longer possible to be picked for the team (like John Garner in 1973) and not play a single match as it was agreed that every team member should play in the singles on the final day. The most significant change was that the contest between the professional golfers of Great Britain and Ireland versus the United States was no more. Players from the mainland of Europe, with the agreement of the PGA of America became eligible. Just as I have used the term 'Britain' as shorthand for 'Great Britain and Ireland' I shall use 'Europe' for 'Great Britain and Europe'.

Only two players from mainland Europe were good enough to be selected in 1979: Seve Ballesteros and Antonio Garrido. Ballesteros had won the Open Championship in July and Garrido had four second place finishes on the Tour during 1979; he had also partnered Ballesteros to win the 1977 World Cup. No other Europeans came close to selection. Spain's José-Maria Canizares was next in ranking but well down in 23rd place.

Captain John Jacobs sent Ballesteros and Garrido out first on 14 September 1979 in the fourball series. They faced some of the most blistering golf ever seen in fourball competition from Larry Nelson and Lanny Wadkins. The Americans reached the turn in a better ball score of 28 made up of 3, 3, 4, 2, 4, 3, 3, 3, 3. Their eventual winning margin of 2 and 1 could have been a lot higher. In the next match, the young and hopeful pairing of Ken Brown and Mark James went down to Fuzzy Zoeller and Lee Trevino. Worse followed when the successful Lytham pairing of Faldo and Oosterhuis lost a close match to Andy Bean and America's first black Ryder Cup player, Lee Elder. One of America's finest golfers was missing; Tom Watson had left the day before play began to be at the birth of his first child. This was a far

better excuse than when Tom Weiskopf had turned down the place he had earned in the 1977 Ryder Cup team because he had wanted to bag a rare species of mountain sheep with his rifle. Oddly, Watson was replaced by another new father of a week, Mark Hayes.

With three of the morning fourballs won by the USA, there followed the only compensation for Europe. The partnership of Brian Barnes and Bernard Gallacher came through against Hale Irwin and John Mahaffey by 2 and 1.

Casper drastically changed his line-up for the afternoon foursomes, reckoning to give most of his players an outing on the first day. He was so pleased with the Nelson/Wadkins performance, however, that he left them together for the last match out, in which they beat Barnes and Gallacher 4 and 3. It was the first match, however, which caused the most controversy — there seems to be a mini-scandal in Ryder Cup matches and most involve the British or Europeans. This time, it was the two young members of the team, Mark James and Ken Brown, who were at the centre of the affair. They almost missed the flag-raising ceremony and they did miss a team meeting. Back in Britain, both James and Brown were fined and Brown was also banned from the 1981 match.

That first afternoon, Brown was paired with Irishman Des Smyth and most thought he was very unhappy at the change. Brown seemed not to exchange a word with his partner throughout the match which didn't last very long as Hale Irwin and Tom Kite beat them by 7 and 6. Fortunately for Europe, this was the nadir of the 1979 Ryder Cup match. Playing second, Ballesteros and Garrido won and Sandy Lyle and Tony Jacklin followed with a halved match. The tried pairing of Barnes and Gallacher, however, lost by 4 and 3 to the strongest US pairing of Wadkins and Nelson. At the end of the day, European prospects were poor and the score sheet had a familiar look: US $5\frac{1}{2}$ Europe $2\frac{1}{2}$.

Right *Hale Irwin*

Above *Seve Ballesteros's first Ryder Cup*

On the second day, the format was changed so that foursomes were played first. Jacklin and Lyle led off and beat Lee Elder and John Mahaffey by 5 and 4; Oosterhuis and Faldo returned to form and won even more comfortably, by 6 and 5. Barnes and Gallacher also won their games so Europe lost only the last match when Ballesteros and Garrido went down by 3 and 2 to Nelson and Wadkins for the second time. As this four were soon out again in the afternoon fourballs, it was about time the Spaniards hit back – but it didn't happen. Wadkins and Nelson trounced them yet again, by 5 and 4 this time. There were mutters that allowing the Europeans in had changed the object of the match and talk that Sam Ryder, who must have turned in his grave when the decision to bring in Europeans was made, might now be chuckling.

When Jacklin and Lyle then lost for the first time to Kite and Irwin after a close match, the European come-back of the morning, which had brought the gap between the teams down to a single point, was checked. However, the rest of the day went well for Europe, with two wins from the very effective pairings of Barnes/Gallacher and Faldo/Oosterhuis. This meant that the teams went into the final day singles with the scores US $8\frac{1}{2}$ Europe $7\frac{1}{2}$. And then there was a little more controversy. With every team member playing, there was no scope for a player being off form or, even worse, injured. Mark James hurt his shoulder and had to withdraw an hour before the start of play. Gil Morgan had a similar problem and was the player whom Casper chose to drop, having only played him once in the series. However, the night before the singles, each captain had placed in an envelope the name of the player they would drop if a member from the other side was injured. Unfortunately, Casper had misunderstood the procedure and decided on and named the man he considered his best player – Lee Trevino. European captain, John Jacobs, allowed him to make a change. Trevino played and Morgan stood down.

Europe made a good start. When Gallacher beat Lanny Wadkins 3 and 2, the teams were level but at number two Seve Ballesteros faced his Nemesis, Larry Nelson, for the fourth time and again he lost. The next four matches in the order also went to the USA though in the meantime Nick Faldo had beaten Lee Elder. In the end, though, only Ken Brown added to the European points total, beating Fuzzy Zoeller. Peter Oosterhuis lost, ending an unbeaten singles record going back to 1971. By this time, he had long been a struggling player on the US Tour but was transformed in Ryder Cup play. It took birdies from Hubert Green on both the 17th and 18th holes to beat him.

Despite losing eight of the singles Europe consoled herself with the fact that four of these games had gone to the last green. Yet a loss is still a loss. The winners were complimentary about the European performance. Though the USA had won by 16–10, Billy Casper said he had never felt confident of victory.

Was the gap in playing standards between the two sides closing at last? Many thought it was but, ominously for Europe, it was the Americans who seemed to sink more than their fair share of vital putts. Even so, in Seve Ballesteros, unsuccessful as he had been at The Greenbrier, Europe had a player who had won all over the world and who would soon win the 1980 Masters at Augusta.

THE GREENBRIER, WHITE SULPHUR SPRINGS, WEST VIRGINIA, USA
14–16 SEPTEMBER 1979

United States		Great Britain and Europe	
Captain Billy Casper		*Captain* John Jacobs	
Fourballs			
Wadkins and Nelson (2 and 1)	1	Garrido and Ballesteros	0
Trevino and Zoeller (3 and 2)	1	Brown and James	0
Bean and Elder (2 and 1)	1	Oosterhuis and Faldo	0
Irwin and Mahaffey	0	Gallacher and Barnes (2 and 1)	1
	3		1
Foursomes			
Irwin and Kite (7 and 6)	1	Brown and Smyth	0
Zoeller and Green	0	Ballesteros and Garrido (3 and 2)	1
Trevino and Morgan (halved)	0	Lyle and Jacklin	0
Wadkins and Nelson (4 and 3)	1	Gallacher and Barnes	0
	2		1
Foursomes			
Elder and Mahaffey	0	Jacklin and Lyle (5 and 4)	1
Bean and Kite	0	Faldo and Oosterhuis (6 and 5)	1
Zoeller and Hayes	0	Gallacher and Barnes (2 and 1)	1
Wadkins and Nelson (3 and 2)	1	Ballesteros and Garrido	0
	1		3
Fourballs			
Wadkins and Nelson (5 and 4)	1	Ballesteros and Garrido	0
Irwin and Kite (1 up)	1	Jacklin and Lyle	0
Trevino and Zoeller	0	Gallacher and Barnes (3 and 2)	1
Elder and Hayes	0	Faldo and Oosterhuis (1 up)	1
	2		2
Singles			
Lanny Wadkins	0	Bernard Gallacher (3 and 2)	1
Larry Nelson (3 and 2)	1	Seve Ballesteros	0
Tom Kite (1 up)	1	Tony Jacklin	0
Mark Hayes (1 up)	1	Antonio Garrido	0
Andy Bean (4 and 3)	1	Michael King	0
John Mahaffey (1 up)	1	Brian Barnes	0
Lee Elder	0	Nick Faldo (3 and 2)	1
Hale Irwin (5 and 3)	1	Des Smyth	0
Hubert Green (2 up)	1	Peter Oosterhuis	0
Fuzzy Zoeller	0	Ken Brown (1 up)	1
Lee Trevino (2 and 1)	1	Sandy Lyle	0
Gil Morgan (match not played)	0	Mark James (injured)	0
	8		3

Final score: United States 16 Great Britain and Europe 10. Two matches halved

1981

By 1981, Ballesteros was firmly established on the world stage and had won the 1980 Masters in dominant fashion. In America he was recognised as a great player; in Britain he was a god. A world-wide poll might well have ranked him behind only Tom Watson among his contemporaries. But Ballesteros did not make the 1981 Ryder Cup team. The problem arose from a dispute with what was then known as the European Tournament Players' Division on the question of appearance money. The result was that Ballesteros played in Europe very little and in those few appearances had not gathered enough points to be one of the automatic ten choices. This left a committee of Neil Coles, Bernhard Langer and John Jacobs, Ryder Cup captain, to choose the final two players. It appears that the discussions mainly centred around Mark James, 11th on the points list, Tony Jacklin, 12th, and Ballesteros and Oosterhuis who had both played little in Europe. Rumour has it that Jacobs wanted Ballesteros (as a great player) and Oosterhuis

(for his Ryder Cup record). He got Oosterhuis, a US Tour and not a European Tour player, but not Ballesteros, mainly because Neil Coles was opposed to his selection.

Oosterhuis was not a controversial choice but what incensed many was that Mark James, the 'bad boy' of The Greenbrier, had been selected ahead of the Spaniard. Giving James preference over Jacklin was also unpopular. Leaks concerning the selection committee choices suggested that Jacklin, at 37, was considered too old. Although the rejection of Ballesteros was undoubtedly a result of the dispute over appearance money, it was also suggested that the Spaniard had not proved a master of matchplay golf. Ballesteros was to make a nonsense of this point by winning the World

The 1981 European team: (left to right) Bernard Gallacher, Des Smyth, José-Maria Canizares, Mark James, Eamonn Darcy, Nick Faldo, John Jacobs (captain), Peter Oosterhuis, Sandy Lyle, Sam Torrance, Howard Clark, Bernhard Langer and Manuel Pinero

Matchplay event which came after the Ryder Cup.

There was less controversy by far regarding the US team; as had quite often been said before, it was considered the strongest line-up the Americans had ever put out. This time there was good reason for saying so; for a start, Nicklaus and Watson were back and Ben Crenshaw was in. Without an apparent weak link the rest of the team was: Larry Nelson, Bill Rogers, Ray Floyd, Jerry Pate, Johnny Miller, Bruce Lietzke, Tom Kite, Hale Irwin and Lee Trevino. Looking back from the perspective of 1989, only Lietzke has failed to become a winner of major championships. Jerry Pate has done little since 1981, as a result of injury, and Bill Rogers has suffered an almost total loss of form since he ranked as the world's best player that year.

The course finally chosen was Walton Heath. The relatively new Belfry just north of Birmingham was the first choice, partly because it was and is the headquarters of the PGA, however, its condition was poor and the decision to move was made. The Belfry is often spoken of as 'an American style' course, meaning that there are several holes where water comes into play. It would have been conceding an advantage to the United States to use it – though the poor fairways might have disconcerted the Americans more than the Europeans, who are well used to complaining about poor conditions, but coping with them.

One of the great courses of the Surrey heathlands, Walton Heath, measured just over 7,000 yards. It is a stern test of golfing ability except that none of the four par 5s is long by modern standards.

John Jacobs pitched two of his young men, Sandy Lyle and the controversial choice, Mark James, straight in to the first foursomes match and they gave him a win over Rogers and Lietzke. This year, three players from continental Europe had made the team – Bernhard Langer, the number one on the Tour in 1981, Manuel Pinero and José-Maria Canizares.

Ben Crenshaw just misses

Jacobs paired Langer and Pinero for his second partnership but they went down to Trevino and Nelson by one hole. Gallacher and Des Smyth, however, had already edged Europe ahead again by beating Ray Floyd and Hale Irwin 3 and 2.

As Jacobs' best bets, Oosterhuis and Faldo were out last but they faced US captain Dave Marr's strongest pairing, Tom Watson and Jack Nicklaus – a player with a surprisingly poor Ryder Cup record. There was little wrong with Nicklaus's game this time, however, and the Americans won very comfortably by 4 and 3. Jacobs responded by leaving Faldo and Oosterhuis out of the afternoon's fourballs. Here Jacobs led off with what some thought

Above *Manuel Pinero and Bernhard Langer debate a putt*

Right *Sam Torrance holes a good one*

his weakest pairing: Des Smyth and José-Maria Canizares. The Spaniard was extremely nervous, suffering that common Ryder Cup complaint where the golfer is not so much afraid of losing as of playing very badly. Against the odds, they trounced Rogers and Lietzke by 6 and 5. James and Lyle then defeated Crenshaw and Pate to put Europe 2 points in the lead. The third match out was halved but Europe went down in the last match of the day as a result of Floyd birdies on the 17th and 18th which neither Gallacher nor Darcy could match.

A point behind, Dave Marr had some thinking to do. On the second day, he dropped Lietzke, Crenshaw and Miller altogether but made greater use of two of his old men, Nicklaus and Trevino. Trevino asked to play with Pate, joking that Pate's swing, combined with his own experience and brains, would be a match for anyone. In the first fourball out, they crushed Nick Faldo and Sam Torrance by 7

Tom Watson and Jack Nicklaus study the line

and 5. The match continued to go in America's favour for the rest of that morning; Nelson and Kite just got home against Mark James and Sandy Lyle, while Canizares and Smyth lost their magic and went down to Watson and Nicklaus. Langer and Pinero, however, managed to beat the tough combination of Floyd and Irwin.

At the lunch break, the United States had moved into a 1-point lead. Nicklaus and Watson, sandwiches in hand, were rushed straight off to the 1st tee for the afternoon foursomes and in due course disposed of Langer and Pinero to maintain their one hundred per cent record. Larry Nelson, too, kept up his remarkable run and increased his Ryder Cup record to played 8, won 8. None of the Americans, in fact, did anything at all to harm either their reputations or career records.

The afternoon was a clean sweep to the United States, with only one match going as far as the 17th tee. As a contest, the 1981 Ryder Cup was virtually over by the end of a day which saw the United States with a 5-point lead with 12 points at stake in the third day's singles.

There was no European fight-back during the singles; four of the first five matches went to the USA and one was halved. The second game on the course which involved Sandy Lyle and Tom Kite was remarkable indeed: Lyle had eight birdies in his round, which was surely enough for a comfortable win? Not so. Tom Kite played the round of his life; he played 16 holes, was ten under par when the match ended and had ten birdies. Kite even had the grace to apologise to Lyle when he holed a very long putt on the 15th to go 3 up.

Left *Johnny Miller had a disappointing Ryder Cup*

Below *One of Larry Nelson's many victories, this time as partner of Tom Kite*

Above *The jubilant US team after their crushing 17–8 win over the Europeans*

The only successes for Europe were individual ones. Howard Clark, who had only been played once on the first two days, was delighted to beat Tom Watson by 4 and 3 and Manuel Pinero beat Jerry Pate equally comfortably. Faldo, who had played both mornings and had been heavily defeated and dropped for the afternoons, may have been consoled by beating Johnny Miller. Perhaps because of Kite's unbeatable golf, the general opinion was that the United States had played too well on the second and third days for any team to challenge them.

How had the continental European contingent fared overall? In the singles, they had held their own with a win and a half to one loss (where Canizares lost to Irwin by one hole). In foursomes and fourballs, Langer and Pinero had been paired in three matches and had lost two and won one. Canizares had played in two fourballs with Des Smyth, winning and losing. With Europe losing 8 to 17 with three halved matches, continental players had achieved better results than the British. Depending on how one juggles the statistics, it was perhaps the worst defeat ever on British soil, rivalled only by the 1937 match where Britain lost 7–3 with two halved games.

WALTON HEATH, SURREY, ENGLAND 18–20 SEPTEMBER 1981

United States		Great Britain and Europe	
Captain David Marr		*Captain* John Jacobs	
Foursomes			
Rogers and Lietzke	0	Lyle and James (2 and 1)	
Trevino and Nelson (1 up)	1	Langer and Manuel Pinero	0
Irwin and Floyd	0	Gallacher and Smyth (3 and 2)	1
Watson and Nicklaus (4 and 3)	1	Oosterhuis and Faldo	0
	–		–
	2		2
Fourballs			
Rogers and Lietzke	0	Smyth and Canizares (6 and 5)	1
Crenshaw and Pate	0	Lyle and James (3 and 2)	1
Kite and Miller (halved)	0	Torrance and Clark	0
Irwin and Floyd (2 and 1)	1	Gallacher and Darcy	0
	–		–
	1		2
Fourballs			
Trevino and Pate (7 and 5)	1	Faldo and Torrance	0
Nelson and Kite (1 up)	1	Lyle and James	0
Floyd and Irwin	0	Langer and Pinero (2 and 1)	1
Nicklaus and Watson (3 and 2)	1	Canizares and Smyth	0
	–		–
	3		1

Foursomes			
Trevino and Pate (2 and 1)	1	Oosterhuis and Torrance	0
Rogers and Floyd (3 and 2)	1	Lyle and James	0
Nicklaus and Watson (3 and 2)	1	Langer and Pinero	0
Kite and Nelson (3 and 2)	1	Smyth and Gallacher	0
	–		–
	4		0
Singles			
Lee Trevino (5 and 3)	1	Sam Torrance	0
Tom Kite (3 and 2)	1	Sandy Lyle	0
Ben Crenshaw (6 and 4)	1	Des Smyth	0
Bill Rogers (halved)	0	Bernard Gallacher	0
Larry Nelson (2 up)	1	Mark James	0
Jerry Pate	0	Manuel Pinero (4 and 2)	1
Bruce Lietzke (halved)	0	Bernhard Langer	0
Johnny Miller	0	Nick Faldo (2 and 1)	1
Tom Watson	0	Howard Clark (4 and 3)	1
Hale Irwin (1 up)	1	José-Maria Canizares	0
Jack Nicklaus (5 and 3)	1	Eamonn Darcy	0
Ray Floyd (2 up)	1	Peter Oosterhuis	0
	–		–
	7		3

Final score: United States 17
Great Britain and Europe 8.
Three matches halved

A NEW BALANCE OF POWER (1983–1987)

1983

In 1989, it is interesting to look back at Tony Jacklin's earlier feelings about the Ryder Cup. He had quarrelled with his captain Brian Huggett in 1977 and been dropped; he was annoyed to miss selection in 1981 and had rejected the offer to be present as an official. Overall, he had really enjoyed only his first Ryder Cup match in 1967 and the 1969 tie, when he had been at the peak of his game. With bitter feelings about his omission in 1981, Jacklin thought no more about the Ryder Cup, anyway, he was nearing the end of his playing career. Then, while on the putting green before the first round of a tournament at Sandmoor, he was asked if he would like to captain the 1983 team.

Jacklin's immediate response was that the team must travel first class to the United States. He felt that in many matches he had played in, the team had felt second class in all respects. The secretary of the European Tour said he would see what he could do. (Was it an omen that Jacklin then went out and shot a 65 to share the lead in the Car Care event?) Ken Schofield then went better than first class travel: the team would travel by Concord and their usual caddies would go as well – something that was perhaps never considered in earlier years.

For the 1983 match at PGA National in Florida, representation from the Continent did not increase. Langer was there again, as was Canizares, from the Walton Heath team. Pinero

was out. Ballesteros of course was in – but only just; the Spaniard still resented the slight of his omission in 1981 and his 'revenge' was to say that he might not play. Ballesteros usually bypassed the World Cup, because of its diminished stature; if he would not play for the greater glory of Spain in that event, the concept of playing for Europe probably had even less appeal. Jacklin approached him at the Open Championship in July. Ballesteros said he would think about it and eventually agreed to play a couple of weeks later. He was the only real world-class star in the team. Major championships were still to come for Langer, Lyle and Faldo, although the latter had enjoyed a superb year in Europe. Two or three of the team were unlikely to do well.

Jacklin began his captaincy on the wrong foot by apparently talking to Gordon J. Brand on the Concorde flight and, so it was reported, warning Brand that he could expect to play only in the singles (where all team members would automatically play). Jacklin had decided on his best pairings and they didn't include Brand who has a highly idiosyncratic swing, and one can assume that Jacklin thought none too highly of him. On Jacklin's part, it was all meant kindly, no doubt, but such words would hardly have inspired Brand to greater heights!

Jacklin intended his team to win; there would be no attempt to give everyone their fair share in the encounter at PGA National, instead, Jacklin's strength lay in getting the best out of his star players. He would tell them, in this and

later years, that they might have to play continually. Faldo and Langer played throughout the first two days as did Ballesteros and Paul Way – the latter was a surprising pairing. Jacklin felt that young Way had talent but must be paired with a very good player, otherwise he could not play him in either foursomes or fourballs. The answer was to tell Ballesteros that only he, the greatest player in the world, could do the job of supporting Way and getting the best out of him. Another of his key pairings worked out less well. This was Bernard Gallacher and Sandy Lyle. Neither of them was in

Above *Tom Watson won the decisive point*

peak form and Lyle can play very bad golf indeed at times. On this visit to America, he had the ball way out of alignment in his stance and could not adjust to the change in time.

US captain Jack Nicklaus's strategy was the reverse; he decided to pair players who were friends and seemed to play well together. Significantly, he wanted to 'ensure that every member of the team gets as near as possible equal golf course time'. There were exceptions, however. He decided, for instance, to play Tom Watson to the maximum because of his psychological impact as the greatest player of big events in the game of golf. Watson was then ranking last among the qualifiers for places in the US team but he had, and still has, that strange talent of being able to raise his competitiveness for the great occasions of golf. For Americans, the Ryder Cup had never really been much more than an enjoyable social event and so it remained in 1983, but increasingly with national pride at stake. The United States' 'worst' player managed to come through with four wins from five games, including, at the end of the singles, the decisive win.

The first foursomes on the opening day saw one of Jacklin's favourite pairings, Bernard Gallacher and Sandy Lyle, facing Tom Watson and Ben Crenshaw. After a close struggle early on, inexorable US holing out upset Jacklin's pre-match calculations. Their 4 and 2 defeat meant that Jacklin didn't play them again until the singles on the last day.

His second pairing, Nick Faldo and Bernhard Langer, were as strong as Lyle and Gallacher had been weak and they trounced the strong US pairing of Craig Stadler and Lanny Wadkins by the same 4 and 2 margin. Nicklaus, content to let everyone have a share of the play, could afford to let the match unfold in that pattern. Jacklin played to his apparent strengths; from that point on, Langer played in all matches as did Faldo.

The next two matches must have bemused Jacklin; Ballesteros and Way lost 2 and 1 yet their opponents, Calvin Peete and Tom Kite, had won partly by holing chip shots. At the end, Way left a putt of about three yards an inch short of the hole while Peete holed from a little closer. Way was distressed; Ballesteros consoled him and told Jacklin that he had also found the burden too heavy. Jacklin told the Spaniard that he was by far and away the world's greatest player and that Seve could undoubtedly do it. Seve agreed. José-Maria Canizares and Sam Torrance had by this time, surprisingly, dis-missed Raymond Floyd, who was looking cross, and his partner Bob Gilder, by 4 and 3. At the end of the morning foursomes, the match stood all square.

Jacklin then introduced his combination of the 'difficult' young man, Ken Brown, paired with the oldest man ever to make a debut in the Ryder Cup, 44-year-old Brian Waites. Brown lacked self-confidence and Waites did not believe he had the ability to compete at tournament level until late in his golf career. However, they put Europe into the lead by beating Fuzzy Zoeller and Gil Morgan 2 and 1, but any euphoria aroused by this result was probably dispelled rather quickly by the fact that Langer and Faldo went down by the same margin. Theirs was the strongest European pairing – the only one which put two sound eggs into one basket. They had seven birdies – but that is often not enough in fourball play.

On the first day both teams wondered whether they had anyone capable of getting up in 2 at the 578-yard 18th which had water all along the right-hand side. Ballesteros couldn't quite do it but he managed to drive around 40 yards further than anyone else in his fourball and then hit a fairway wood just short of the front edge of the green. This meant a 4 for Ballesteros which the Americans, after good third shots, couldn't quite match. With a half in the other match, Crenshaw and Peete versus Torrance and Woosnam, the Europeans went into the second day with a 1-point lead.

Jacklin was pleased that his men had taken $2\frac{1}{2}$ points from the 4 available and decided to use the same pairings in the repeat fourballs which opened the match on the second day. Brown and Waites again led the way, beginning with four birdies in the first six holes to go a commanding 3 up after seven holes. At about this time, the first three European pairings out on the course were all in the lead. Last came Ian Woosnam and Sam Torrance facing Tom Watson and Bob Gilder. In this last match, the Americans took the first three holes with birdies, were never threatened thereafter, and went on to win very convincingly indeed by 5 and 4.

Waites and Brown, on the other hand, failed to exploit a similar position. They lost two holes with neither being able to produce a par and a couple of US birdies then put them behind before Brown squared with a birdie of his own on the 13th. That was the position on the 18th tee. Waites parred this 578-yard hole; Brown grazed the hole with his attempt at a birdie putt. Craig Stadler had gone through the green with his third shot into light rough but was not very far from the hole – perhaps six or seven yards. He flicked a sand-iron shot into the air and watched with increasing interest as it ran true to the hole – and fell in. It was an unexpected blow for the Europeans but Stadler is one of the great short game exponents and he had simply played one of his best shots when it was needed.

For Europe, the second pair out was Faldo and Langer against Calvin Peete and Ben Crenshaw, the only pairing Jack Nicklaus

hadn't changed from the previous afternoon. Langer, distressed at his form when losing with Faldo on the first afternoon, suggested to Jacklin that he be dropped. The captain pointed out to the German that he was a player who had the knack of putting a good score together when below his best. Langer played and he and Faldo were 3 up at the turn on the Americans and went on to win by 4 and 2. With the other matches finished, this left just Gil Morgan and Jay Haas facing Paul Way and Seve Ballesteros. Having been ahead early, the European pair lost both 16th and 17th to birdies and came to the last 1 down. Could Ballesteros get up in 2? He drove well past the other three players and then lashed a 3-wood not only to the green but on through the back, about 20 yards from the pin. With the other three on in three shots, Ballesteros then ran up to a few feet. The others

Below *Calvin Peete, America's finest black golfer, Jack Nicklaus and Bob Gilder*

missed their birdie putts, Ballesteros didn't. The match was halved and the teams were level at 6 points each. There had been no signs of a European weakness in fourball play as there had been in the past when two good Americans had often seemed to be playing no more than one-and-a-half opponents.

In the afternoon foursomes, Faldo and Langer gave Europe a good start with a comfortable 3 and 2 win, the German holing a chip shot of nearly 20 yards to finish the match on the 16th. The United States hit back by winning the next two matches, in one of which the European pair were disgraced. Torrance and Canizares were 4 over par and without a birdie on their card when they went down by 7 and 5 to Gil Morgan and Lanny Wadkins. But a final point which would leave the match level at the end of the second day was always sure to come from the Way/Ballesteros pairing, which faced

Above *Rivals Tony Jacklin and Jack Nicklaus share a joke*

Tom Watson and Bob Gilder. They won five holes in a row from the second and were 5 up with only six holes left to play. Then the Americans made a splendid come-back, throwing birdies at Way and Ballesteros but they were just a little too late and lost on the 17th green by 2 and 1.

The score stood at 8 points all. Not only was this the first time that the result of a Ryder Cup match on American soil had been in real doubt as it went into the final day, but it was also the first time that the scores had been level at this point. Jacklin's words were, 'I'm happy and numb'. He must have known, however, that the odds were in the United States' favour.

Jacklin apparently had little trust in a couple of his players and one or two others were not in good form. In what order should he send out his 12 men? He sensibly decided that he needed a good start more than strong men out at the end – when the match could well have been over. He put his best man, Ballesteros, at number one, followed by the in-form Faldo and Langer. In last place, he put Bernard Gallacher, a proven matchplayer. There was probably no particular logic in the order of places four to 11. In the pairs matches, Jacklin had to choose the best combination of players; in the singles, when every one of his team had to play, all he could do was hope that each man would perform as well as he was able.

Nicklaus put his strength at the bottom of the order and sent his weakest man out first. This was Fuzzy Zoeller, who had played just one match because of recurring back trouble. Zoeller had asked to go first as he, like Nicklaus, reckoned that Jacklin would put his strength at the bottom of the order.

I think that it is about time that, at least for the singles, Ryder Cup captains agree to send out their men in true order so that in 1983 we would have had the spectacle of a Ballesteros versus Watson match. Instead, though Watson had wanted to play the Spaniard and Nicklaus had agreed, they were at opposite ends of the order!

Ballesteros went behind at the 2nd but then produced four birdies in a row, none from short putts. Zoeller, bad back or not, was by no means done for. He won four holes in a row, twice needing only a par to win the hole. Ballesteros was behind though he squared on the 16th with a putt of several yards in length. The 17th was halved and the odds favoured Ballesteros, the man who had shown he could get up in 2 on this 578-yard hole. He hit what he later called 'one of the worst drives of my life'. From deep rough, he could make no more than a pitching wedge shot which, disastrously, he sent into a fairway bunker, just 20 yards further on. He was still nearly 250 yards from the green but Zoeller had been doing none too well either. He was also in the rough from the tee and had to

Above *Curtis Strange during the 1983 Ryder Cup*

play out with a lofted club. He needed a 2-iron for his third.

Ballesteros's ball lay well in the fairway bunker, on an upslope, but close to the face. He decided to try to play a high slicing 3-wood when, it was said, most golfers would have settled for a sand iron onto the fairway. In both imagination and execution it was the shot of the 1983 Ryder Cup and it came to rest on the fringe of the green. Zoeller responded with a 2-iron of the highest quality to about three yards. Eventually both hole and match were halved in 5s.

As the first match finished, the last – Watson versus Gallacher – was well into the first nine. Overall, things were going well for Europe. Five matches were all square but Europe led in four and were down in only two. Jacklin's tactics also seemed to be succeeding. Maybe Ballesteros hadn't brought in the expected point but in quick succession both Faldo and Langer had won to give Europe a 2-point lead. Brand then lost, as did Lyle. The latter player, though off form, had played well enough but Ben Crenshaw had produced seven birdies when he won on the 17th green. The sixth match, Waites versus Peete, also went to the United States, and Woosnam lost to Stadler 3 and 2. However, with things going very much America's way, there came a welcome surprise for Jacklin; young Paul Way exceeded all hopes by beating Curtis Strange 2 and 1 when the American had played par golf.

Playing well down the field at number 11, Ken Brown handed Ray Floyd a heavy defeat by 4 and 3, ending with a string of birdies. It had been a disastrous Ryder Cup for Floyd, one of the best US players. He had played and lost four times, arguably the worst performance ever in these matches by an American. More importantly, the encounter as a whole was levelled at $12\frac{1}{2}$ each. Three matches were still

out: Torrance versus Kite, Canizares versus Wadkins and Gallacher versus Watson. After all, it had come to a test of the Jacklin and Nicklaus tactics.

Playing the 16th, Torrance was 2 down but Kite dropped a shot here. After a half at the 17th, they came to the last with Kite holding a one-hole lead. For his pitch to the green at the last, Torrance was playing from the rough. Though he played the shot well he needed luck – and got it. His ball finished dead. The result was a halved match and the Ryder Cup was still level. At the time, this seemed likely to be the final score of the 1983 Ryder Cup competition. Canizares had been 3 up with seven to play on Wadkins and held a one-hole advantage playing the last. Alas, though never in trouble he made a sad mess of it; his pitch to the green was short in the rough just before the fringe. With Ballesteros watching his fellow Spaniard from a few paces away, Canizares sent his next right to the back of the green. By this time the real damage had been done. Wadkins, from about 60 yards, had put his third shot almost dead and when Canizares putted back wide and too strong he conceded the hole for a halved match.

The failure even to par the 18th would mean the loss of the 1983 match – unless Bernard

Below *The US team celebrates scraping home*

Gallacher could now produce a miracle. Against a very determined Watson, thwarted in his wish to face Ballesteros, Gallacher was 3 down after seven holes and always struggling to get back into the match. However, when Watson dropped a stroke on the 16th, he had done it, though still 1 down with two to play. Both missed their tee shots to the 192-yard 17th; both also failed to make the putting surface with their next shots. Running chips caught in the semi-rough. Alas for Europe, Gallacher then took 3 more, missing a putt from about five feet while Watson did rather better. Watson won the Ryder Cup, in a sense, with his bogey 4 to a double bogey 5.

So ended a Ryder Cup match as exciting as those close finishes in 1933, 1953 and 1969. Surely Europe would win in 1985, especially as the Americans hadn't a logical selection system. In 1983 the US Open champion Larry Nelson couldn't play as he hadn't accumulated enough points from other tournaments. Nor could the US PGA champion Hal Sutton as he wasn't yet a full member of the US PGA.

PGA NATIONAL, PALM BEACH GARDENS, FLORIDA, USA
14–16 OCTOBER 1983

United States

Captain Jack Nicklaus

Great Britain and Europe

Captain Tony Jacklin

Foursomes

United States		Great Britain and Europe	
Watson and Crenshaw (4 and 2)	1	Gallacher and Lyle	0
Wadkins and Stadler	0	Faldo and Langer (4 and 2)	1
Kite and Peete (2 and 1)	1	Ballesteros and Way	0
Floyd and Gilder	0	Canizares and Torrance (4 and 3)	1
	2		2

Fourballs

Morgan and Zoeller	0	Waites and Brown (2 and 1)	1
Watson and Haas (2 and 1)	1	Faldo and Langer	0
Floyd and Strange	0	Ballesteros and Way (1 up)	1
Crenshaw and Peete (halved)	—	Torrance and Woosnam	0
	1		2

Fourballs

Stadler and Wadkins (1 up)	1	Brown and Waites	0
Peete and Crenshaw	0	Faldo and Langer (4 and 2)	1
Morgan and Haas (halved)	—	Ballesteros and Way	0
Watson and Gilder (5 and 4)	1	Torrance and Woosnam	0
	2		1

Foursomes

Floyd and Kite	0	Faldo and Langer (3 and 2)	1
Haas and Strange (3 and 1)	1	Brown and Waites	0
Wadkins and Morgan (7 and 5)	1	Torrance and Canizares	0
Gilder and Watson	0	Ballesteros and Way (2 and 1)	1
	2		2

Singles

Fuzzy Zoeller (halved)	0	Seve Ballesteros	0
Jay Haas	0	Nick Faldo (2 and 1)	1
Gil Morgan	0	Bernhard Langer (2 up)	1
Bob Gilder (2 up)	1	Gordon J. Brand	0
Ben Crenshaw (3 and 1)	1	Sandy Lyle	0
Calvin Peete (1 up)	1	Brian Waites	0
Curtis Strange	0	Paul Way (2 and 1)	1
Craig Stadler (3 and 2)	1	Ian Woosnam	0
Tom Kite (halved)	0	Sam Torrance	0
Lanny Wadkins (halved)	0	José-Maria Canizares	0
Ray Floyd	0	Ken Brown (4 and 3)	1
Tom Watson (2 and 1)	1	Bernard Gallacher	0
	5		4

Final score: United States 12 Great Britain and Europe 11. Five matches halved

1985

When Dave Thomas designed The Belfry in the 1970s, one of his aims was to produce an American-style course. This it certainly is, with shots over water to some of the greens. It is a course whose design favours the Americans' style of play and its choice did not seem to bode well for an European victory. Commercial considerations, however, dictated its choice for the 1981 match, but as we have seen, its poor condition forced the organisers to change their minds.

Re-seeding, tree planting and fertilising meant that it was in excellent condition for the 1985 match, even if it will never be an excellent course. Like so many courses currently being developed in Britain, an impressive building was already there and a golf course was built later. It is far better to find a good stretch of duneland or heath and then build a clubhouse, country club, hotel – or whatever else the profit motive may dictate.

Captain Tony Jacklin was not happy with the choice. He would have preferred a links course with the happy prospect of some chill autumnal winds and rain to unsettle the Americans. Of course, many Americans – Tom Watson, for instance – grew up playing in bad weather but for tournament players really cold weather is exceptional rather than almost the norm as it is on the European Tour.

Though still numerically dominated by the British, this Tour had an increasing number of Continental players rising to the top. This was reflected in the make-up of the 1985 Ryder Cup team. There were four Spaniards – Seve Ballesteros, Manuel Pinero, José-Maria Canizares and José Rivero – and one West German, Bernhard Langer. The British players were Ken Brown, Howard Clark, Nick Faldo, Sandy Lyle, Sam Torrance, Paul Way and Ian Woosnam. Although Ballesteros remained the acknowledged number one on the team, he had

Below *The clubhouse at The Belfry*

been joined by the other major champions Bernhard Langer and Sandy Lyle, winners of the Masters and Open Championship respectively in 1985. The winners of the other major championship that year were both in the US team and were Andy North (US Open) and Hubert Green (US PGA). Other winners of the majors on the US team were Ray Floyd, Craig Stadler, Hal Sutton, Lanny Wadkins and Fuzzy Zoeller. Tom Watson had needed to par the last hole in the US PGA that year to reach the points total to qualify for the team and hadn't managed it. He could still have played in the next and final qualifying tournament but chose not to. His presence would have provided a psychological boost to the American team. Ironically, the changed selection procedures which brought in the US Open and PGA champions did not automatically strengthen the US team.

The European captain on the other hand had the option of choosing the last three players himself. Those who got the nod were Nick Faldo, Ken Brown and José Rivero. Their performances in the 1985 match went some way towards demonstrating that the money list, contrary to popular belief, is a reasonable basis for choosing members of Ryder Cup teams. This, in spite of the fact that results in 72-hole tournaments really ought to be a poor guide to how a man will play over 18 holes of matchplay.

Wanting a good start, Jacklin picked perhaps his strongest pairings for the foursomes of the first morning. Ballesteros and Manuel Pinero were first off, facing Mark O'Meara and Curtis Strange. At 8.15 a.m., the first shot of the 1985 Ryder Cup was struck by O'Meara. It was a push to the right, which left his partner to play over young trees. Pinero's drive was just off the fairway and Ballesteros bunkered the second shot. Pinero played a fair sand shot and his partner holed the putt to halve the hole in 4s. A scrappy start but the trial of the new European strength was under way.

Early on, the Spanish players didn't need to do anything spectacular as the Americans took

Mark O'Meara was out of form during the match

28 strokes to play the first six holes and go 4 down. Their first win came at the 7th, a par 3 of 183 yards where Pinero missed the green and the six-foot putt which Ballesteros's chip left him. When they birdied the next, to win, Strange and O'Meara were back in business and were only 2 down after the first nine holes. Then came that very odd Belfry golf hole, the 10th. Throughout this Ryder Cup, it was played from a forward tee which shortened it from around three hundred yards to 275. Every player on either side had the length to carry the lake and fly over trees to reach the green – if they cared to chance it. The sensible route was to knock a mid-iron short of some fairway bunkers and then turn half right to play a short

pitch to the green. Trevino had told his men to play safe on this hole in the foursomes; Jacklin left it to the individuals' choice.

Ballesteros, with the tee shot, had a go, made the carry and finished right at the back of the green, something like 30 yards from the hole. Curtis Strange, obeying orders, just contented himself with a 7-iron up the fairway. Pinero, left with the huge putt, got it to about two yards and Ballesteros holed for the birdie and a 3-up lead. Though the Americans were playing much better by this time, they lost the 235-yard 12th to a par 3 but won another par 3, the 14th, with par. At the 16th, O'Meara's pitch came to rest a couple of feet from the hole to reduce the gap to two holes. But that was that for the Americans; the long 575-yard 17th was halved in 5s and the match went to Europe by 2 and 1.

The best foursomes golf from either side came in the next match from the American pairing of Calvin Peete and Tom Kite. They reached the turn in 33 to an approximate 37 from Nick Faldo, off form, and Bernhard Langer. On the 10th, the German went for the green, but just failed to carry the water to be three down. At the next, he missed quite a short putt for a half and, at 4 down, that was very nearly that: United States 1 Europe 1. Behind them came Sandy Lyle and Ken Brown against Lanny Wadkins and Ray Floyd, perhaps the most formidable US pairing. They had relatively little to do; although they took 38 for the first nine holes, they were 3 up and when the Europeans found the water on the 10th, the match seemed over. Although Lyle and Brown won their only hole with a par on the 13th the match went to the United States by 4 and 3 soon afterwards.

At 11.30 a.m. the US led 2–1 and were 2 up with 4 to play in the only match still out, Clark and Torrance versus Craig Stadler and Hal Sutton. This had been a close match, with much scrambling play. The feature shot had come from Clark when he sent his team's second shot to about a foot for an eagle on the 579-yard 4th. A little later, the Europeans were able to win the 396-yard 6th with a 5 when Stadler put the US ball in the lake. One up at the turn, the US were brought back to square when Torrance faded his tee shot onto the 10th green and a birdie resulted. The US won the next but a vast Clark putt for a 2 on the 12th again levelled the match. On the 13th, Clark drove into the rough and Torrance's attempted recovery went out of bounds and a succession of poor British shots lost the 14th to a par. The US then won the 15th to be dormy, and a half then saw them home by 3 and 2.

Predictions of a European victory and a shift in the balance of world golfing power were looking rather silly at the lunch break. What was Jacklin to do? With the exception of Pinero, brought in because Rivero had played poorly late on in practice, he had chosen his best eight men, those he had counted on to bear the burden in the pairs play. Should he drop his Open champion and Masters champion? And who to bring in? Way, weakened by tonsillitis after the good early season form which had earned him his place? Rivero, who had the least impressive record? Canizares, whose nerves were shaky? At this point, Jacklin may well have been wishing he had chosen Gordon Brand Junior who was highly experienced in match-play golf from his days as a top amateur. In the end, Jacklin dropped Lyle, Brown and Faldo and started off his fourball line-up with Paul Way and Ian Woosnam. He brought in Canizares to replace Faldo as Langer's partner, thus breaking up his very successful pairing from the 1983 match.

Trevino, with no real problems, kept two of his successful pairs – Stadler/Sutton and Floyd/Wadkins – and then ensured that everyone played on the first day by bringing in Fuzzy Zoeller, Hubert Green, Andy North and Peter Jacobsen.

The first match out was Way and Woosnam against Zoeller and Green. Woosnam began with a birdie from about three yards on the 2nd to win the hole and further birdies from him on the 4th and 6th put the US 2 down. That

Left *Britain's mighty atom, Ian Woosnam*

Right *Andy North, whom many blamed as the man who lost the Ryder Cup*

remained the position after nine holes and at the 10th Woosnam went for the green and failed; Way didn't, but pitched and putted for a winning birdie. At 3 up, this match looked fairly safe for Europe but Green then had a birdie 2 on the 12th and Zoeller a birdie 3 on the 13th to get back to only 1 down. Another Zoeller birdie on the 16th squared the match which was to have a brilliant finish. A Woosnam birdie on the long 17th was matched by Green.

The 18th is a very long par 4 indeed at 474 yards. There is a lake to carry with the tee shot but the secret in playing the hole is a draw following the line of the fairway and shortening the shot to the green, also over water, which needs to find the correct level of the three tiers. Zoeller and Woosnam drove through the fairway into sand; Green and Way played very safe; all four, however, found the green with their second shots, Way the closest, about four yards past the flag. Green, from the top tier with the flag set on the second came very close to holing as did Woosnam from closer. Way then holed his putt for the match and received the accolade of a kiss from the captain. They were round in 64 – one better than the Americans.

Behind them were Ballesteros and Pinero, facing North and Jacobsen. The US Open champion was in relatively poor form throughout, troubled by a hook, but he started well enough, holing from seven feet on the 1st for a birdie and a win. Ballesteros squared on the 5th with a birdie and put his side ahead at the next with another. At the turn, however, the match was back to all square. And so to the 10th. Shortening the hole had been a huge spectator success. Again Ballesteros made the green, this time hitting a 3-wood to seven or eight yards. So did little Pinero. He putted up stone dead for a birdie while Ballesteros nearly holed for a 2. The 3 was good enough.

Pinero then birdied the 11th to put the Spanish pair 2 up until Jacobsen reduced the gap with a 2 on the 14th. The next two holes were halved with pars. Then, from the 17th tee, Ballesteros went full out with his driver, trying to cover the 575 yards in two blows. He was just in range, perhaps 280 yards away. Pinero and North were both forced to play short of the ditch which crosses the fairway with their seconds. Ballesteros went for the green with a long iron but was still left with a pitch of about 60 yards. His sand iron came to rest less than three yards away and, when he holed the putt, the Americans were beaten by 2 and 1.

The morning's deficit had now been wiped out, with two matches featuring the strongest US pairings still out on course. Langer, with his new partner Canizares, reached the turn in level par 36. Only one hole had changed hands, the 4th, won by a Stadler birdie 4. On the 10th, everyone seemed to be either in trees or water but Langer pitched close both here and on the 11th to go 1 up. Stadler squared at the 13th with a putt of several yards and the remaining holes were all halved, leaving the two teams still level at 3½ points each.

The day's last match saw Torrance and Clark given a second chance, this time against Floyd and Wadkins. After four holes, the British pair were two down, having lost one hole to a par, but Clark won the 6th with a birdie and Torrance the 9th to square the match. The next six holes were all halved and then Wadkins struck what proved the decisive putt from as far away as ten yards for a birdie. Both Clark and Torrance missed from closer to the hole. With the last two holes halved, the match went to the United States by 1 up.

At the end of play, both teams had cause for satisfaction. The Americans led by 4½ to 3½ but Europe, after a bad morning, were back in the match. Both teams knew they were in a fight.

To lead off on the second day, in the four-balls, Jacklin decided to persist with his pairing of Clark and Torrance, even though their record was played two, lost two. They faced Andy North, in poor form, and the ever reliable Tom Kite. With wins at the 3rd and 5th, the British pair quickly went 2 up but lost the 8th when neither could par the hole. A Clark birdie on the 10th, a hole where the European team shone throughout, restored their lead. Successive birdies from first Kite and then North on the 12th and 13th levelled the match. The long 550-yard 15th was a turning point. All four

players were on the green in 3 with Kite the nearest but still with one tier to putt up. It was Torrance to putt first and he got his ball close – but by no means dead. From not far short of 20 yards away Clark proceeded to hole out for a fifth and vital birdie. On the next he chipped the ball into the hole from off the green, though from about half the distance. If the Americans were deflated, it would hardly have been surprising as they were dormy 2 down. Although Kite birdied the long 17th, so did Torrance and the match was over.

Behind them there was a repeat fourball with Way and Woosnam again facing Green and Zoeller, whom they had beaten by 1 up on the first day. This time the match went very differently. Woosnam began by holing a long putt for a birdie on the 1st and the British pair went quickly on to win the 3rd, 4th and 5th. The match was to all intents over when neither American could par the 8th and they went 5 down. However, the British dropped the 9th to a par and Green nearly succeeded in dragging the Americans back into the match with a long winning birdie putt on the 11th. Zoeller followed on the 12th, a 235-yard par 3, with an excellent tee shot to a couple of yards or so. Green was bunkered and Way not close. Woosnam then played the decisive shot, his tee shot came to a halt almost dead, about two-and-a-half feet away. When Zoeller missed his birdie putt, the British pair were 4 up again with 6 to play. The next three holes were halved in pars and the match went to Europe by 4 and 3.

Next out for Europe was the unbeaten pairing of Ballesteros and Pinero. They reached the turn in a very respectable 36, with no shots dropped to par but it was nowhere near good enough. Wadkins had begun with a long putt to birdie the 1st and later he and O'Meara began to race away with the match as they birdied three of the four holes before the turn. They were 4 up. It was becoming a matter of routine for Ballesteros to drive the 10th green. He did so again but caused a flutter of apprehension

Ballesteros with team member Manuel Pinero watching play on the 18th green

when his first putt stopped a good six feet from the hole. Then, though he holed it, he was matched by Wadkins who had played the hole for safety but pitched close and holed for his 3 also. It was Wadkins again on the 13th. He holed from about three yards. The Americans were dormy 5 up and birdies from the Spanish pair on both the 14th and 15th only narrowed the margin of defeat. The Europeans lost by 3 and 2.

The competition was now square at 5½ points each. Still out on the course was the match between Langer and Lyle and Craig Stadler and Curtis Strange. Lyle had been angry and disappointed at being dropped from the four-balls on the previous afternoon. However, he

is understood to have been angry with his standard of play rather than his captain. Perhaps he was embarrassed too: he had reigned as Open champion for just a couple of months.

Although Lyle played very well throughout this match, it was Langer who shone first, his birdie putting the European pair ahead after the 1st for what was to prove the only time in the match. On the 2nd, after Lyle had missed for a birdie from less than a couple of yards, Strange holed out from close range to square the match. Thereafter, the match swung to and fro, the Americans going into a one-hole lead and then being brought back to square. On the 13th, however, after both Strange and Lyle had almost birdied, Stadler holed from about three yards to put the United States 2 up. That this lead was hardly immutable was shown when Lyle was the only player to par the 14th. Not long after this came what seemed to be the decisive shot. On the 16th, a par 4 of 410 yards, Curtis Strange's long approach finished stone dead: United States 2 up and dormy 2 at that.

On the long 17th, Sandy Lyle kept his partnership in the match. First he took a bold line over the angle of the dogleg but some of the resultant length was lost when his ball caught a spectator's umbrella. Even so, his second shot found the green. He was pin high but a long way from the hole – about eight yards. Stadler also hit a fine second through the back of the green. His chip for an eagle was just a touch short but it looked as if a birdie would be good enough but it wasn't. Lyle holed his eagle putt and he and Langer played the last 1 down. Lyle drove safely, Langer particularly well. Stadler also drove safely but Strange went across the fairway into a bunker. He had no hope of reaching the green at this 474-yard par 4. He played out and Lyle then hit a long iron to the bottom level of the three-tier green with the flag in the middle. Langer followed with a 3-wood to half a dozen yards. The Europeans were now certain of at least a par between them. The pressure was on Stadler and he responded with a moderate shot, to the right of the bottom level. However, his putt of nearly 20 yards up a big slope was very good and it finished about 18 inches away. Strange had a try at chipping in for his 4 and neither Lyle nor Langer could hole for a winning birdie. There remained the formality of Craig Stadler's tap-in to give the Americans the match. Incredibly, he pulled it wide of the hole and the match was halved; Europe had caught up and the score stood at United States 6 Europe 6.

That tiny putt of Stadler's, which failed even to touch the hole, has remained fixed on many a retina. Alas for Stadler that he didn't get it over with at, say, around 10 a.m. on the 4th. All would soon have been forgiven and forgotten. As it was, anyone with a tongue who could find an ear to listen declared it to be a decisive moment in Ryder Cup history.

Although Stadler's failure would have been quickly forgotten had the United States prospered in the afternoon foursomes, the near landslide against them inevitably suggested they had been shaken and European morale lifted. It began with the play of José-Maria Canizares paired with José Rivero. Jacklin must have felt that he had to bring in the latter, with only the singles of the final day remaining, and he also wanted to rest Torrance and Clark. He probably sent out this Spanish pair first with some confidence that his next three pairs would be able to stage a recovery when and if they lost.

But Canizares and Rivero found the strong Kite/Peete pairing no trouble at all. After three holes the match was square but the Spaniards then produced a run of 4, 3, 4, 2, 3 against par of 5, 4, 4, 3, 4. To put it another way, they had four birdies in five holes and played them in 16 strokes. In the same run, the Americans had no birdies and used 23 strokes. They were also 4 down, went on to lose the 10th to a par, and the 12th and 13th. The match was over, the Spaniards winning 7 and 5.

All in all, it was rather a Spanish afternoon. Next out were a pair of whom more was expected – Ballesteros and Pinero – against the shamefaced Stadler and Hal Sutton. Although they dropped a shot on the 9th and lost the hole they did little else wrong. The rest were pars plus three birdies and after eight holes they were 6 up. On the 10th, Sutton managed to find the green to win the hole with a 2. Stadler drove out of bounds on the 13th to give the hole to the Spaniards and Ballesteros then almost holed his tee shot on the 14th. It was all over. The official result was 5 and 4 but 6 and 4 was the unofficial score.

Europe now held a 2-point lead at 8–6. Were the United States about to collapse as on that far-off day at Lindrick, 28 years before? It was up to Curtis Strange and Peter Jacobsen to hold Way and Woosnam, the two mighty atoms. The early exchanges favoured the British players, but the Americans went ahead with a birdie on

Right *Seve Ballesteros: the world's greatest golfer*

Jacklin, Langer and Brown watch the result of a shot anxiously

the 9th and then quickly pulled away with wins on both the 10th and 11th. (The 10th didn't favour Europe this time. Woosnam put their tee shot in water and Way then thinned his chip up the bank at the rear of the green.) No holes changed hands thereafter until Curtis Strange pitched dead for his 3 and the match, by 4 and 2 on the 16th.

The Langer/Brown versus Floyd/Wadkins match was close for much of the way though the Europeans were never behind. In fact, they were quickly 2 up after three holes but could not get away from the American pair, who squared the match at the 10th. Here Wadkins hit the American tee shot 'safely' miles to the left into the crowd, but Floyd sent the long pitch to about three yards. Meanwhile, Langer had cut his tee shot and Brown put the Euro-

pean ball in the water. The European pair regained the lead with a par 3 on the 12th. The match ended rather suddenly. After two holes halved in par, Langer holed a very long putt to win the 15th and on the next hole Ken Brown hit an 8-iron to four inches. When Wadkins couldn't hole from several yards the match was Europe's by 3 and 2. Surprisingly, it was Langer's first win and Wadkins' first defeat in his fourth match.

From their disastrous first morning, when the European team were 3–1 down, they would go into the final day with a 2-point lead. Anything could happen with 12 matches still to play, but Europe seemed on the rise and the crushing defeats suffered by two of Trevino's pairings in the afternoon foursomes were bad omens for the captain.

The contribution of the Spanish players had been remarkable. Success had been expected, even demanded, of Ballesteros but Pinero, Canizares and Rivero had all raised their games. In all, the four Spanish players had been in six matches on the first two days. Only one of those matches had been lost and four Spanish players had been involved in winning $4\frac{1}{2}$ of Europe's 9 points. A half of the successes from a third of the team was respectable indeed.

It was a Spaniard who led off in the final singles, Manuel Pinero. Jacklin guessed that Trevino would lead off with his strong players to try to draw level and then put more strength at the bottom of his list, which is what Trevino actually did. In response, Jacklin put his main strength in the middle of the order. Pinero was the sacrificial lamb who had to face the American with the sharpest teeth: Lanny Wadkins. The match was close over the first nine holes though Wadkins twice managed to get to 1 up before Pinero squared at the 8th, when Wadkins 3-putted. There was a dramatic shift of fortunes on the 10th. Here, while Wadkins seemed to have a holeable putt for a birdie, Pinero, not on in 2, suddenly holed his chip of a dozen yards for his birdie 3. Wadkins missed and then followed by hitting into both sand and a bush on the next while Pinero struck a long iron safely to the heart of the green. The next three holes were halved but a birdie 4 from Pinero on the 15th put Wadkins 3 down with three to play and almost out. The American managed to birdie the 16th for a win. Then he made rather a mess of the long 17th and Pinero's par 5 was enough to win both hole and match. Europe were 3 points clear at 10–7.

Next out were Woosnam and Stadler in a match of mixed quality. Woosnam began 4, 5, 5, 6 yet was only 1 down and went on to be 1 up after the 7th. The pair finished the first nine all square with Woosnam out in 39 to Stadler's 37.

Woosnam went 1 down at the 10th and seemed to have lost another hole when he hooked his 1-iron tee shot out of bounds on the 13th but a birdie with his second ball enabled him to halve the hole with Stadler's bogey 5. It looked like Stadler was about to pay dearly for his error when the Welshman birdied the 14th to again draw level, but the unlikely is always happening in golf. Stadler won the next two holes with birdies and when Woosnam failed with a birdie attempt on the 17th the match was over, 2 and 1 to Stadler.

In Ray Floyd, Paul Way faced another of Trevino's top men, yet Floyd was to play as badly as anyone on either team. With five 5s, he reached the turn in 41 and was lucky to be only 4 down. When Floyd won both 11th and 12th, however, the pressure was back on Way but his position looked impregnable when the next three holes were halved. The situation looked even better for Way on the 16th. Floyd drove into thick rough along the left while Way was lucky when his ball came out of the deep rough into semi-rough and a good lie. Floyd thought long and hard before deciding on his choice of club and the kind of shot he would attempt; it was a hack out which finished well short of the green. With dreams of glory dazzling him, Way then thinned his approach right through the green and from there, he fluffed his next shot and Floyd ran his ball up dead. Instead of shaking hands, winner by 3 and 2, Way was back to 1 up with two to go. On the next, both bunkered their tee shots but in the end holed short putts for a half in par 5s.

At the last hole, though it is a par 4 of maximum length, the main problem is not the shot to the green but the tee shot, where a well placed draw or a bold straight shot down the left edge of the fairway shortens the next one to the green. But the better that tee shot, the nearer it comes to the lake which lies along the left-hand side. Although a straighter shot can seem safer, with no water problem, it is easy to run across the fairway into one of two bunkers. This is exactly what Floyd did.

Paul Way hit a perfect draw shot. Floyd, at 1 down, could only go for the green with a wood. Not surprisingly he topped it and found the arm of the lake which swings around the front of the green. Way now simply had to avoid putting his second shot in the same place, so he over-clubbed a little with a 3-iron and his ball came to rest at the back of the green. Three putts would surely mean a halved hole and victory in the match itself. In the event, he didn't have to putt at all. Though Floyd played a precise fourth shot it spun back down the slope and he walked forward to concede the hole.

One can probably put far too much stress on the magic of captaincy. In golf, one's players either perform or they don't. Let's just say that Jacklin's tactics had worked out very well; his players had taken 2 points out of 3 from America's finest and Way's victory brought his team to the brink of victory at 13–8 with $14\frac{1}{2}$ needed to win the Ryder Cup. However, at this point other matches had already finished, the first of these being the Langer/Sutton encounter 20 minutes earlier. This was the sixth game whereas Way and Floyd had gone out third.

Sutton began with some poor golf so Langer found himself 2 up after opening with four straight pars and then won the 6th with a birdie to go further ahead. Sutton made his only real fight on the 7th and 8th, winning both holes with a couple of pars. He then lost four holes in a row to go 4 down with seven to play. On the last of these holes, the par-3 12th, Sutton's game had reached its nadir when he took 6 after a penalty drop. Sutton did win the 13th with a par and then struck his tee shot to the 14th to the rear edge. With a 5-iron for the 194 yards, Langer came close to holing in 1, his ball stopping a little over a foot away. He had won by 5 and 4 and, at just after 3 p.m., Europe had moved 3 points clear with the score 11–8.

The next match to finish was between Sandy Lyle and Peter Jacobsen, who were out fifth. It was a close battle all the way, until the sudden ending, and the scoring was good. Lyle was out in 34 to be 2 up and then won the 11th with a par. After holing a good putt on the 12th to remain 2 up he then drove out of bounds on the 13th and eventually conceded the hole. It was the only shot he dropped to par in the match. On the long 15th, Lyle bunkered his tee shot but recovered well, put his third shot about three yards from the hole and wasn't asked to putt when Jacobsen took 3 putts from the front fringe. The end came with one of those freak shots that seemed always to come from the European team. Lyle sent his approach at the 16th to the back of the green, perhaps a dozen yards past the hole. His putt from there hung on the edge before falling in. The time was about 3.10 p.m. and Lyle's 3 and 2 win brought the points score to 12–8. The second phase of Jacklin's master plan was also going well for him. The apparent strength of his middle order was proving no illusion.

Meanwhile, where was his superstar, the man he had introduced at the flag-raising ceremony as 'the greatest golfer in the world'? Seve Ballesteros was in fact heading the middle order at number four and was in trouble against Tom Kite in a match of charisma versus faceless competence. Ballesteros began with a couple of pars to go 1 down and then failed to match Kite's par 5 on the 4th. The 7th went to the Spaniard with a birdie but Kite hit back with one of his own on the 9th to end the first half 2 up. The next three holes were halved, the 11th in birdies. Then came disaster for Ballesteros on the 13th when he managed to hit his wedge second shot into a greenside bunker. Although he recovered to three or four yards he didn't get the putt and went 3 down with five to play in a mean mood.

At the 14th, Ballesteros played the better tee shot. With Kite just off the green, Ballesteros finished at the rear. When Kite then came up to a full five feet it looked as if Ballesteros might get one hole back if he could get down in 2 from perhaps as far as 15 yards. Instead he holed it –

Sam Torrance manages to get his ball out of a stream during the match

one of the longest putts of the 1985 Ryder Cup. Again, it was a European who did it.

At the par-5 15th, Ballesteros was pin high in 2 but only managed to get his third shot to about six yards. Never mind, he holed it to claw back to only 1 behind. Kite looked like a man who was wondering what was going to hit him next – a holed long iron perhaps? There were no dramatics on the 16th, however. The hole was halved in 4s.

The tee shot at the 17th gives a great advantage to the man who shortens this par 5 by cutting across the angle of the dogleg. Ballesteros launched a big one and finished some 60 yards ahead of Kite. He could reach the green, Kite was out of range. Ballesteros then hit a 3-wood just through the green. With Kite eight yards short of the hole with his third shot, the chances were that all Ballesteros had to do was chip and putt for a win, which is what he

did. He added to the interest of the occasion, however, by fluffing his chip shot but then holed his putt from about four yards. He was 3 under par for the last four holes and the match was all square.

Tom Kite, who had done hardly anything wrong with his four pars in a row, ought to have been shaken to the tips of his toes but he played the last hole beautifully with a long drive that flirted with the lake along the left but rewarded him with a 9-iron shot to the green. Both players found the correct tier of the green, with Kite much nearer the hole. He had a realistic chance of winning as Ballesteros was perhaps 18 yards away. Seve then coasted his ball close to the hole and Kite had a putt for the hole and the match. His attempt was certainly a bold one which ran about five feet past. Kite to play again. His next putt was missing all the way but, like Ballesteros's last putt in the 1984 Open Championship, it contrived to fall in. Hole and match halved. Europe 13½ United States 8½. (Since taking that 3–1 lead on the first morning, the Americans had added just 5½ points as against 12½ for Europe. One more point was needed for Europe to win the cup back.)

At times it looked as if that point might be hard to find. All the remaining six matches were close except the last between Trevino's strong man, Curtis Strange, and Ken Brown. Strange played splendidly from the start, while Brown had a very poor spell in the middle holes of the first nine to go 4 down and then lost the 10th to a par to go 5 behind. His fight-back was matched by Strange who eventually won by 4 and 2. By then, the outcome of the competition was decided.

Trevino had placed his weakest players (those off form) in his middle order while Jacklin gambled on the match being over as a team contest before Faldo, Rivero, Canizares and Brown were needed to bring in points. This meant that the two men who might bring in the decisive points once Ballesteros had finished were Sam Torrance and Howard Clark, playing Andy North and Mark O'Meara respectively.

The first of these matches saw some poor golf from both Torrance and North. Torrance, after topping his drive into the lake and conceding the 9th, was out in an approximate 40, with North a couple of shots better. The Scotsman then made a mess of the little 275-yard 10th hole. Taking 6, he went 3 down but immediately got 1 back when North missed the green on the 11th. The next three holes were halved in par and Torrance was then able to win the 15th with a par when the American missed a putt of less than three feet. At the 16th, Torrance almost squared when his birdie putt shaved the hole. At the 17th, North was in a plantation while Torrance hooked his second to the par 5 into thick rough. From there, he repeated his 1983 effort with a pitch to six feet. In both of these Ryder Cup singles he had no chance of finishing near the hole but the shot happened to work. Of such hit-and-hope shots are legends made, and Torrance was about to go into legend. He holed for a birdie and had caught North.

Behind Torrance, Clark looked in command

against O'Meara from the early holes, with the American playing the first five in 4 over par to be, not surprisingly, 3 down. He then won the 9th and 12th to be right back in the match. Hole after hole was then halved with O'Meara having a chance to square when he pitched close on the 16th but missing the putt. At about 4.03 p.m. Howard Clark had a putt to win the Ryder Cup. He bunkered his second shot to the 575-yard 17th but splashed out to four feet, perhaps a little more. His putt for the hole, his match and the Ryder Cup hit the hole and spun away. Dormy 1 up, he would have to play the 18th. At that moment, Torrance was on the 18th green waiting to make sure of the golden chalice. First, let's briefly retrace the play of North and Torrance on this last hole.

After the honour of winning the 17th, Torrance pushed aside memories of his top from the 9th tee and produced the ideal drive, very, very long with draw. It was well over three hundred yards. As North stepped up to play, he knew Torrance had just a pitch with, say, a 9-iron to the green. Should he go for a big draw or a safe line which would leave him a more testing long iron to the green? In the event, he produced neither shot; appearing to collapse in the hitting area, North ballooned his shot. Ripples spread. The crowd cheered. Torrance burst into tears; he had won the match and with it the 1985 Ryder Cup.

There were some formalities to complete. Playing 3, North cleared the water and then pitched to the right tier of the green. He could get a 5. Too many people were clustering round Torrance, congratulating him, telling him the match was won – and much else. But Sam still had to get the ball onto the green. Clearing his eyes, he did so. His ball lay half-a-dozen yards from the hole. North didn't get his 5 so as Torrance stood over his putt he actually needed four putts for a 6, a halved hole and match and a Europe points total of 14½ (Clark was already assured of a half at dormy 1). Instead he holed his first putt and a hundred motor drives whirred. Torrance had joined the immortals.

Perhaps he deserved to but for the majestic tee shot rather than the putt. The time was 4.04 p.m.

Now the other matches didn't matter any more – except to the individuals involved, who had all thought that their result might be vital throughout the competition. Clark halved the last hole to win his match. Faldo, playing uneven golf against Hubert Green, led early on but lost by 3 and 1 when he bogeyed both 16th and 17th. José Rivero looked in charge of Calvin Peete at 2 up after 14 but Peete then birdied the next three holes and won by 1 up. The Canizares/Zoeller match was square after nine holes and the next seven holes were all halved. Canizares then won the 17th with a par and, eventually, won his match 2 up. With $2\frac{1}{2}$ points from his three matches, he was the only

Left *Sam Torrance's win against Andy North guaranteed a European victory*

Below *Tony Jacklin and Lee Trevino with Mrs Joan Ryder-Scarfe, daughter of Samuel Ryder*

undefeated player on either side, expunging memories of his singles failure in 1983. His fellow Spaniard Manuel Pinero had the best record, however, with three wins out of four in pairs play followed by that unlikely win over Lanny Wadkins.

Some thought the villains of the piece were the vast crowds who cheered such American errors as Stadler's missed putt and North's ballooned drive. Torrance had once to remind one section that they weren't at a football match. Ray Floyd remarked on the second day as a Langer shot headed for trees, 'Somebody will probably kick it back into play'. Ray hadn't enjoyed himself at Walton Heath in 1981 either. For Peter Jacobsen the villain was his captain, Trevino of whom he said, 'Lee seemed to have nothing to say about anything at any time'. He thought Jacklin worthy of an invitation to captain the United States but he also condemned the partisan British crowd. There were no villains for the British spectators whose only complaint was that the PGA might have put up a few more scoreboards.

THE BELFRY, SUTTON COLDFIELD, ENGLAND 13–15 SEPTEMBER 1985

Great Britain and Europe		United States	
Captain Tony Jacklin		*Captain* Lee Trevino	
Foursomes			
Ballesteros and Pinero (2 and 1)	1	Strange and O'Meara	0
Langer and Faldo	0	Peete and Kite (3 and 2)	1
Lyle and Brown	0	Wadkins and Floyd (4 and 3)	1
Clark and Torrance	0	Stadler and Sutton (3 and 2)	1
	1		3
Fourballs			
Way and Woosnam (1 up)	1	Zoeller and Green	0
Ballesteros and Pinero (2 and 1)	1	North and Jacobsen	0
Langer and Canizares (halved)	0	Stadler and Sutton	0
Torrance and Clark	0	Floyd and Wadkins (1 up)	1
	2		1
Fourballs			
Torrance and Clark (2 and 1)	1	Kite and North	0
Way and Woosnam (4 and 3)	1	Green and Zoeller	0
Ballesteros and Pinero	0	O'Meara and Wadkins (3 and 2)	1
Langer and Lyle (halved)	0	Stadler and Strange	0
	2		1
Foursomes			
Canizares and Rivero (7 and 5)	1	Kite and Peete	0
Ballesteros and Pinero (5 and 4)	1	Stadler and Sutton	0
Way and Woosnam	0	Strange and Jacobsen (4 and 2)	1
Langer and Brown (3 and 2)	1	Floyd and Wadkins	0
	3		1
Singles			
Manuel Pinero (3 and 1)	1	Lanny Wadkins	0
Ian Woosnam	0	Craig Stadler (2 and 1)	1
Paul Way (2 up)	1	Ray Floyd	0
Seve Ballesteros (halved)	0	Tom Kite	0
Sandy Lyle (3 and 2)	1	Peter Jacobsen	0
Bernhard Langer (5 and 4)	1	Hal Sutton	0
Sam Torrance (1 up)	1	Andy North	0
Howard Clark (1 up)	1	Mark O'Meara	0
José Rivero	0	Calvin Peete (1 up)	1
Nick Faldo	0	Hubert Green (3 and 1)	1
José-Maria Canizares (2 up)	1	Fuzzy Zoeller	0
Ken Brown	0	Curtis Strange (4 and 2)	1
	7		4

Final score: Great Britain and Europe 15 United States 10. Three matches halved

1987

In 1987, the Ryder Cup matches went to the best venue they have yet enjoyed: the Augusta of the north, the course that Jack built. In other words, Muirfield Village, Columbus, Ohio. To add to the sense of occasion, Nicklaus, who was captaining the US team, was not keen on being the first such to preside over defeat on American soil. He was faced by the same rival as in that decisive 1969 final singles, Tony Jacklin. Their styles of captaincy were to be in strong contrast.

On paper, the European team was a little stronger than in 1985. Ballesteros was still Ballesteros; Faldo had become the holder of the Open Championship with his win at Muirfield two-and-a-half months earlier; Lyle had won the 'fifth major', the Tournament Players' Championship earlier in the US season; Woosnam was having the best season of anyone in the world; Langer had won the PGA Championship and the Irish Open with two of his most brilliant performances. Thereafter, the superlatives no longer apply but nevertheless both Clark and Gordon Brand Junior had won twice in Europe during the season and Torrance, Rivero and Darcy had one win each. Olazabal and Ken Brown had none and were the personal selections of Tony Jacklin, along with Sandy Lyle, who would not have qualified on his European Tour performances.

As only Langer, Ballesteros, Lyle and Faldo had won in America, there was a tendency for Nicklaus, his players and the US press and public to think the European team lacked all-round strength. All forgot that the European Tour had become almost as competitive as the US circuit and the team had more Ryder Cup experience. Only the 21-year-old Olazabal and Brand, with international experience as an amateur, were new to the match. For the USA, on the other hand, Mark Calcavecchia, Larry Mize, Dan Pohl, Scott Simpson and Payne Stewart were newcomers. And, though no one mentioned it, precious few had won in Europe.

Their players with the best Ryder Cup records were Lanny Wadkins with 12 wins and four losses, Tom Kite with eight wins and four losses and Larry Nelson who had played nine and won the lot.

There was talk that the Europeans would be unable to cope with hot and humid weather, just like the players of the 1930s and 1950s who almost invariably performed in the British Isles only. Today's European Tour players compete on a world-wide basis. Then there was the speed of the greens at Muirfield Village which are among the fastest in the United States and in great contrast to the slow surfaces so often found in Britain. (Where are those glassy surfaces of Open Championships of long ago?) In the event, the Europeans, many with American experience in plenty, rejoiced in the Muirfield greens. They adjusted to the speed and enjoyed the true surfaces. It helps to know that a putt rolling true at the middle of the hole will not jiggle away as the pace dies.

The competition began with the Ohio State University marching band, more than a hundred strong, parading up the 18th fairway. Tony Jacklin, his team announced by the bagpipes, presented his players by name and country only, lapsing into the sentimentality of 'Little Woosie' but having a good attempt at the correct pronunciation of 'Olazabal'. Perhaps he strove for the dramatic impact of leaving 'Severiano Ballesteros' till last. Jack Nicklaus contented himself with simply announcing his team in alphabetical order and declaring, 'I couldn't have 12 finer players or 12 finer gentlemen'.

Jacklin had again decided to put the main burden on those he considered his best players; it was rumoured that he had told Darcy, Brand and Rivero they might not play till the singles on the third and last day. In the foursomes on the first morning he decided also not to use Lyle, a player he thinks performs below his best in this kind of golf. His line-up, in order, was therefore Clark/Torrance; Brown/Langer; Faldo/Woosnam; Ballesteros/Olazabal.

Nicklaus probably began with the intention of giving all his players a blooding early on. Curtis Strange and Tom Kite were paired because they wanted to play together. Nicklaus put them out first because rumour had it that Jacklin intended to start with two of the world's slowest players, Bernhard Langer and Ken Brown, hoping to unsettle the Americans behind. Strange is said to have claimed he could play even more slowly than them. Strange lead off but Jacklin sent the tortoises of Europe out second. The rest of the US line-up was: Sutton/Pohl; Wadkins/Mize and Nelson/Stewart.

Play began in mist with dew on the ground. For Europe, Howard Clark bunkered the first

Right *A cheerful Larry Nelson*

(Front, l to r) Lanny Wadkins, Larry Nelson, Tom Kite, Payne Stewart, Larry Mize, Ben Crenshaw. (Standing) Curtis Strange, Hal Sutton, Andy Bean, Jack Nicklaus, Dan Pohl, Mark Calcavecchia, Scott Simpson

Above *Ballesteros goes for the green from sand*

tee shot. This pair continued to miss fairways and were quickly 3 down. The other European pairings did little better and, after about a couple of hours play, the United States led in every match. Worst of all was the apparently strong pairing of Faldo, the Open champion, and Ian Woosnam, perhaps the best player in the world during the year, who went out in 40 and were 4 down. Was the foursomes debacle of The Belfry about to be repeated? Suddenly Faldo and Woosnam won the 10th and 12th. They were back in their match with Wadkins and Mize and, with Wadkins faltering, first drew level and then went into the lead, reaching the 18th tee 1 up and then won that hole as well. There was no recovery from Clark and Torrance, however, and they went down on the 16th green by 4 and 2 to Curtis Strange and

Tom Kite. Langer and Brown also lost, by 2 and 1.

Still out on course were Ballesteros and Olazabal against Larry Nelson and Payne Stewart. At this point, Nelson had played in nine Ryder Cup matches over the years and had won the lot. Stewart had received his share of publicity by declaring that the United States would win. The Spanish pair reached the 18th tee 1 up and in sight of levelling the series as a whole. Then Olazabal bunkered their tee shot but Ballesteros managed to find the green with his long second shot. He was a long way from the hole, however. At this point, Stewart, with none too difficult a shot, cut his ball well wide of the green, leaving Larry Nelson an almost impossible little running shot which had to be pitched in the semi-rough. It came off perfectly. In his turn, Olazabal managed to get his long, swinging putt to four or five feet and Ballesteros did the rest. It was Nelson's first defeat in a Ryder Cup match and it came against Ballesteros, who had lost a remarkable four times in matches where the two were opposed.

To end all square at lunch was a huge boost for Europe and an equal disappointment for the United States. It was going to be difficult to defend that record of never having lost a Ryder Cup on home soil. The captains had to re-think. Nicklaus did the obvious and sent out his two foursomes winners for the afternoon fourballs and dropped the losers. Payne Stewart was reported not to have been informed. Jacklin scrapped his master plan of banking on the players he respected most. Out went the losers though he made an exception of Bernhard Langer and merely brought in Sandy Lyle to partner him. Otherwise, he did much the same as Nicklaus in dropping his other losers, Clark and Torrance. Instead, he brought in two players not expecting to play so early, José Rivero and Gordon Brand Junior. Having relatively little faith in them, he sent them out first where they would probably have to face a good pair.

The afternoon went far to settle the destiny

of the Ryder Cup. Rivero and Brand, playing Ben Crenshaw and the US Open champion Scott Simpson, cruised through their match. Playing the 12th, they were 4 up. Though they lost that hole to a Crenshaw birdie, Brand immediately countered on the next hole, with a birdie of his own. On the 16th, Rivero, narrowly missed a putt for the match, but it was all over seconds later as Simpson missed from around three feet.

Behind them was a tough match between Lyle and Langer and Andy Bean and Mark

Below *Hal Sutton*

Calcavecchia. Playing the 14th, the European pair were 2 down but a 3 from Langer won that hole and a 4 from Lyle levelled the match on the 17th green after poor American play on the hole. On the next both Lyle and Langer drove well. The German bunkered his second shot, Lyle hit the green while both Americans went through to the rear fringe. From there, neither could get down in 2 more while Lyle struck his long swinging putt to a couple of feet and holed for the match. People began to comment that the Americans were looking fallible in the crunch of the last couple of holes, the last particularly. Of Calcavecchia and Bean, captain Nicklaus remarked, 'They threw it away!' and so they had. In fourball play neither had managed a par on either the 17th or 18th.

Next came the men who had struck the biggest psychological blow of the 1987 Ryder Cup by playing so well in the morning, Faldo and Woosnam. After 11 holes this match was all square but then came a severe blow for the US on the difficult short 12th. Hal Sutton played much the best of the tee shots to about four feet. Faldo then raced his long putt into the hole for a 2 while Sutton missed. However, the sequence was reversed on the next when Sutton holed a good putt and Woosnam missed from very much closer. Both putts were cheered by the American crowd who had mostly been strangely quiet. Perhaps they were still not involved in the Ryder Cup and the hooting and hollerin' of earlier years had come mostly from supporters of Arnold Palmer. There was also the factor that the average American golf follower had no suspicion that the balance of power in world golf might be moving in Europe's favour.

On the 14th, Woosnam hit a superb iron to some two feet to win the hole and go 2 up, a position maintained to the 17th green, where the match ended with a 2 and 1 victory for the British pair.

The Spanish pairing of Ballesteros and Olazabal were always in command against Strange and Kite. After ten holes they were 4 up but a Strange birdie 4 won the 11th and the

Above *The brilliantly successful pairing of Balles-teros and José-Maria Olazabal*

Spanish pairing then lost the next hole as well. However, there were no further signs of weakness with birdies needed to halve holes. The end came on the 17th. Here both Strange and Kite were much closer to the hole with their second shots than Ballesteros but the Spaniard holed a long putt for his seventh birdie of the round and a 2 and 1 victory.

After that tremulous start, Europe ended the day leading by 6–2 and had a clean sweep of the fourballs. Jacklin was ecstatic; Ballesteros confessed to having had a good day and praised the

Muirfield Village course highly saying that it had the best greens he had ever played on. Nicklaus said that the Europeans had played the best golf and conceded an American weakness, 'I do not have a Seve Ballesteros on my team'. He would put out his best eight in the foursomes the following morning. Stars and stripes flags were handed out a day early; the US team needed more crowd support. Nicklaus commented that the 2,000 or so fans from Europe were making far more noise. Any distant cheer he heard meant a birdie for Europe.

For the time being, Jacklin had no problems. In the morning foursomes he decided simply to send out the eight men who had brought him all four points from their afternoon matches on the first day. Brand and Rivero led off against Strange and Kite and seized the initiative when Brand birdied the 1st hole from as far away as 15 yards. This was immediately answered by a long birdie putt from Strange on the 2nd. The match stayed level until the European pair lost the 6th after being bunkered. However, they squared with a birdie on the very next hole before eventually, and finally, going behind when they lost both 8th and 9th to pars. With the US pair getting three birdies on the second nine, there was no way back for Rivero and Brand. Curtis Strange, winner of about $700,000 at that point on the 1987 US Tour, made sure of victory with a 7-iron to about five feet on the 17th to win by 3 and 1.

The second match between Faldo/Woosnam and Sutton/Mize brought the first halved match of the series. It was a game Europe should have won. Woosnam seemed to have won it on the 17th when he hit a short iron to about five feet of the hole but Mize answered with a good putt. The match went to the last with Europe 1 up but they proved unable to par the hole.

After Ballesteros's splendid performance on the first day, it was Olazabal's turn to excel in their match with Crenshaw and Stewart. The Americans were 3 down with five to play but won the 14th when Ballesteros found the

Nick Faldo got this one close to the hole

stream to the right of the green. They also won the 17th when Crenshaw put his approach shot dead. The US crumbled on the last, however. First Crenshaw drove into a fairway bunker; Stewart then recovered poorly while Crenshaw, trying to get the pitch close, slightly underhit his shot and finished in sand. He made amends eventually by holing a good putt for a bogey 5.

The finish from Ballesteros and Olazabal was also hardly perfect; after a good tee shot from Olazabal into the middle of the fairway, Ballesteros pulled his iron shot into a greenside bunker. After the US errors the Spanish pair needed to get down in two putts from eight feet. Easy? Well, it was a very fast putt, Ballesteros coasted it at the hole but the ball continued about six feet past. Seve was mortified. However, Olazabal, a superb putter from this distance, rolled it in and was rewarded by a hug from the much relieved Ballesteros.

The last match really turned in Lyle and Langer's favour when Lyle cracked a 2-iron about 250 yards on the 11th for an eagle and the lead. Langer then struck a blow for the cause with a putt of some eight yards on the 13th for a lead of 2 up. When they won the 15th after US errors, the result was virtually settled and the match ended on the 17th by 2 and 1. Europe had won the second series of foursomes by $2\frac{1}{2}$ to $1\frac{1}{2}$ and had the very secure looking lead of $8\frac{1}{2}$–$3\frac{1}{2}$.

Payne Stewart plays a shot from the edge of a bunker

The pattern of the first day was repeated with the series of four fourballs in the afternoon. Jacklin sent his apparently weakest pair out first – Gordon Brand and Eamonn Darcy, whose first appearance this was. They faced Payne Stewart who was paired with the out-of-form Andy Bean, who was only playing in the Ryder Cup because of a good season in 1986. In fact the Americans were unbeatable. Bean birdied the first three holes and Stewart the next two to lead 4 up. Out in 29 they were 5 up and went to 6 a little later. There was no way back but Darcy managed to win both the 13th and 14th before the match ended on the 16th.

Playing second, Faldo and Woosnam were equally destructive; they too birdied the first five holes, reached the turn in 29 and led by 4 up. At this point Woosnam hit a drive and wedge to three feet on the 441-yard 10th. Strange did manage to get one hole back with a 2 on the 12th but Faldo holed from about four yards on the very next hole for yet another birdie. The 14th was halved in birdie 3s – but the match was over, 5 and 4 to Europe. Although the US pair were 5 under par for the 14 holes played, Faldo and Woosnam were ten under.

Behind them, the Spanish pairing of Ballesteros and Olazabal showed signs of strain. They were 3 down after nine but Olazabal began a fight-back with a birdie at the 12th for a win. They also birdied the next three holes but their opponents, Sutton and Mize, had birdies of their own at the 14th, 15th and 16th and they won by 2 and 1.

Last came the match which had the most impact of all on the watching television audience, in part because it was the climax of the day as the shadows lengthened. The first half of the match was closely contested with Langer and Lyle holding a lead of one hole on the 12th over Wadkins and Nelson. Langer holed a good putt on this par 3 to go 2 up and Lyle eagled the 15th to go dormy 3. Wadkins then birdied the par-3 16th to reduce the lead to two holes and then birdied the 17th as well to win the hole. The

18th was memorable because all four players were unfaltering. After all had hit good tee shots, Lyle hit his approach to not much more than a couple of yards. He turned to Langer and said, 'Get inside that and we'll be all right'. But first Nelson and Wadkins had to play. Nelson's shot seemed to be going right at the flag but the draw eventually made it settle perhaps seven yards to the left. Wadkins struck right at it also, his ball pitching a foot or two from the hole before running about five yards past. And then came Langer with an 8-iron. He did indeed get inside Lyle's ball, stopping about a foot away.

Jacklin was ecstatic. For some tastes, there was rather too much jubilation; Nicklaus continued to act as a model captain. As Langer's ball came down, he turned away impassive, realising in that moment that the match was as good as over. He was gracious as he saw defeat impending, there were handshakes and a smile. Later he said, 'I've seen superior golf played by the European team. We fought to the end but our best simply was not good enough today.'

The standard of golf over the very testing Muirfield course had indeed been remarkable. In the fourballs, 260 holes of golf were played.

One eagle was recorded and 58 birdies. At the end of play on the second day, Europe led $10\frac{1}{2}$–$5\frac{1}{2}$; they needed $3\frac{1}{2}$ points from the 12 singles to retain the trophy, 4 points to win outright for the first time on American soil. For the United States, the prospects were bleak: they needed 9 points from the singles. The task was almost impossible – but they were to come very close to succeeding.

The line-up of both teams for the singles reinforces my argument that it would be better for the captains to decide on their orders before play begins on the first day and to let the man playing number one enjoy the glory. As it was, it was difficult to see the reasoning behind Jack Nicklaus's order of play. Needing a good start he placed Calcavecchia and Pohl in his first four, men who had played, respectively, one and two games out of the four possible. Nicklaus's expected strength seemed to lie towards the end where Kite, Strange, Sutton and Wadkins completed the line-up.

Jacklin's policy was varied. He had two in-form men, Faldo and Woosnam, in his top four, the reliability of Langer, Lyle and Ballesteros at eight, nine and ten and Ken Brown, who had not played since the first morning, 'hidden' in the last place when, hopefully, the contest would be over. In the first match out, there was a foot difference in the contestants – five foot four inch Ian Woosnam versus six foot four inch Andy Bean. The outcome of this match looked like a sure thing for Europe but in fact Bean played as well as anyone. Bean was out in 34 but should have been brought back to square at the 14th where Woosnam missed from about six feet for his birdie while Bean holed a considerably longer putt to save his par. On the 15th, Woosnam had the chance of an eagle but the hole was halved in birdies eventually. On the next, Woosnam was let off when Bean pushed a putt wide of the hole from quite close. The Welshman should have squared at the 17th

Bernhard Langer holes a fine shot

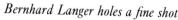

when Bean drove into trees but the hole was eventually halved in bogey 5s. On the 18th, both drove safely. Woosnam hit his second shot to about seven yards and there was then a pause while Bean consulted captain Nicklaus. (Advice from the captain is permitted in Ryder Cup matches and Nicklaus had earlier complained that his team had never consulted him about a shot. At a vital point in one earlier match when Bean went through a green Nicklaus would have liked to have knocked the club out of his hand!)

Eventually Bean played safely to the heart of the green and a halved hole meant that one of Jacklin's aces had gone down. Overall, the United States, though still with little chance of saving the Ryder Cup, were having easily their best day. As Woosnam lost to Bean, the position in the 11 matches out on the course showed the US up in five, while three were all square and Europe led in the remaining three.

With Woosnam losing, a loss by Howard Clark in his match against Dan Pohl might cause some alarm to spread through the team. Their play on the 18th went some way towards settling the outcome of the 1987 Ryder Cup. Clark had missed fairly short putts on the 16th and 17th but launched a long drive down the 18th. It was three hundred yards plus but slightly hooked. However, a television tower obstructed his shot to the green and Clark could drop into a better position. His 7-iron was out of the middle of the club, bit into the green and spun back to the fringe. Even so, a 4 looked a near certainty.

Pohl, however, was in trouble; his tee shot caught a bunker at the angle of the dogleg to the right and his second didn't make the green but came down short in semi-rough at the foot of the upslope leading to the green. Then came one of the shots which helped to ensure that the Ryder Cup would return to PGA headquarters at The Belfry: Dan Pohl thinned his third into the back of a bunker behind the green. Pohl took 6 and Clark was conceded his 4 – and the match.

Elsewhere, the European position had deteriorated slightly: down in five, up in only two and square in two. If that position were maintained, Europe would just scrape home to victory, but with not even half a point to spare. The actual match score at this point looked much more promising however: Europe $11\frac{1}{2}$ US $6\frac{1}{2}$.

In the third match, Sam Torrance had just gone 1 down to Larry Mize at the wrong time – the 17th green. It was Mize, however, who cracked on the 18th, hooking his drive onto the bank of a stream. He could claim line of sight relief from an obstruction but this entailed his dropping into the stream itself. A quarter of an hour passed. Torrance had driven well. Eventually Mize, who had taken a penalty drop, attempted to force a 3-wood somewhere near the green but finished in the left front bunker. Greatly encouraged, Torrance then hit to about ten feet – he had to get down in 2 to halve his match and did so. Mize was the second American to play the 18th poorly. The lead for Europe was an emphatic 5 points but match after match now went the United States' way. Could Europe be about to endure one of the worst collapses on record?

Yes, it really was as bad as that. First Faldo lost to Calcavecchia, then Olazabal to Stewart – both by just 1 down on the final green – that made the score 12–9. Then Rivero lost on the 17th and Lyle lost to Kite on the 16th and the United States had almost closed the gap at 12–11.

An unlikely hero was in the wings. He had an abysmal Ryder Cup record, a ridiculous swing and his captain had no confidence in his ability. In other words, Eamonn Darcy was playing Ben Crenshaw – and making a good job of it. He took 34 to the turn and was 3 up after the 11th. In the meantime, Ben had broken his faithful putter. The story was that Crenshaw had smashed the club in a fit of temper on the 6th. My own theory is that Crenshaw felt he had to show some spirit when he missed the putt and gave it a rap on the turf. That was enough to sheer the aged shaft (Crenshaw has stayed faithful to his Wilson 8802 throughout a career in which he has often been ranked as the best putter in the world). But Crenshaw was proving that it's the man not the putter that matters. He seemed to be able to do just as well with the leading edge of a pitching club or the face of a long iron. On the 12th, a very shaky second putt from Darcy reduced his lead to two holes and on the 13th Crenshaw produced a splendid second shot to about six feet and holed out for a 3. He won the next as well and Darcy's lead was gone. At all square with four to play, few would have cared to bet on Darcy's chances.

On the 15th, Crenshaw again had the better of the play but Darcy holed a very good putt indeed, about five yards, for the birdie which kept him level with Crenshaw. The American then hit an excellent tee shot to the 204-yard 16th, about six feet past the flag. When Darcy could do no better than a 4, Crenshaw went 1 up with two to play. Gloom for the European camp; a levelling of the team scores at 12 points apiece was imminent.

Darcy had one of the worst Ryder Cup records ever; this was his fourth selection for the team since 1975. His match against Crenshaw was his eleventh and as he moved to the 17th tee he had lost all his matches except for a couple of halved games. But it was Crenshaw who cracked. On the 430-yard 17th, Darcy hit his second shot to about six feet. Crenshaw, however, missed the green on the right and then, trying to play a precise shot, succeeded in flopping his ball into a bunker. Match all square. Darcy drove safely but Crenshaw certainly didn't, and sent his ball left into water. He took a penalty drop and then could do no better than force his third shot into a bunker to the left of the green. Behind them, José Rivero shook hands with Scott Simpson on the 17th green, loser by 2 down. The Ryder Cup score was Europe 12 United States 10. But Darcy's position had vastly improved from minutes before; Crenshaw could now hardly do

better than a 5. From the middle of the fairway, Darcy had to hit the green and 2-putt for his match – a 3-iron and 195 yards to go. Darcy, his right elbow flying up, pulled his shot slightly. He was in Crenshaw's bunker – but he had played one shot less than his opponent.

Behind them, Ballesteros holed a testing putt on the 15th to remain 2 up on Curtis Strange; on the 16th, Sandy Lyle was losing to Tom Kite by 3 and 2. Even as Darcy walked towards the green, the United States had drawn even closer at 12–11. But this was the official score; the match as a whole was swinging towards Europe. Langer, once 3 down, had drawn all square with Larry Nelson. Gordon Brand was 2 up on Hal Sutton; Ballesteros was looking in command.

Below *Ben Crenshaw seen after he had broken his putter*

Only Ken Brown's cause was lost at 4 down to Lanny Wadkins. Europe had 12 points; 14½ were needed for victory.

Crenshaw delicately sliced under his ball. It came to rest about six feet from the hole to a roar from the crowd but Crenshaw wasn't pleased. He had expected to be closer and it was Darcy's turn to play. His bunker shot was good, about four-and-a-half feet from the hole, but leaving him a downhill putt. His ball would roll on if he missed. Crenshaw gently rolled his putt in with a 3-iron. Darcy, with a little jab, holed and he had won his first Ryder Cup match and made the capture of the trophy almost – but not quite – certain. Congratulations in abundance came in from his team-mates who had finished and a friendly arm round the shoulders from Jack Nicklaus. The match score was 13–11 and 1½ points were needed from a combination of Langer, Ballesteros and Brand to guarantee the first European win in the United States.

On the par-3 16th, Ballesteros played a superb tee shot to little more than six feet. Strange's shot was also good, a little under four yards away leaving a putt with a pronounced right to left swing. His putting stroke was not smooth and his ball was never far enough right. Ballesteros had a putt for his match and a score of 14–11 which would at least mean the trophy was retained by Europe. He narrowly missed on the right but was now certain of a half at worst, at 2 up with two to play. Surely he would not lose the last two holes? Which is what Ben Crenshaw had just done.

The pride of both Ballesteros and Strange must have been a factor in their match; who was the best player in the world at the time? Was it Norman, Langer, Woosnam or Ballesteros? Many Americans would have none of this. The answer, for them, was Curtis Strange. So, whatever Nicklaus and Jacklin had intended, the result was this Ballesteros/Strange encounter. Going out in 33, the Spaniard had the better of it all the way.

Gordon Brand had been even more in command of his match, 4 up after ten holes but by

Jack Nicklaus is fondly known as the Golden Bear

these closing minutes, Sutton was well back in the match, though still 1 down playing the 17th. Ahead of him, Ballesteros had found the heart of the green with his second shot while Strange, after a poor tee shot, had run his second through the green.

Langer and Nelson were finishing ahead. The German had a putt of eight or nine yards while Nelson had chipped up to about three feet. After much thought and study of the line, Langer was not dead in his turn but a touch closer. He suggested a half; Nelson agreed. With Ballesteros certain of a half, the European Ryder Cup points total had reached 14 and the trophy would return to Europe. Moments later Ballesteros halved the 17th to win his match, making the score 14½–11½. Jack Nicklaus, perhaps the greatest competitor golf has seen, had become the first US captain to lose on American soil and only the fifth overall.

Ballesteros first exulted at his personal win and was more excited when he was told that Langer had just halved. The match was won; the $14\frac{1}{2}$ point target had been reached.

Behind, Brown lost to complete a poor match for him personally (though he went on to win the Southern Open in the USA just over a week later) and Gordon Brand halved a match with Hal Sutton few were watching. The final score was Europe 15 United States 13.

Those present at Muirfield Village had seen some unforgettable golf but television coverage had failed. The BBC, presented with a potential spectacle rivalled only by the Open Championship, largely muffed the opportunity. Perhaps The *Observer*'s Peter Dobereiner was right when he wrote, 'The BBC has always had a niggardly attitude towards the golfing public, preferring to devote its budget to packaged non-golf involving Bruce Forsythe's non-jokes to the real thing'.

The BBC was taking American network coverage which failed to handle the problems of covering 12 matches on the final day. Some games were hardly shown at all – just a putt or two from a pair of players playing 36 holes between them. The US network had also decided not to show the morning play and the BBC went along with this decision and decided not to buy the cable coverage available. Yet occasionally they will devote hour upon hour to *(Back, l to r) Eamonn Darcy, Sam Torrance, Nick Faldo, Tony Jacklin, Sandy Lyle, Gordon Brand Jnr, Seve Ballesteros. (Front) Howard Clark, Bernhard Langer, Ian Woosnam, Ken Brown, José-Maria Olazabal, José Rivero*

relative nonentities playing in a run–of–the–mill tournament because once the engineering is done and the cameras are in place, it makes for cheap television programming.

The hero of the competition was Seve Ballesteros, the only player to take 4 of the 5 possible points from his matches. Langer, Woosnam, Faldo and Olazabal played every match with the first three taking $3\frac{1}{2}$ points and Olazabal 3. Sandy Lyle also brought back 3 points, from one game less. Only two US players won 3 points – Hal Sutton and Tom Kite. These two were sent out by Nicklaus for every match, as was Curtis Strange – the 'best player in the world' – who won twice. No one on either side was undefeated. Statistically the worst performances came from Ken Brown with two matches and two defeats and Ben Crenshaw who lost all three of his games. Larry Nelson performed badly; he played four times and gained just one half in his match with Bernhard Langer.

For Jacklin, making the shortest speech possible, it was 'the greatest week of my life'. Nicklaus's judgement was, 'They played the better golf. The Europeans were tougher coming down the last hole today.'

So they were; times had changed.

MUIRFIELD VILLAGE, COLUMBUS, OHIO, USA 25–27 SEPTEMBER 1987

Great Britain and Europe		United States			
Captain Tony Jacklin		*Captain* Jack Nicklaus			
Foursomes					
Torrance and Clark	0	Strange and Kite (4 and 2)	1		
Brown and Langer	0	Sutton and Pohl (2 and 1)	1		
Faldo and Woosnam (2 up)	1	Wadkins and Mize	0		
Ballesteros and Olazabal (1 up)	1	Nelson and Stewart	0		
	2		2		
Fourballs					
Brand and Rivero (3 and 2)	1	Crenshaw and Simpson	0		
Lyle and Langer (1 up)	1	Bean and Calcavecchia	0		
Faldo and Woosnam (2 and 1)	1	Sutton and Pohl	0		
Ballesteros and Olazabal (2 and 1)	1	Strange and Kite	0		
	4		0		
Foursomes					
Rivero and Brand	0	Strange and Kite (3 and 1)	1		
Faldo and Woosnam (halved)	0	Sutton and Mize	0		
Ballesteros and Olazabal (1 up)	1	Crenshaw and Stewart	0		
Lyle and Langer (2 and 1)	1	Wadkins and Nelson	0		
	2		1		
Fourballs					
Darcy and Brand	0	Bean and Stewart (3 and 2)	1		
Faldo and Woosnam (5 and 4)	1	Strange and Kite	0		
Ballesteros and Olazabal	0	Sutton and Mize (2 and 1)	1		
Lyle and Langer (1 up)	1	Wadkins and Nelson	0		
	2		2		
Singles					
Ian Woosnam	0	Andy Bean (1 up)	1		
Howard Clark (1 up)	1	Dan Pohl	0		
Sam Torrance (halved)	0	Larry Mize	0		
Nick Faldo	0	Mark Calcavecchia (1 up)	1		
José-Maria Olazabal	0	Payne Stewart (2 up)	1		
José Rivero	0	Scott Simpson (2 and 1)	1		
Eamonn Darcy (1 up)	1	Ben Crenshaw	0		
Bernhard Langer (halved)	0	Larry Nelson	0		
Sandy Lyle	0	Tom Kite (3 and 2)	1		
Seve Ballesteros (2 and 1)	1	Curtis Strange	0		
Ken Brown	0	Lanny Wadkins (3 and 2)	1		
Gordon Brand Junior (halved)	0	Hal Sutton	0		
	3		6		

Final score: Great Britain and Europe 13 United States 11. Four matches halved

EPILOGUE

As this book goes to press, 68 years have passed since the first international contest between professionals of Britain and the United States. The early British superiority at matchplay (although Americans were carrying off the Open Championship) was followed by level-pegging up to World War II. Thereafter, the Americans dominated the Ryder Cup until the turning point came in 1983; true, Britain did win in 1957 and tied in 1969 but that was all there was to show for the high hopes of many years' competition.

During the 1980s, the presence of Seve Ballesteros has arguably had more impact on the game than that of any of the great American stars of the past – men such as Walter Hagen, Sam Snead, Ben Hogan and, more recently, Jack Nicklaus and Tom Watson. The Europeans have been buoyed up by having the man they consider to be the best golfer in the world on their side. Whether he is the best or not is debatable but there has certainly never been a better matchplayer.

The alterations in the rules in 1978 which allowed continental Europeans to qualify for selection have made little real difference – apart from Pinero's inspired play in 1985 and the presence of the always rock-like Bernhard Langer. Choosing players only from the British Isles would not have significantly weakened the teams. However, a substantial change has been brought about by the soaring playing standards on the European Tour where golfers are driven by the need to emulate Greg Norman, Seve Ballesteros, and Bernhard Langer. Also, the emergence of British top-class stars such as Nick Faldo, Sandy Lyle and Ian Woosnam has boosted national pride.

So far predominantly Spanish players and a lone German have joined the European side, but with the boom in golf in Europe I believe that the make-up of the teams will inevitably change. Swedish players have come close to selection in the past and no doubt some of them will contend at The Belfy in 1989. However, I doubt that there will be any French, Italian, Portuguese or Danish representatives or any new Spanish or German players.

The situation will surely change in the near future as Europe now has a larger golfing population than the United States. Perhaps the European team will become as dominant as the American team was for more than 30 years after World War II. However, the United States is determined to win but the strengths of the two teams are much the same as they were in 1987.

The PGA will be allowing just 20,000 spectators into The Belfry. The maximum attendance for any one day at the Open is 43,000 which was set at Lytham in 1988. The R and A have not found it necessary to set a limit at all, let alone one as low as 20,000. The 1989 and future Ryder Cup contests will be great sporting occasions and I believe that more people should be able to watch the matches.

PLAYERS' RECORDS
1921–1987

(Note that players who were selected for teams but did not compete and players selected for teams which, on account of war, did not compete, are not included.)

UNITED STATES

	Played	Won	Lost	Halved
Tommy Aaron 1969, 1973	6	1	4	1
Skip Alexander 1949, 1951	2	1	1	0
Tommy Armour 1926	2	0	2	0
Jerry Barber 1955, 1961	5	1	4	0
Miller Barber 1969, 1971	7	1	4	2
Jim Barnes 1926	2	0	2	0
Herman Barron 1947	1	1	0	0
Andy Bean 1979, 1987	6	4	2	0
Frank Beard 1969, 1971	8	2	3	3
Homero Blancas 1973	4	2	1	1
Tommy Bolt 1955, 1957	4	3	1	0
Julius Boros 1959, 1963, 1965, 1967	16	9	3	4
Gay Brewer 1967, 1973	9	5	3	1
Billy Burke 1931, 1933	3	3	0	0
Jack Burke 1951, 1953, 1955, 1957, 1959	8	7	1	0
Walter Burkemo 1953	1	0	1	0
Mark Calcavecchia 1987	2	1	1	0
Billy Casper 1961, 1963, 1965, 1967, 1969, 1971, 1973, 1975	37	20	10	7
Bill Collins 1961	3	1	2	0
Charles Coody 1971	3	0	2	1
Wilfred 'Wiffy' Cox 1931	2	2	0	0
Ben Crenshaw 1981, 1983 1987	9	3	5	1
Jimmy Demaret 1947, 1949, 1951	6	6	0	0
Gardner Dickinson 1967, 1971	10	9	1	0
Leo Diegel 1927, 1929, 1931, 1933	6	3	3	0
Dave Douglas 1953	2	1	0	1

	Played	Won	Lost	Halved
Dale Douglass 1969	2	0	2	0
Ed Dudley 1929, 1933, 1937	4	3	1	0
Olin Dutra 1933, 1935	4	1	3	0
Lee Elder 1979	4	1	3	0
Al Espinosa 1927, 1929, 1931	4	2	1	1
Johnny Farrell 1927, 1929, 1931	6	3	2	1
Dow Finsterwald 1957, 1959, 1961, 1963	13	9	3	1
Ray Floyd 1969, 1975, 1977, 1981, 1983, 1985	23	7	13	3
Doug Ford 1955, 1957, 1959, 1961	9	4	4	1
Emmett French 1921, 1926	4	1	2	1
Ed Furgol 1957	1	0	1	0
Marty Furgol 1955	1	0	1	0
Al Geiberger 1967, 1975	9	5	1	3
Bob Gilder 1983	4	2	2	0
Bob Goalby 1963	5	3	1	1
Johnny Golden 1927, 1929	3	3	0	0
Lou Graham 1973, 1975, 1977	9	5	3	1
Hubert Green 1977, 1979, 1985	7	4	3	0
Ralph Guldahl 1937	2	2	0	0
Fred Haas 1953	1	0	1	0
Jay Haas 1983	4	2	1	1
Clarence Hackney 1921	2	0	1	1
Walter Hagen 1921, 1926, 1927, 1929, 1931, 1933, 1935	13	7	3	3
Bob Hamilton 1949	2	0	2	0
Chick Harbert 1949, 1955	2	2	0	0
Chandler Harper 1955	1	0	1	0
Dutch Harrison 1947, 1949, 1951	3	2	1	0
Fred Hawkins 1957	2	1	1	0

	Played	Won	Lost	Halved
Mark Hayes 1979	3	1	2	0
Clayton Heafner 1949, 1951	4	3	0	1
Jay Hebert 1959, 1961	4	2	1	1
Lionel Hebert 1957	1	0	1	0
Dave Hill 1969, 1973, 1977	9	6	3	0
Charlie Hoffner 1921	2	0	2	0
Ben Hogan 1947, 1951	3	3	0	0
Jock Hutchison 1921	2	0	1	1
Hale Irwin 1975, 1977, 1979, 1981	16	11	4	1
Tommy Jacobs 1965	4	3	1	0
Peter Jacobsen 1985	3	1	2	0
Don January 1965, 1977	7	2	3	2
Herman Keiser 1947	1	0	1	0
Tommy Kerrigan 1921	2	0	2	0
Joe Kirkwood 1926	2	0	2	0
Tom Kite 1979, 1981, 1983, 1985, 1987	20	11	6	3
Ted Kroll 1953, 1955, 1957	4	3	1	0
Ky Laffoon 1935	1	0	1	0
Tony Lema 1963, 1965	11	8	1	2
Bruce Lietzke 1981	3	0	2	1
Gene Littler 1961, 1963, 1965, 1967, 1969, 1971, 1975	27	14	5	8
Jerry McGee 1977	2	1	1	0
George McLean 1921	2	0	2	0
Fred McLeod 1921, 1926	4	1	2	1
John Mahaffey 1979	3	1	2	0
Tony Manero 1937	2	1	1	0
Lloyd Mangrum 1947, 1949, 1951, 1953	8	6	2	0
Dave Marr 1965	6	4	2	0
Bill Maxwell 1963	4	4	0	0
Dick Mayer 1957	2	1	0	1
Bill Mehlhorn 1921, 1926, 1927	6	2	4	0
Cary Middlecoff 1953, 1955, 1959	6	2	3	1
Johnny Miller 1975, 1981	6	2	2	2
Larry Mize 1987	4	1	1	2
Gil Morgan 1979, 1983	6	1	2	3
Bob Murphy 1975	4	2	1	1
Byron Nelson 1937, 1947	4	3	1	0
Larry Nelson 1979, 1981, 1987	13	9	3	1
Bobby Nichols 1967	5	4	0	1
Jack Nicklaus 1969, 1971, 1973, 1975, 1977, 1981	28	17	8	3
Andy North 1985	3	0	3	0

	Played	Won	Lost	Halved
Mark O'Meara 1985	3	1	2	0
Ed 'Porky' Oliver 1947, 1951, 1953	5	3	2	0
Arnold Palmer 1961, 1963, 1965, 1967, 1971, 1973	32	22	8	2
Johnny Palmer 1949	2	0	2	0
Sam Parks 1935	1	0	0	1
Jerry Pate 1981	4	2	2	0
Calvin Peete 1983, 1985	7	4	2	1
Henry Picard 1935, 1937	4	3	1	0
Dan Pohl 1987	3	1	2	0
Johnny Pott 1963, 1965, 1967	7	5	2	0
Dave Ragan 1963	4	2	1	1
Henry Ransom 1951	1	0	1	0
Wilfred Reid 1921	2	1	1	0
Johnny Revolta 1935, 1937	3	2	1	0
Juan 'Chi-Chi' Rodriguez 1973	2	0	1	1
Bill Rogers 1981	4	1	2	1
Bob Rosburg 1959	2	2	0	0
Mason Rudolph 1971	3	1	1	1
Paul Runyan 1933, 1935	4	2	2	0
Doug Sanders 1967	5	2	3	0
Gene Sarazen 1927, 1929, 1931, 1933, 1935, 1937	12	7	2	3
Denny Shute 1931, 1933, 1937	6	2	2	2
Dan Sikes 1969	3	2	1	0
Scott Simpson 1987	2	1	1	0
Horton Smith 1929, 1931, 1933, 1935, 1937	4	3	0	1
Jesse Snead 1971, 1973, 1975	11	9	2	0
Sam Snead 1937, 1947, 1949, 1951, 1953, 1955, 1959	13	10	2	1
Ed Sneed 1977	2	1	0	1
Mike Souchak 1959, 1961	6	5	1	0
Craig Stadler 1983, 1985	8	4	2	2
Joe Stein 1926	2	0	2	0
Payne Stewart 1987	4	2	2	0
Ken Still 1969	3	1	2	0
Dave Stockton 1971, 1977	5	3	1	1
Curtis Strange 1983, 1985, 1987	12	5	6	1
Hal Sutton 1985, 1987	9	3	3	3
Lee Trevino 1969, 1971, 1973, 1975, 1979, 1981	30	17	7	6
Jim Turnesa 1953	1	1	0	0
Joe Turnesa 1927, 1929	4	1	2	1
Ken Venturi 1965	4	1	3	0

	Played	Won	Lost	Halved
Lanny Wadkins 1977, 1979, 1983, 1985, 1987	21	13	7	1
Cyril Walker 1926	2	0	2	0
Art Wall 1957, 1959, 1961	6	4	2	0
Al Watrous 1926, 1927, 1929	5	2	3	0
Tom Watson 1977, 1981, 1983	12	9	3	0
Tom Weiskopf 1973, 1975	10	7	2	1
Craig Wood 1931, 1933, 1935	4	1	3	0
Lew Worsham 1947	2	2	0	0
Fuzzy Zoeller 1979, 1983, 1985	10	1	8	1

GREAT BRITAIN AND IRELAND/EUROPE

	Played	Won	Lost	Halved
Jimmy Adams 1947, 1949, 1951, 1953	7	2	5	0
Percy Alliss 1933, 1935, 1937	6	3	2	1
Peter Alliss 1953, 1957, 1959, 1961, 1963, 1965, 1967, 1969	30	10	15	5
Seve Ballesteros 1979, 1983, 1985, 1987	20	10	7	3
Harry Bannerman 1971	5	2	2	1
Brian Barnes 1969, 1971, 1973, 1975, 1977, 1979	26	11	14	1
Maurice Bembridge 1969, 1971, 1973, 1975	16	5	8	3
Aubrey Boomer 1926, 1927, 1929	6	4	2	0
Ken Bousfield 1949, 1951, 1957, 1959, 1961	10	5	5	0
Hugh Boyle 1967	3	0	3	0
Harry Bradshaw 1953, 1955, 1957	5	2	2	1
James Braid 1921	2	1	0	1
Gordon Brand Junior 1987	4	1	2	1
Gordon J. Brand 1983	1	0	1	0
Eric Brown 1953, 1955, 1957, 1959	8	4	4	0
Ken Brown 1977, 1979, 1983, 1985, 1987	13	4	9	0
Dick Burton 1935, 1937, 1949	5	2	3	0
Jack Busson 1935	2	0	2	0
Peter Butler 1965, 1969, 1971, 1973	14	3	9	2

	Played	Won	Lost	Halved
José-Maria Canizares 1981, 1983, 1985	9	4	3	2
Alex Caygill 1969	1	0	0	1
Clive Clark 1973	1	0	1	0
Howard Clark 1977, 1981, 1985, 1987	9	4	4	1
Neil Coles 1961, 1963, 1965, 1967, 1969, 1971, 1973, 1977	40	12	21	7
Archie Compston 1926, 1927, 1929, 1931	8	2	5	1
Henry Cotton 1929, 1937, 1947	6	2	4	0
Bill Cox 1935, 1937	3	0	2	1
Fred Daly 1947, 1949, 1951, 1953	8	3	4	1
Eamonn Darcy 1975, 1977, 1981, 1987	11	1	8	2
Bill Davies 1931, 1933	4	2	2	0
Peter Dawson 1977	3	1	2	0
Norman Drew 1959	1	0	0	1
George Duncan 1921, 1926, 1927, 1929, 1931	9	5	3	1
Syd Easterbrook 1931, 1933	3	2	1	0
Nick Faldo 1977, 1979, 1981, 1983, 1985, 1987	22	14	7	1
Johnny Fallon 1955	1	1	0	0
Max Faulkner 1947, 1949, 1951, 1953, 1957	8	1	7	0
George Gadd 1926	2	2	0	0
Bernard Gallacher 1969, 1971, 1973, 1975, 1977, 1979, 1981, 1983	31	13	13	5
John Garner 1971	1	0	1	0
Antonio Garrido 1979	5	1	4	0
Malcolm Gregson 1967	4	0	4	0
Tom Haliburton 1961, 1963	6	0	6	0
Arthur Havers 1921, 1926, 1927, 1931, 1933	10	6	3	1
Jimmy Hitchcock 1965	3	0	3	0
Bert Hodson 1931	1	0	1	0
Tommy Horton 1975, 1977	8	1	6	1
Brian Huggett 1963, 1965, 1967, 1969, 1971, 1973, 1975	24	8	10	6
Bernard Hunt 1953, 1957, 1959, 1961, 1963, 1965, 1967, 1969	28	6	16	6
Geoff Hunt 1963	3	0	3	0
Guy Hunt 1975	3	0	2	1

	Played	Won	Lost	Halved
Tony Jacklin 1967, 1969, 1971, 1973, 1975, 1977, 1979	35	13	14	8
John Jacobs 1955	2	2	0	0
Mark James 1977, 1979, 1981	10	2	7	1
Ted Jarman 1935	1	0	1	0
Herbert Jolly 1926, 1927	4	2	2	0
Michael King 1979	1	0	1	0
Sam King 1937, 1947, 1949	5	1	3	1
Arthur Lacey 1933, 1937	3	0	3	0
Bernhard Langer 1981, 1983, 1985, 1987	19	10	5	4
Arthur Lees 1947, 1949, 1951, 1955	8	4	4	0
Sandy Lyle 1979, 1981, 1983, 1985, 1987	18	7	9	2
Jimmy Martin 1965	1	0	1	0
Peter Mills 1957	1	1	0	0
Abe Mitchell 1921, 1926, 1929, 1931, 1933	10	6	2	2
Ralph Moffitt 1961	1	0	1	0
James Ockenden 1921	2	2	0	0
Christy O'Connor Junior 1975	2	0	2	0
Christy O'Connor Senior 1955, 1957, 1959, 1961, 1963, 1965, 1967, 1969, 1971, 1973	35	11	20	4
John O'Leary 1975	4	0	4	0
José-Maria Olazabal 1987	5	3	2	0
Peter Oosterhuis 1971, 1973, 1975, 1977, 1979, 1981	28	14	11	3
Alf Padgham 1933, 1935, 1937	6	0	6	0
John Panton 1951, 1953, 1961	5	0	5	0
Alf Perry 1933, 1935, 1937	4	0	3	1
Manuel Pinero 1981, 1985	9	6	3	0
Lionel Platts 1965	5	1	2	2
Eddie Polland 1973	2	0	2	0
Ted Ray 1921, 1926, 1927	6	3	3	0
Dai Rees 1937, 1947, 1949, 1951, 1953, 1955, 1957, 1959, 1961	18	7	10	1
José Rivero 1985, 1987	5	2	3	0
Fred Robson 1926, 1927, 1929, 1931	8	4	4	0
Syd Scott 1955	2	0	2	0
James Sherlock 1921	2	2	0	0
Des Smyth 1979, 1981	7	2	5	0
J. H. Taylor 1921	2	0	1	1
Josh Taylor 1921	2	2	0	0
David Thomas 1959, 1963, 1965, 1967	18	3	10	5
Sam Torrance 1981, 1983, 1985, 1987	15	3	8	4
Peter Townsend 1969, 1971	11	3	8	0
Harry Vardon 1921	2	2	0	0
Brian Waites 1983	4	1	3	0
Charlie Ward 1947, 1949, 1951	6	1	5	0
Paul Way 1983, 1985	9	6	2	1
Harry Weetman 1951, 1953, 1955, 1957, 1959, 1961, 1963	15	2	11	2
Charles Whitcombe 1927, 1929, 1931, 1933, 1935, 1937	9	2	3	4
Ernest Whitcombe 1926, 1929, 1931, 1935	8	2	4	2
Reg Whitcombe 1935	1	0	1	0
George Will 1963, 1965, 1967	15	2	11	2
Norman Wood 1975	3	1	2	0
Ian Woosnam 1983, 1985, 1987	12	6	5	1

INDEX